School of American Research
Advanced Seminar Series

DOUGLAS W. SCHWARTZ,
GENERAL EDITOR

SCHOOL OF AMERICAN RESEARCH
ADVANCED SEMINAR SERIES

Published by Cambridge University Press

Published by the University of New Mexico Press

The Evolution of Political Systems

THE EVOLUTION
OF POLITICAL
SYSTEMS

Sociopolitics in Small-Scale Sedentary Societies

EDITED BY
STEADMAN UPHAM

A SCHOOL OF AMERICAN RESEARCH BOOK

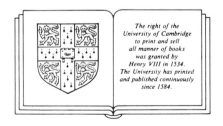

The right of the
University of Cambridge
to print and sell
all manner of books
was granted by
Henry VIII in 1534.
The University has printed
and published continuously
since 1584.

CAMBRIDGE UNIVERSITY PRESS
Cambridge
New York . Port Chester . Melbourne . Sydney

Published by the Press Syndicate of the University of Cambridge
The Pitt Building, Trumpington Street, Cambridge CB2 1RP
40 West 20th Street, New York, NY 10011, USA
10 Stamford Road, Oakleigh, Melbourne 3166, Australia

© Cambridge University Press 1990

First published 1990

Printed in Great Britain by The Bath Press, Avon

British Library cataloguing in publication data

The evolution of political systems : sociopolitics in
small-scale sedentary societies. – (School of American
Research Advanced Seminar Series). – (A School of
American Research book).
1. Agricultural communities. Political development, history
I. Upham, Steadman   II. Series   III. Series 320

Library of Congress cataloguing in publication data

The evolution of political systems: sociopolitics in small-scale sedentary societies
edited by Steadman Upham.
    p.   cm. – (School of American Research advanced seminar
series)
"A School of American Research book."
Bibliography.
Includes index.
ISBN 0-521-38252-1
1. Political anthropology – Congresses. 2. Communism and
anthropology – Congresses.   I. Upham, Steadman.   II. Series.
GN492.E96 1990
306.2–dc20 89–35789 CIP

ISBN 0 521 38252 1

wv

326635

To Peggy, Erin, and Nathan

Contents

Contents

PART II THE ROLE OF DECISION-MAKING, PRODUCTIVE, AND ENVIRONMENTAL PROCESSES IN POLITICAL CHANGE

PART III MARXIST VIEWS OF POLITICAL CHANGE

Figures

Tables

Contributors

BARBARA BENDER, Department of Archaeology, University College London

DAVID P. BRAUN, Department of Anthropology, Northern Arizona University

CHRISTINE A. HASTORF, Department of Anthropology, University of Minnesota

ARTHUR S. KEENE, Department of Anthropology, University of Massachusetts – Amherst

RICHARD B. LEE, Department of Anthropology, University of Toronto

ROBERT McC. NETTING, Department of Anthropology, University of Arizona

STEPHEN PLOG, Department of Anthropology, University of Virginia

DEAN J. SAITTA, Department of Anthropology, University of Denver

BRUCE G. TRIGGER, Department of Anthropology, McGill University

STEADMAN UPHAM, The Graduate School and Department of Sociology and Anthropology, New Mexico State University

Foreword

Over the past fifty years there has been a tremendous amount of research focused on the agricultural revolution. Scholars have examined the causes of the domestication of plants and animals in great detail and have come up with increasingly sophisticated models to explain the processes of domestication. Our understanding is not so secure, however, of the social revolution that accompanied the changes in technology, economy, and settlement of the agricultural revolution.

The transformation from hunting and gathering to agricultural subsistence strategies resulted in dramatic changes in the nature of social relations between human groups. Among nomadic hunters and gatherers, neighbors tended to be temporary and ephemeral, and relations between groups to be transitory and based on ad hoc circumstances. There were few long-lasting relationships between groups to dictate patterns of interaction and intergroup behavior. With agriculture came greatly increased sedentism and investment in fields, crops, and herds. Sedentism in turn meant that one was likely to have neighbors, *permanent* neighbors, and investment meant that one had to get along with those neighbors. The exigencies of sedentary life demanded more stable and predictable patterns of relationships between neighboring groups. With the emergence of sedentism, new forms of social interaction proliferated. Political relationships, in particular, underwent a major transformation as people struggled to adapt to the demographic and economic realities of sedentary life.

The chapters in this volume address the political revolution that took place in concert with the development of agriculture and a more sedentary lifestyle. They examine the causes behind the evolution of political systems in "middle-range" societies and the nature of political relationships within these societies. "Middle-range" in this context refers to those societies in between the relatively simple band organization characteristic of many known hunting and gathering societies and the centralized, hierarchical, and bureaucratic state. Although Steadman Upham wants to steer away from typological models, the chapters largely deal with what would traditionally be called tribes and simple chiefdoms. In looking at the evolution of political systems in such societies, they are in fact looking at the beginnings of true political relationships.

In looking to the beginnings of politics, the contributions in this volume offer insight not only into the historical societies associated with the agricultural revolution but also into the basic nature of human politics. They explore fundamental questions about the origins and development of political relationships: How do people come to forsake local autonomy and equality for broader, hierarchical political units? What are the costs and benefits of entering into political relationships with other people? To what extent do economics, demographics, and ideology affect the nature of political organization? These are questions not just about simple societies of the past but about all human groups across time and culture.

Several chapters discuss general models of change that can be used to explain the evolution of emergent political systems in early sedentary societies. These models could be applied just as well to explain patterns of local-level change in any society. David Braun, for example, argues that cultural evolution proceeds through a process of selection from a pool of variability. This argument can be used explicitly to explain the formation of early tribal alliances in the face of severe environmental stress; however, it might equally be applied to the evolution of a pattern of tenant-ownership in urban public housing projects. Similarly, Dean Saitta and Arthur Keene demonstrate the parallels between political relationships in the prehistoric American Southwest and the Israeli kibbutzim.

A number of chapters address a fundamental issue of culture and human nature – autonomy. Along with the agricultural revolution around the world people are found to have lost their autonomy as social and political hierarchies developed. Although, as Robert Netting points out, hierarchies are not an inevitable outgrowth of agricultural intensification, agriculture does set the stage for the widespread emergence of political centralization and social ranking. Decision-making authority comes to be delegated to a central leader, and the prevailing egalitarianism gives way to social and economic inequalities. Although several alternate theories are offered to explain these changes, a central consensus of the seminar and this volume is that people in egalitarian societies actively resist trends toward political hierarchy and social inequality. Hierarchy and inequality emerge in spite of such resistance; political centralization and social hierarchies are imposed on egalitarian systems. People do not quietly give up their autonomy in willing exchange for the inherent benefits of political leadership and social stratification.

This volume attempts to integrate theory and substance in an effort to understand the evolution of political systems in small-scale sedentary societies. The seminar from which it originated produced no rousing statement of conclusions, for the participants reached differing and sometimes contradictory conclusions about the nature of political organization and change in such societies. But participants do all recognize the broader anthropological importance of studying emergent political systems in early sedentary societies. They push the field of political anthropology in new directions and offer alternative avenues for exploring the foundations of political relationships in human society.

JONATHAN HAAS

Preface

The idea for this book, and the Advanced Seminar on which it was based, developed through correspondence and in conversations with Jonathan Haas during 1984 and 1985. Haas, director of programs and research at the School of American Research, had corresponded with me about a variety of issues during this time. Most of our letters and phone calls revolved around interpretive positions that were being taken by archaeologists seeking to reconstruct the political prehistory of different world areas. Haas and I agreed that a forum was needed to bring scholars with different views and different data together. To formalize our ideas we met in Denver at the 84th annual meetings of the American Anthropological Association. Out of our discussions came the idea for an Advanced Seminar at the School of American Research. That seminar, "The Development of Political Systems in Prehistoric Sedentary Societies," was convened in April 1986, and the present book represents the findings of those deliberations.

Many people contributed their time and energy to make the Advanced Seminar a success. The staff at the School of American Research especially made the week in Santa Fe productive and enjoyable. As coordinator of the Advanced Seminar series, Jonathan Haas is to be especially acknowledged. His organization and management of pre- and post-seminar details has enabled the present project to be completed in such a timely fashion.

The participants, who left their academic and administrative responsibilities behind for an entire week, deserve enormous credit. Although such opportunities for scholarly debate as those provided by the School of American Research are rare, it can be a burden to leave one's commitments behind in the midst of a demanding schedule. I want to acknowledge the wit and wisdom of the participants, to thank them for their time, and to let it be known that even scholars with widely divergent (and sometimes doctrinaire) viewpoints can come together for meaningful exchanges. The camaraderie that developed among participants during the course of the week was perhaps the most enjoyable aspect of the seminar.

The Advanced Seminar was supported by a grant from the School of American Research. Additional funding was provided by the Research Center, College of Arts and Sciences, New Mexico State University. I want to thank Dean Thomas M. Gale, and Associate Deans Dennis Darnall and John J. Monagle for their support and encouragement. Without their assistance and cooperation, this project would not have been possible.

I would also like to acknowledge in this endeavor my colleagues and students in the Department of Sociology and Anthropology at New Mexico State University. I have been fortunate to work with an exceptional group of anthropologists, demographers, and sociologists during the past several years, and I particularly want to thank Bradley Blake, Ronald A. Farrell, Richard S. MacNeish, Fred Plog, Joseph Rogers, Scott Rushforth, Edward Staski, Cookie Stephan, Wenda Trevathan, Richard Wilk, and James Williams for the intellectual atmosphere they create in the work place. I am also indebted to my students. They are too numerous to mention, but during the past decade, they have kept me on my toes and, fortunately, one step ahead.

The manuscript was typed by Beverly J. Brady and Guadalupe Crespo. Their unflagging efforts and conscientious work are greatly valued. Editorial assistance was offered by Maggie Greenlaw, who looked after the typescript in the midst of helping to administer graduate education at New Mexico State University. I would also like to acknowledge the extremely acute editorial advice of Jane Kepp of the School of American Research. Her help with the typescript has allowed for a much clearer presentation of ideas.

Finally, I acknowledge my family. Their forbearance throughout this effort has been appreciated in ways that cannot be easily communicated.

STEADMAN UPHAM

1
Decoupling the processes of political evolution

STEADMAN UPHAM

New Mexico State University

Men would be Angels, Angels would be Gods.
Aspiring to be Gods if Angels fell,
Aspiring to be Angels men rebel.

Alexander Pope, *An Essay on Man*

How many angels can sit on the head of a pin? For archaeologists and cultural anthropologists studying political evolution, the answer appears to be far fewer than was previously thought. For years, social, political, and economic variables and processes have been linked together in positive feedback models in an attempt to explain the evolution of different political systems. These feedback loops are often perilously joined; the resulting welter of processes and variables appears to perch precariously (as if on the head of a pin), balanced in a kind of unholy equilibrium. Now, however, social and economic variables and processes linked by traditional models of political development have been *decoupled*. What has fallen out of that decoupling suggests that a major change is afoot in anthropology that will result in fundamentally different views of the human political past. Such statements capture the consensus view of authors represented in this volume and provide a foundation for reexamining the past forms of human political organization.

This book has its roots in an unusual scholarly forum, an Advanced Seminar at the School of American Research, that brought together leading scholars of political evolution from England, Canada, and the United States. The focus of the seminar, political evolution in small-scale sedentary societies, underscores a major theme in anthropological research and writing during the last decade. Much of that research, however, has followed the systems model popular during the late 1960s and 1970s, with researchers seeking to link social and economic processes together through positive feedback loops. In such frameworks, processes like population growth, competition over resources, agricultural intensification, and political centralization are seen as a suite of processes that consistently covary. Other processual loops (for example circumscription, intensification, warfare) have likewise been invoked in models seeking to explain the evolution of political systems from communal hunting and gathering bands to centralized chiefdoms and states. Through an indepth analysis of case material, as well as a general rethinking of theoretical issues, seminar participants resoundingly rejected such an approach. That rejection is now evident in the chapters of this book, chapters that were fashioned during five days of serious introspection and scholarly cross-examination at the seminar, and several months of contemplation and rewriting afterward.

This book is structured around the analysis of both living and extinct cultural systems. The union of cultural anthropologists and archaeologists here is not merely fortuitous. Rather, archaeological and ethnographic case studies provide a point of departure for rethinking our political past. These data are used to illuminate aspects of political structure and political development in a variety of small-scale, traditional societies. Modern Kofyar farming communities of the Jos Plateau and adjacent lowlands (Netting, chapter 2), !Kung bands of the Kalahari (Lee, chapter 9), archaeologically and ethnohistorically documented Iroquois communities of northeastern North America (Trigger, chapter 5), Eastern and Western Pueblo groups of the American Southwest (Plog, chapter 7, and Saitta and Keene, chapter 8), and data from the Wanka horizons in highland Peru (Hastorf, chapter 6) provide important perspectives with which to examine broader theoretical issues related to political evolution and the origins of social and economic inequality.

The seminar, and now this book, are the products of a plan I developed and formalized in a seminar proposal submitted to the School of American Research. Because many of the chapters reflect on this initial formulation, and because the questions posed in the proposal now serve as theoretical and analytical foils for the contributors, parts of that proposal are presented below. As an initial statement, the proposal reflects the weaknesses of untested argument. Yet as it passed through the week of discussion and debate, the proposal fostered incisive, trenchant analyses that led each contributor to identify and define modes of existence that were essential parts of the human experience in prehistory and to analyze and evaluate political systems that represented the fundament from which subsequent political systems evolved. In this sense, the proposal presented below (modified slightly for publication) stands as untempered metal before being tested at the forge. Following exposition of key elements of the proposal, however, I summarize what emerged from discussion and debate. Each reader can then determine, from the chapters that follow, whether the deliberations in Santa Fe forged a theoretical and analytical mode of analysis with sufficient hardness, flexibility, and resilience.

A PROPOSAL FOR THINKING ABOUT POLITICAL DEVELOPMENT IN SMALL-SCALE SEDENTARY SOCIETIES

Around the world, the agricultural revolution produced dramatic changes in human cultural systems. People began to settle down, population grew rapidly, subsistence and technology underwent major transformations. Accompanying these changes in economy, settlement, and demography were fundamental changes in the nature of social relations. The familial relations of the kin-oriented band were no longer adequate to accommodate the interaction between increasingly sedentary agriculturalists, and new forms of intergroup political relationships began to develop. The emergence of these new political systems proved to be the first step toward evolution of the state in the classic civilizations of the world. From an historical perspective, the nature and evolution of emergent political systems in small-scale sedentary societies is thus of elementary anthropological interest. The goal of this book is twofold: (a) to identify the general evolutionary processes that led to the development of a "middle range" of societies between the communally organized band and the stratified and centralized chiefdoms and states, and (b) to isolate the sociopolitical and

3

productive structures that make these middle-range societies a distinct class of organizational and evolutionary phenomena in prehistory.

Although the processes leading to the evolution of civilization have been an anchor of research for the past several decades in anthropology, most of this research has been conducted within the context of state-level polities. Much less attention has been paid to the evolutionary and political antecedents of civilization. Those middle-range societies preceding the state have not been examined as intensively or with an eye toward identifying the kinds of historical and developmental processes that resulted in a particular constellation of organizational features. Six general issues structure inquiry into the emergence of political systems.

1. What are the general organizational properties of small-scale sedentary societies and what terms, definitions, and analytical strategies can be used to describe them?

2. As people began to settle into a sedentary lifestyle around the world, what were the common cross-cultural processes that allow generalization about the marked advances in socio-political complexity that occurred at that time?

3. What are the demographic characteristics of emergent sedentary societies?

4. To what extent are there asymmetrical social relationships, or social ranking, in small-scale sedentary societies? Do such relationships occur only in the context of emerging political centralization, or can they also be found in communal modes of existence?

5. Does the natural environment condition, limit, or select for the kinds of social responses that result in emergent multi-community political systems, or are factors of social production and technology more important in determining variables in political evolution after the adoption of sedentary horticultural lifestyles?

6. How does the organizational structure of emergent "tribal" political systems provide a foundation for subsequent political evolution?

There are at least five major topical areas that must be addressed in dealing with the emergence of political systems in small-scale sedentary societies. The topical areas define a "field of view" for each of the above questions, framing the theoretical and methodological issues with necessary historical background.

Terms, definitions, and analytical strategies

Many different terms and definitions have been employed to describe and explain the properties of emergent political systems. In many respects, the terminological and definitional morass that presently exists in studies of small-scale societies is so serious that the entire book could be devoted to this topic. Thankfully, this strategy is not employed. It is, nevertheless, important to have a common understanding of terms, definitions, analytical and interpretive strategies, and the implications that are embodied in the use of these and other anthropological approaches.

The definition of terms used to describe the origin and development of political systems have been characterized by two divergent alternatives. One, the typological approach, has sought to classify societies by type. Key societal and organizational attributes are identified and grouped into monothetic divisive categories. The traditional "band, tribe, chiefdom, state" and "egalitarian, ranked, stratified, state" schemes fall within this approach. The other, the processual approach, has attempted to deal with organizational diversity by identifying suites of covarying processes. The latter approach might be considered a polythetic alternative to the typological schemes noted above, and it provides a basis for studying organizational phenomena like centralization, productive intensification, or sedentarization.

Both approaches have advanced the study of political systems, but both have limitations. The typological approach, derived from cross-cultural studies, often cannot account for the range of variation found in organizational forms; the types are too rigid in their construction and the transformation from one organizational form to another is not addressed. The processual approach, on the other hand, can be used to account for the variation missed by the typological approach. But in identifying suites of covarying processes, this approach has often reduced the study of political evolution to the identification of intuitively obvious positive feedback cycles. To suggest that the organization of craft production intensifies, for example, as the demand for craft goods increases does not advance our understanding of the *organizational mechanisms* required either to intensify craft production or to explain the increased demand for craft goods. Although there are some exceptions to the pitfalls of typological and processual approaches outlined above, to date a synthetic alternative has not been identified. I address these issues in chapter 4 in an attempt to clarify the issues and resolve the dilemma posed by typological and processual alternatives. Other contributors represent practitioners of both approaches. Consequently, the remaining chapters in this book provide a forum for alternative perspectives and offer sometimes contradictory views on key aspects of organizational and political development.

Technology and social production

New interpretive trends in the discipline today are concerned with identifying theoretical frameworks that are appropriate for studying the development of organizational complexity in prehistory. Perhaps nowhere has this trend been more clearly evident than in the recent writings of Marxist and neo-Marxist cultural anthropologists and archaeologists. Not surprisingly, this interpretive movement is also most clearly framed in issues that deal with technology and social reproduction. The following excerpt from Bender (1985:53) illustrates this fact:

Technology in the larger sense of the word – that is, not only implements, but also work production – is structured by social relations. There is no simple response to the environment: what is extracted, the degree of productive specialization and intensification, the division of labor, and the form of distribution and circulation are all socially mediated, and are all reproduced by symbolic and ideological means.

Here, the Marxist perspective identifies clear alternatives. If the anthropological goal is to explain the development of political systems by identifying a series of general processes that are valid cross-culturally, then the above concept must be treated as an hypothesis. If, on the other hand, all forms of sociopolitical organization are "socially produced," only ideographic interpretations are possible, since the unique social history of each group will condition its socially mediated response to the environment. The latter idea is analogous to the life-history phenomenon noted by evolutionary biologists to explain the purely idiosyncratic adaptations of some organisms to generalized environmental conditions faced by all organisms in a biome. Each

6

course requires vastly different data acquisition and analytical strategies. Contributors again represent both perspectives and address this issue to identify different theoretical orientations while seeking common ground between the two positions. Readers should compare, for example, the differing views of Netting (chapter 2) and Bender (chapter 10) on this important topic.

Human responses to the physical environment

If Bender's approach epitomizes the importance attributed to social processes by Marxist anthropologists, a clear alternative has been postulated by several ecologically oriented archaeologists (for instance, Braun and Plog 1982; Dean et al. 1985). In its purest form, this alternative formulation attributes great significance to variation in the amplitude, frequency, temporal, spatial, and durational aspects of critical environmental variables. Human response to this variation is seen as determining the form, structure, and organization of human societies (see also Dean et al. 1985). A somewhat less rigid approach that still retains the importance attributed to the natural environment has been set forth by Braun and Plog (1982). In their formulation, environmental risk and human adaptive responses for dealing with risk and uncertainty are emphasized, but the "centralization of decision-making and boundary formation and maintenance, among other details of organizational form, are analytically distinct societal properties subject to potentially different sets of ecological constraints" (1982:502). The dichotomization suggests that divergent processes serve to structure different spheres of society, and that the effects of the natural environment on different dimensions of political organization are variable. A number of the contributors to this book address the impact of environmental factors on the development of small-scale political systems in several distinct world areas, including Europe, Africa, the American Southwest, and highland Mesoamerica. Readers are especially referred to chapter 7, where Plog outlines an alternative to the deterministic scenarios of the past, and shows how social and political structures can be both wedded to and independent of environmental constraints. Braun (chapter 3) also approaches this issue, but from a theoretical position that emphasizes selectionism.

Demographic variables, organizational form, and emergent political systems

Since the publication of Boserup's classic study, *The Conditions of Agricultural Growth* (1965), anthropologists have been aware of the importance of demographic variables, but have been unable to specify precisely what role population growth plays in the development of political systems. Moreover, a few recent studies suggest that demographic variables other than those related solely to increasing population size may be of equal or greater importance in explaining organizational change (Feinman and Neitzel 1984; Upham 1987). It has been argued, for example, that regularities in the population density of individual communities and the size and spacing of regionally integrated populations on the landscape account for much of the organizational variation seen in what Feinman and Neitzel identify as *middle-range societies*. It must be said, however, that the demographic characteristics of middle-range societies are largely undefined. A number of the contributors focus on this issue to clarify the demographic characteristics of middle-range societies and the role of demographic variables in explanations that seek to account for increasing political complexity. Readers are referred to chapter 2 by Netting and chapter 4 by Upham for insights into arguments about demographic preconditions.

Productive specialization, surplus production, and exchange

If demographic variables have been a focus of research during the last several years, exchange and the formation of surplus economies have occupied an equal share of cultural anthropologists' and archaeologists' attention. The latter research has served as a primary means for making inferences about past political organization. Often, reconstructions of prehistoric exchange systems have emphasized elite exchange networks and the movement of exotic goods over long distances. In such studies, the existence of preciocities in the archaeological record has been used as an indication of surplus production, since the production of "nonutilitarian" commodities often indicates that nonagricultural productive specialists could be supported. As Saitta and Keene have noted:

The presence of "surplus" goods in the archaeological record in the form of exotica, preciocities, or non-utilitarian items is frequently treated as a bar-

8

ometer of social "complexity," while changes in the degree of energy or labor investment in these categories of material culture is often taken as a sign for *organizational change*. In the absence of such obvious material indicators, surplus production is seen as nonexistent or limited, an absence explained with reference either to environmental impoverishment or, more commonly, organizational "simplicity" (1985:3).

Saitta and Keene go on to point out that conceptualizing surpluses only as a measurable phenomenon short-changes an archaeologist's ability to perceive organizational change in a variety of different social dimensions: variability in the amount of surplus *labor* in a society, the rules according to which surplus labor is distributed, and the social mechanisms by which such labor is appropriated. This formulation focuses attention back to basic demographic issues and away from indirect measures of surplus production, productive specialization, and exchange. Surplus production is examined in chapter 8 by Saitta and Keene in an effort to identify and explain its role in the evolution of political systems in small-scale sedentary societies. The role of productive specialization and exchange is examined by Hastorf (chapter 6) in the context of Sausa culture history and the broader arena of pan-Andean sociopolitical development.

THROUGH THE FORGE: ASSESSING CONSENSUS VIEWS

The modified excerpts from the seminar proposal presented above identify the central themes of this book. Yet the manner that each contributor treats these themes departs in significant and remarkable ways from more traditional anthropological discourse. That is because discourse in this book proceeds on a variety of different levels. At the highest level of generality, major discussions are presented regarding the appropriate theoretical "point of entry" for analyses of political organization. Do social relations prevail over technological and environmental considerations, or do these latter "ecological" domains pose primary constraints on the evolution of political systems and social structures? This question is not resolved in the chapters presented here, but cultural ecologists and structural and classical Marxist theorists move closer to an understanding of the interplay (dialectic, if you will) between the traditional base–superstructure dichotomy. As a result, the notion of *infrastructure* emerges, not as a base–superstructure fusion, but as a dynamic that identifies social relations as a key element of broader ecological–materialist formulations.

A second level of discourse proceeds in tandem with theoretical discussions and deals with identifying structural regularities of form and development for small-scale sedentary societies as a class of political phenomena. Case material proves essential here, and four broad areas of consensus emerge: resistance, power and information closure, the scale of systems, and productive forces.

Resistance

Societies exhibit strong internal forces of cohesion that are manifest as resistance to social and political change, especially when such change threatens to use the relations of power to create dominant and subservient groups in a population. Resistance to power and to cooptative control of decision-making is a common feature of all small-scale communal societies. In the economic sector, the idea of resistance is manifest in a communal ethos. In communally organized groups, for example, there is a commonly perceived notion about sharing and accumulation that can be translated by the metaphor "the floor through which no one will fall and the ceiling through which no one will rise" (see Lee, chapter 9). Change out of the communal mode of production occurs when the concept of floors and ceilings is distorted either to enlarge the distance between floor and ceiling, or to create multiple floors and ceilings that are hierarchically arranged in terms of increasingly disparate distributions of basic resources. Among the !Kung, for example, resistance resides in the use of rough humor and derogation that is used to counteract achievement. In Iroquois society, which at a maximum size of 20,000 stresses the upper limits of the communal ethos, resistance is formally articulated into the system of decision-making checks and balances. Iroquois leaders must seek permission from followers to lead (i.e., to speak for the group), and must report frequently to their constituents on the nature of decision-making at higher levels of the political bureaucracy (see Trigger, chapter 5). The concept of resistance thus stands in marked contrast to some recent ideas set forth by structural Marxists about the inherent tendency of cultural systems to develop inequalities in the distribution of power and resources *and* to traditional processual notions about positive feedback relationships and increasing social and political complexity.

10

Power and information closure

All societies exhibit relations of power. In many small-scale societies, the relations of power are manifest in the idea of "general will," a concept Rousseau identified more than 200 years ago. In contrast to Rousseau, however, the contributors to this book conclude that power relations revolve around the uncertainty, insecurity, and ambiguity associated with access to material and information. The evolution of power relations in small-scale societies occurs when decision-making becomes linked to the use and possession of basic resources. This rupture of reciprocity involves more than the simple ability to give orders. It involves the cooptation of access to natural and social resources: A gives orders to B; B does not give orders to A. B gives food to A; A does not give food back to B. In the first part of the above sequence A and B can be viewed as equals, even though decision-making authority distinguishes A from B. In the second part, however, the relations of power become linked to economy, and profound inequalities result.

Case material presented in this book indicates that such change can only occur when relationships and institutions are disembedded from the kinship networks that prevail in many pre-state societies. Demographic considerations, especially the way increasing population size and density affect social distance, are of obvious importance in such a process. Because power relations also involve access to information, the concept of information closure and the creation of *esoterica* are also important dimensions of power in all societies. Many archaeologists and anthropologists have identified how information carried through unique stylistic criteria demarcates boundaries and signals group identity (Wobst 1974, 1978; Plog 1987; Wiessner 1983; Sackett 1985). In a fundamental manner, stylistic identities are a manifestation of a broader process of information closure that results in social marking. When information closure occurs *within* a given society, segmentation results. Ultimately, such segmentation provides the basis for social and economic differentiation. Consequently, information closure is intimately related to the evolution of inequality.

Scale of systems

Political evolution is ultimately a matter of scale. Fundamental to understanding issues related to the scale of cultural systems are *thresholds*. Case material reviewed by seminar participants indicates that several significant thresholds can be identified that, when met or exceeded, result in major internal organizational change. All of the thresholds are empirically derived from cross-cultural data. The strongest correlations are found in density-dependent relationships: population densities of 150 per mi.^{2} requiring intensive agriculture, villages between 300 and 500 inhabitants requiring more coordinated political leadership, administrative units larger than 1,500 people (e.g. five villages or kinship units of 300) requiring more centralized political control, more than six equivalent administrative units requiring vertically specialized political integration, circumscribed regions of more than 10,000 people requiring both centralized political control and vertically specialized political integration.

Threshold values are not magic numbers, but should be viewed in relation to the social and technological parameters of the system under study. These parameters act as filters that both constrain and channel change and render threshold values more a matter of close approximation than inviolable reality. More important, however, thresholds are not tied to positive feedback models, but are fundamentally decoupled from that kind of linkage. Consequently, it may be that population densities of 150 or more per mi.^{2} necessitate the adoption of intensive agriculture, but that these important changes in subsistence and labor are not necessarily related to encompassing political change, especially political centralization. Similarly, administrative units of 1,500 may require more centralized political control, but political leaders may have no privileged claim to strategic economic resources.

Productive forces

The productive forces in any society are ultimately linked to the division of labor, the relations of property, technology, and the mode of subsistence. Historically, the most controversial of these has been the relations of property and the process of privatization, since private property is usually associated with more complex, centralized forms of government. Review of case material, however, indicates that the

12

existence of private property, especially land, is not incompatible with other aspects of communal organization. Such a situation is especially true among intensive agriculturalists who live in dispersed household units. Here, the holding of private plots of land is not conjoined with other forces of political centrality, even though the process of privatization may result in some economic inequalities and some status differences.

The privatization of land, as discussed above, is analogous to Dyson-Hudson and Smith's (1978) notion of territoriality. They have rejected both the "pop" ethological notion of the "territorial imperative" and more traditional definitions linked to boundary formation. Instead, they have sought to show that territories, to the extent that they exist, are resource specific; that when resources are dense and predictable in time and space, they will be defended in a manner akin to more traditional notions of territoriality. Land for the intensive agriculturalist satisfies these criteria, perhaps being the densest of all usable resources. Consequently, land *and* the inheritance rights to land and other property can be part of a communal society's portmanteau (to use Netting's term). The decoupling of these productive processes based on the analysis of case material again is a major theme of this book.

My view of the consensus

As with any group endeavor that seeks accommodation of disparate theoretical positions, participants often feel both enthusiasm and ambivalence about "views" arrived at by "consensus." Such an exercise at an Advanced Seminar must in some respects resemble the intellectual acceleration that accompanies the close of high-level political talks, just before issuance of the joint communiqué. Invariably, one feels stronger about some aspects of a formulation struck by committee, and I see the consensus view discussed in the sections above in this light. One of the great benefits of being the organizer of an Advanced Seminar and editor of the ensuing volume, however, is the license that one receives to develop a personal view of the consensus and, precipitous as it may be, to offer that view for public consumption.

Despite the firm commitment of seminar participants to the generalist goals of anthropology, I believe it is fair to say that reconciliation of the disparate views of social and political change held by the participants did not occur. These different views of social and political change, of

13

course, derive from the different theoretical perspectives each participant brought to the seminar. Among the seminar participants, who were
selected precisely because they represented different theoretical
"schools," there was important give-and-take: a serious scholarly discourse took place that gave birth to the idea of infrastructure discussed
above. But reconciliation of major theoretical differences did not occur.
In fact, it is probably fair to say that only the slightest movement and
reassessment of theoretical positions occurred among the participants at
the seminar (although the long-term effects of this kind of week-long
discourse cannot be measured easily). This is neither surprising nor an
indictment of the seminar process. It is rather a statement about the
process of research and scholarship; a statement about the commitment
to years of field work, the development of extensive data bases, carefully
thought-out analytical strategies, and the written word which become
vested interests of scholars, stemming from and underlying their
theoretical positions.

What does this mean in terms of the consensus view described above?
Specifically it means that discussion and debate could not resolve the
most important question raised at the seminar: "What is the appropriate
point of entry for the analysis of social and political systems?" The idea
of infrastructure discussed earlier represents an attempt to mediate the
divergent theoretical views. But like all attempts at mediation, it fails to
address adequately the litany of concerns voiced by proponents of
different theoretical schools. Moreover, each seminar participant
brought specific and often deterministic perspectives to the seminar.
Cultural ecologist Netting places primary emphasis on a modified
Boserupian demographic framework; cultural evolutionist Braun argues
that use of a selectionist approach is the key to explaining variability in
political systems. Classical Marxists emphasize modes and relations of
production as elemental to explanation of political evolution, while
structural Marxists place primary emphasis on social structure, social
reproduction, and the role of ideology as an active force in fostering
political change.

As a materialist *and* processualist, I find discomfort in notions of
"determinism" writ any way. Consequently, I cannot accommodate
easily ideas that posit a deterministic role for specific forces or variables.
In this book (chapter 4) I outline what I call the "generic framework,"
and it represents the explanatory framework I find most appealing. My

Marxist counterparts, however, view this framework as too "malleable," lacking connections between base and superstructure. The seminar's voice for selectionism sees the generic framework as teleological and mechanistic. Ironically, I believe our seminar's cultural ecologist sees my generic framework as too deterministic, because of the importance I impute to thresholds! Thus, we come full circle.

My own view is that it matters less what theoretical perspective one uses to define a point of entry for the analysis of social and political systems than if one identifies, describes, and explains variation in a phenomenon under observation. Some theoretical and methodological flexibility is thus crucial to the extent that it prevents the establishment of immovable intellectual positions and doctrinaire arguments. Consequently, despite the importance of unresolved theoretical differences, I believe that more fundamental progress was made at the seminar in identifying the central axes of political variation. Explaining such variation leads to the identification of structural regularities of form and development for small-scale sedentary societies as a class of political phenomena. I believe this progress is summarized above in my discussion of resistance, information closure, the scale of systems, and the process of privatization in relation to broader notions of productive forces. More importantly, these themes are found within the remaining chapters of this book and are developed by the contributors using archaeological and ethnographic data. That the contributors approach these themes from different theoretical perspectives provides a kind of texture and variation to the chapters that I find anthropologically appealing. A unifying theme throughout is the idea that social and economic variables and processes must be decoupled. This decoupling is empirically grounded by the contributors in case studies and holds perhaps the greatest promise for future attempts to explain the evolution of political systems in small-scale societies.

CONCLUSION

Defining new axes of political variation and decoupling formerly linked processes promise to redirect thinking on important issues in political evolution. Evolution out of a communal mode is a relatively recent phenomenon in human history (*ca.* the last 10,000 years); the formation of state-level polities more recent still. Understanding how political institutions form and are transformed and identifying the regularities of such change will allow anthropologists and other social scientists to reconstruct the essential patterns of our political past.

While small-scale sedentary societies have long been the subject of general anthropological research, it is only within the past five years that a few archaeologists and cultural anthropologists have begun to examine systematically the nature and evolution of political organization in these middle-range societies. The contributors to this book are a fundamental part of this new research. They reflect the theoretical diversity present in the field and represent expertise in a broad spectrum of middle-range societies in different world areas. At the core of each succeeding chapter is the commonly perceived problem of how and why complex political systems and inequality begin to emerge in small-scale sedentary societies. At this exciting stage of progressive research, the inevitable problems of definitions, causality, data recovery, theory, and methodology will require redefinition in the future. But the contributors seek a clearer understanding of the evolution of politics in small-scale societies by explaining the political foundations underlying the rise of increasingly complex social and political forms, and the evolution of that impalpable anthropological entity, civilization.

This book is divided into three parts, each consisting of three chapters. In the first, Netting, Braun, and I outline in successive chapters evolutionary perspectives and frameworks for explaining political change. These papers provide a baseline for the rest of the volume in that they focus on decoupling demographic, productive, and social processes from the political and economic milieu and emphasize the mosaic quality of political evolution.

The second part contains three studies of political change based on ethnographical, ethnohistorical, and archaeological data. These studies are intended to provide a perspective on the role of decision-making, productive, and environmental process in both the maintenance and dissolution of political equality. Here, too, the contributors emphasize the mosaic quality of political evolution, identify key processual disjunctions between economic, political, and social processes, and explore how and why political and economic inequality arise in different world areas.

The final part contains the works of Marxist and neo-Marxist anthropologists. The diversity of thought represented by Saitta and

16

Keene, Lee, and Bender in these chapters underscores the eclectic character of modern Marxist research and writing. These authors deal not only with the traditional Marxist concepts of production and labor, but grapple with new formulations that emphasize the important role of surplus and ideology in political change. Together, the three parts of this book provide current anthropological perspectives on the evolution of political systems in small-scale sedentary societies.

PART I

Evolutionary perspectives and explanatory frameworks

2
Population, permanent agriculture, and polities: unpacking the evolutionary portmanteau

ROBERT McC. NETTING

University of Arizona

No one is today a nineteenth-century unilinear evolutionist, and even the term *neo-evolutionism* sounds old-fashioned. Indeed "the bulk of the history of sociocultural anthropology is written from points of view critical of sociocultural evolutionism" (Stocking 1987:1982). At the same time, few of us would·deny the minimal regularities of polity, economy, and social organization that an earlier generation referred to as periods or stages. At the very least there are some cross-cultural statistical associations of traits (Carneiro 1926) that Tylor called adhesions that still fall out when one shakes the HRAF.

Ethnologists, with their small, distinctively patterned case study carpet bags, may ignore evolutionary issues entirely. Archaeologists, however, necessarily carry large diachronic portmanteaus whose internal dividers still bear the labels of unreconstructed evolutionism. For example, this intellectual baggage might separate preindustrial food producers into two loose pockets, as shown in tabular form on p. 22. Such a dichotomy approaches caricature, but it follows in the great tradition of *societas/civitas*, status/contract, mechanical/organic that we have all absorbed.

Let me modestly propose that we try unpacking these capacious and somewhat dusty categories, using some recent ethnographic and com-

21

	Earlier	Later
Population	Sparse	Dense
Settlement	Dispersed, impermanent	Nucleated, sedentary
Agriculture	Shifting	Intensive
Productive group	Kin group, lineage	Neighborhood, village groups
Occupations	Undifferentiated	Specialized crafts, trade, government
Rights to resources	Communal, egalitarian	Individual, unequal
Political organization	Acephalous, tribal	Centralized chiefdom, state
Dependency status	Local autonomy	Tributary relations

parative findings to suggest where functional connections actually exist and what material things and processes go with what social and political behaviors. This exercise is not intended to prescribe a set of neat analogies for the past. Rather, it is an effort to narrow the range of possibilities so that the archaeologist who finds evidence of dense, sedentary populations practicing intensive agriculture can make, and perhaps even test, a few inferences about how the social organization worked.

I will claim that there is a strong probability that a dense local population of farmers will (a) practice intensive cultivation, (b) substitute labor and capital for scarce resources, (c) produce and consume in family households rather than unilineal descent groups, (d) maintain individualized, heritable, rights to property, and (e) have unequal access to resources, including the possibility of nonagricultural means of support. The economic/demographic system does *not*, however, correlate with the absence or presence of political centralization, dependency relationships, or warfare.

It is perhaps the better part of wisdom for an inveterate cultural ecologist to begin a discussion of the great themes of cultural evolution with some ethnographic observations that suggest a pattern and some cross-cultural comparisons that support it. Here, this procedure may elicit provisional agreement on the regular association of population density and intensive agriculture, or at least an acceptance of common definitions for our key terms. The debates over how the relationships came to be and what the directions of causality have in fact been will be no less fierce for having, at least initially, a firm empirical grounding.

Our cases will be drawn from farming peoples, sedentary agricultural food producers in rural communities, who rely primarily on human and animal energy sources, and who raise a substantial portion of their own food. They will include agricultural communities in market and nonmarket economies as well as in states and stateless societies in order to demonstrate systematic links among population pressure, intensive agriculture, labor organization, land tenure, and inequality that are *not* contingent on descent group structure, political centralization, or capitalism. I will use as illustrative examples some self-sufficient intensive cultivators with simple tool kits who live in small, autonomous villages in hilly terrain in Africa and the Philippines, but I will also draw from contemporary peasant groups in China, Java, Nigeria, and the Swiss Alps.

DEMOGRAPHY AND AGRICULTURAL INTENSITY: SOME CROSS-CULTURAL REGULARITIES

Population has the advantage of being a straightforward variable that you can count on, simple enough so that anyone (with the exception of some sophisticated demographers) can get the same quantitative results from the same kind of census. We will use population as a density variable – people per unit of land (both total available land and arable land) – and, to a lesser extent, as it is manifest in community size, population structure by age, sex, and wealth, and population change through time. The relations of rural population density to agricultural intensification in preindustrial societies shows an uncomplicated logic, an intuitively obvious and satisfying geometrical relationship. If a certain number of people must derive their subsistence from a limited area of land, they can no longer utilize it by extensive means (foraging, pastoralism, shifting or swidden cultivation with impermanent fields planted with crops for shorter periods of time than they are fallowed [Conklin 1961]). They must, perforce, make more frequent use of land and increase its production by annual cropping and multicropping (Boserup 1965).

Regional cross-cultural comparisons show consistent association between population density and agricultural intensity, despite varying local climate, rainfall, soils, crops, and tools. For West Africa, the geographers Gleave and White (1969) found that shifting cultivation, rotational bush fallowing, and permanent agriculture coincided with successively higher local population densities, and then realized belatedly that their observations fit the Boserup model. An overall

23

density of 290 Kofyar per mi.[2] (Netting 1968:110) with regional agricultural land (excluding rocky slopes and wasteland) densities of 93, 174, and 238 people per mi.[2] (Stone et al. 1984:92) in the intensively farmed hills contrasted with the neighboring Chokfem, who practiced shifting cultivation at densities of 82 per mi.[2] (Netting 1968:115). In eastern Nigeria, Igbo tropical forest horticulturalists use intensive plots of tuber, grain, and tree crops in areas with population densities of 400 to 1,000 per mi.[2] but maintain bush fallow of ten or more years where populations are below 150 per mi.[2] (Morgan 1953; Udo 1965).

A statistical comparison of twenty-nine groups of tropical subsistence cultivators (without plows and draft animals) indicated that variations in population density accounted for 58 percent of the variation in agricultural intensities. The addition of constraining environmental variables, representing length of dry seasons and presence of alluvial and hydromorphic soil, increased the explanatory power to 79 percent (Turner, Hanham, and Portararo 1977). People living at densities up to 64/km.[2] (166/mi.[2]) practiced forest fallowing and bush fallowing predominantly; those above this demographic line relied on more intensive farming (Boserup 1981:21). Shifting dry rice cultivators in Asia lived at densities averaging 31/mi.[2] (range 8–91), but the groups who practiced the most intensive multi-cropping with irrigation and transplanting averaged 988/mi.[2] (range 260–1,300 [Hanks 1972:57]).

Even when one examines samples that classify modern nations by population density, frequency of cropping (average cultivated area expressed as a percentage of cultivated plus fallow area), and technology level (per capital energy consumption, telephones per 1,000, life expectancy, and percentage of literates), higher agricultural intensity is positively related to population density (Boserup 1981:19). Cropping frequency above 80 implies raising one or more crops per year on the same land. This practice occurs uniformly in countries with population densities from 166 to 1,326/mi.[2], regardless of technological level (Boserup 1981:20).

Although population density is a standard, readily measurable, and easily scaled variable, agricultural intensity is often treated as multiplex, partly qualitative, and subject to different evaluations by different observers. The original Boserup model (1965:15–16) specifies five categories of land-use, defined by years of cropping, years of fallow, and fallow vegetation. As population increases and local density rises, the farming technology passes from slash-and-burn to forest fallow, to bush

24

fallow, to short fallow with grass, to annual cropping, and finally to multicropping. "This sequence of cropping systems represents an 'intensification' of subsistence production since most of the fallowing methods lie within the technological horizon of the society at a given time; the one which is chosen depends primarily on the population and the available land" (Pryor and Maurer 1982:325). This continuum has been numerically scaled (Boserup 1981:19) depending on the frequency of cropping. Pryor (1985:737) defines the cropping index (CI) as the ratio of land used annually to total land used primarily for plant agriculture. Such a variable, despite its appearance of precision, is often based on rough estimates.

Because farming peoples can achieve more frequent and sustained land-use only with a greater number and variety of agricultural techniques, observers measure relative intensity by the presence or absence of specific methods (Brookfield and Hart 1971). Turner and Doolittle (1978) provide a weighted index of farming technology including ground and crop protection, erosion and hydraulic controls, soil fertility maintenance, and plant preparation. Boserup (1981:45) lists operations according to their occurrence in a wide variety of systems (planting, scaring wild animals, harvesting), or their appearance in successively more intensive systems (weeding, soil preparation, fertilizing, watering crops, feeding domestic animals, producing fodder). Indirect labor and capital investments in future production, such as (a) more complete clearing, leveling, and terracing of land, (b) constructing irrigation, drainage, and flood control facilities, (c) training and maintaining draft animals, and (d) providing better tools, equipment, storage, and shelter buildings, become increasingly important with intensification (Boserup 1985:45; Pryor and Maurer 1982:327).

Though the particular devices may change in material, shape, and mechanical complexity, intensive agriculture was present in prehistory and is sometimes absent in the high-tech contemporary world. A raised ridge or mound with an accompanying depression for drainage or irrigation can be created with a flattened wooden digging stick, a hoe of shell, bone or metal, a spade, or a plow, either scratch or moldboard. The spectrum of land-use we are discussing is not an artifact of technological evolution.

All the basic means of intensification were available in prehistory. Intensification does not require a particular invention or a diffused technique. Farmers who must, for a variety of reasons, get higher yields and prevent their hill slope fields from washing away will terrace them; and so they do (or did) in highland Luzon, Bali, the Jos Plateau, the Alps, Yucatan, and the Andes. They could grow more rice, sorghum, rye, maize, or potatoes on less land if they did, and they could improve yields with or without irrigation, draft animals, and plows. Such convergence on a common technique, just as in the case of independent centers of plant domestication, suggests both the existence of common problems of intensification and a selective advantage for the terrace solution.

LABOR COSTS AND TECHNOLOGICAL PROGRESS

The existence of a correlation between population density and agricultural intensity may seem simple to the point of triviality, though its wide applicability across environments, culture areas, and historical periods has not been generally appreciated. When, however, we link the two factors in cause-and-effect relationships, when we look for them in systems of "specific evolution" based on predictable economic processes, we encounter fundamentally opposed views on change. The Boserup breakthrough challenged the prevailing paradigms of cultural evolution because it denied the primary causal role of technological change in raising the quantity and energy efficiency of food production, thereby allowing an increase in human population. Though Malthus's "dismal science" emphasized the speed with which human population expanded to fill (and overshoot) the environmental carrying capacity as enlarged by technology, and Childe (1951) and White (1959) both stressed the successive revolutions that captured more energy, increasing the size and presumed evolutionary fitness of the population, they all posited the same causal sequence of technology to demography. Boserup countered by pointing out the *costs* of intensification, the declining marginal returns to labor as it encountered resource scarcity. The economic needs of a larger population pushed farmers to use techniques that demanded more work for every unit produced. If migration is not a viable option, "the increase of population within an area provides an incentive to replace natural resources by labor and capital" (Boserup 1981:5). The dynamic element in Boserup's system of change is demographic.

"Labor demands of agricultural intensification" is an abstract, bloodless phrase that can, in the hands of economists, be further formalized into an arid equation bristling with Greek algebraic signs. Archaeologists have only begun to do time allocation and agricultural production studies with living subjects, but ecological anthropologists and agricultural economists have described the extra tasks that intensive farmers perform. The Niger ian Kofyar increase yields and limit risk by intercropping early millet, sorghum, and cowpeas that mature at different times and share light and soil nutrients with oil palms and other perennial tree crops. Such permanent horticulture demands the skills and discipline to provide elaborate terracing and ridging, repeated weeding, stall-fed livestock for manure, and carefully guarded fields (Netting 1968). Chinese cultivators build and maintain irrigation systems, crop nurseries, leveled fields with optimally spaced transplanted rice seedlings, and elaborately processed fertilizers of oilseeds, nightsoil, and carbon-impregnated bricks (Yang 1965:24). Clearly labor carried to the *n*th degree can have only the most marginal of economic returns. When alternatives such as cheap chemical fertilizer appeared in northern Portugal, old practices like collecting gorse and brush from the untillable pine forests to provide stall bedding for cows (and hence manure for the cornfield) were happily dropped (Bentley 1986). But intensification with all its drudgery is often the only way for a group to survive.

To assess the increased work inputs and declining returns on labor that accompany intensification, we need controlled comparisons with population density as the independent variable. In three nearby Hausa villages (Norman 1972; Norman, Simmons, and Hays 1982) with differing demographic pressure on land, declining average farm size and higher production per ha. occurred along with a substantial increase in total hours of farm work and declining per-hour return (table 2.1). Permanent agriculture supports densities of 200 people/km.[2] in the vast "close-settled zone" surrounding Kano City (Mortimore 1972; Netting, Cleveland, and Stier 1980) where urban wastes were purchased to fertilize fields.

In the very different tropical forest environment of southeastern Nigeria, where farming depends on the tuber crops of yams, cassava, and coco yams along with beans, maize, and a large variety of tree crops, a similar contrast has been found among Igbo villages with populations ranging from 250 to 1,200 per km.[2] (Lagemann 1977; Netting 1977). In these cases of extremely high rural densities, the adaptations hypo-

Table 2.1. *Hausa populations, farm sizes, and returns*

Village	Population density	Farm size (ha.)	Ha. per resident	Returns per ha.	Total returns	Annual person-hours on family farm	Returns to labor per hour
Dan Mahawayi	30/km.²	4.8	0.8	₦47.9	₦229.9	1,516	₦0.14
Doka	147/km.²	4.0	0.5	₦60.5	₦242.0	1,634	₦0.12
Hanwa	264/km.²	2.9	0.25	₦66.7	₦193.4	2,257	₦0.11

Note: The symbol for the Nigerian national currency, the naira, is ₦.
Source: Norman et al. 1982:104, 107.

Table 2.2. *Igbo populations, farm sizes, fallows, and fragmentation*

Village	Population density	Farm size (ha.)	Length of fallow (years)	No. plots per Farm	Plot size	Domestic animals
Okwe	250/km.^{2}	2.4	5.30	4.4	880 m.^{2}	11.7
Umuokile	500/km.^{2}	1.0	3.87	4.4	620 m.^{2}	19.3
Owerre-Ebeiri	1,200/km.^{2}	0.40	1.38	6.6	340 m.^{2}	24.4

Source: Lagemann 1977: 23, 24, 42.

thesized by Boserup were obviously occurring. Nevertheless, although intensification may have slowed the Malthusian process of impoverishment, it was not sufficient to halt declining return to labor and deteriorating agricultural production (Lagemann 1977:6). Table 2.2 indicates that an average farm size of 2.4 ha. in the most thinly settled area was reduced to a mere 0.4 ha. as population exceeded 1,000 km., and, predictably, while average plot size declined, fragmentation into more and more widely scattered plots took place. A length of fallow of 5.3 years (barely enough to regenerate land fertility) was cut to just over a year, and increasing reliance was placed on compound kitchen gardens that received some fertilization from household waste products, animal dung, and compost. Farm production was further diversified and labor intensified by increasing the number of domestic animals (table 2.2).

Historically, such intensification in areas of growing population density has been accompanied by a breakdown of sectorial fallowing and nucleated communities in favor of dispersed compounds of permanently tilled fields (Udo 1965; Morgan 1953; Netting 1969, 1977; Lagemann 1977:28–29). Though denser planting, multi-storied interplanted gardens, fertilization, and a proliferation of horticultural tasks were used to make up for land scarcity, they could not fully compensate for declining soil fertility. Compound cultivation (the mixed gardening of land immediately adjacent to the residence) began only when the yields of distant and near bush fallow fields fell precipitously (table 2.3), and even the compound became less productive under maximum pressure (Lagemann 1977:59). As the ratio of yields to labor declined in shifting cultivation, the option of intensification in the medium-density village became more economically attractive (see Barlett 1976), and efficiency may even improve temporarily (table 2.3), but continuing

29

Table 2.3. *Igbo crop yields and labor input by field type*

Village	Crop yields (kg. dry matter per ha.)			Labour input (person-hours per cultivated ha.)	
	Compounds (intensive)	Near fields	Distant fields (shifting)	Compounds (intensive)	Outer fields (shifting)
Okwe (low density)	—	4,677	4,436	—	3,010
Umuokile (medium density)	4,540	1,945	1,763	2,772	2,023
Owerre-Ebeiri (high density)	3,348	1,042	949	3,353	3,388

Source: Lagemann 1977: 59, 93.

impaction in the high-density village forces labor input up even though yields are declining.

Though both Hausa and Igbo show substantial internal variation in land availability, yields, and labor productivity according to population density, real shifting cultivators with plentiful land and occasional physical movement of village habitations fall at the other end of the spectrum. The Gbaya in the upland savanna of central Cameroon live at densities of 4/km.[2] in the region that they entered within the last century or so (Burnham 1980:2, 77). Their staple manioc (cassava) can be planted at any time during the eight-month rainy season and in almost any type of soil. It requires no preparatory breaking of the soil and is merely stuck in a dibbled hole. The tubers mature in eighteen months and can be dug up as needed over a period of two and a half to three years, with no necessity for further storage. At a mean manioc field size of 0.22 ha. per adult cultivator, a husband and wife could produce a minimum of 2,200 kg., or more normal yields of 6,600 kg., over sixteen months. An average Gbaya household of 4.36 persons requires only 1,760 kg. of manioc per year, so a surplus is possible (Burnham 1980:134). This return is achieved with field preparation and planting times of 10–14 days by one person, followed by 3 weedings. Both manioc and maize fields can be fallowed for up to fifteen years, and it is apparent that the Gbaya density is far below the potential numbers that might be supported with minimal intensification (Burnham 1980:162). Though peanuts, yams, sorghum, and fruit trees grow well in their area, the Gbaya appear to lack interest in such crops because of the deep hoeing and continued care required (Burnham 1980:151). In a manner seemingly characteristic of shifting cultivators everywhere, the sparse Gbaya population can be prodigal of land and economize on labor, producing a secure subsistence by simple means and with a relatively small expenditure of work.

It is easy to contrast the annual labor inputs of shifting and intensive cultivators at opposite ends of the population density spectrum. This exercise should not obscure the quite variable level of efficiency in return per hour of work. As the number and diversity of farming tasks expands, so too does the range of marginal returns. Investments in new tools, seeds, and draft animals, in the long-term benefits of irrigation or terracing, and in the acquisition of increasingly valuable land can keep productivity per hour constant, or even increase it substantially. Such investments are not simple to calculate, and they must be amortized by higher total per capita production over the long term. In Southeast Asia, average person days spent in the field for a single crop of rice rise from 241 for shifting cultivation to 292 for intensive transplanting, but output more than doubles, and efficiency (rice per labor day) increases by 81 percent (Hanks 1972:54–66). But whereas the shifting cultivator has negligible cash expenses and abundant free time for fishing, collecting, and other non-agricultural activities, the wet-rice farmer must pay indirect costs equivalent to a minimum additional 138 days of labor time per year (Hanks 1972:62). Though intensification seems inevitably to raise total labor input, its effect on labor efficiency is not necessarily negative and must be empirically determined for particular agricultural operations.

MALTHUS, BOSERUP, AND CAUSALITY

The debate over the interaction of population density, intensification (as a type of technological change), and economic returns to labor has focused less on the fact of their association than on the causal relationships, the limits and trajectory of the system, and the functional alternatives, such as migration or military coercion, that might affect the system. Though ethnographic and archaeological examples supporting the Boserup position have accumulated (Netting 1974a; Cohen 1977), it is the recent economic theory literature that most effectively confronts the priority of technology or population and the positive or negative aspects of population growth.

A consensus is emerging that Malthus and Boserup are not contradictory but complementary, and that indeed a formal synthesis of their theories is possible (Pryor and Maurer 1982; Robinson and Schutjer 1984; Lee 1986a, 1986b). It is plain that both authors recognize processes that lead to scarcities of resources, but the demographic and technological reactions to disequilibrium, the rates of change in system variables, and the nature of new equilibria are at issue. Neither would deny the law of diminishing returns. "The heart of all economic theory of population, from Malthus to *The Limits of Growth*, can be stated in a single sentence: The more people using a stock of resources, the lower the income per person, if all else remains equal" (Simon 1981:257). For Malthus, the supposed inherent potential of human beings to increase geometrically could outrace even growing production so rapidly that income would fall to starvation levels. In 1798, during the very real expansion of eighteenth-century European populations before the benefits of the Industrial Revolution had taken hold, his theory was conceptually appropriate to a major ecological transition (Wilkinson 1973:22). But the inevitability of rapid population growth and the rates of potential changes in food supply were conjectural and wrong. Those like the anthropological neo-evolutionists who were bullish on technology also portrayed human history as a Malthusian progression, but they emphasized the technological revolutions preceding the expansion of population to new and higher equilibrium levels (Lee 1986a:121).

In a simplified Malthus-type model, we assume a constant technology and a constant amount of land. As population expands, the marginal and average productivities in agriculture fall; after some point, the birth rate begins to fall, the death rate rises, and the population growth rate falls, and the society eventually achieves a relatively constant population level. Thus, this type of model assumes an exogenous level of technology and an endogenous population response. Boserup proposes a much different mechanism: the population rises (exogenously) at a given rate and the technology employed in agriculture adapts to the ratio of land to population (Pryor 1985:731).

For Malthus, an exogenous improvement in productive technology would lead directly to more food, a higher general level of welfare, and more people. Such a technological change was random, and thus was no more likely to emerge if population pressure existed (Hammel and Howell 1987). As Simon points out (1981:200), innovations of the "invention pull" type, such as a better calendar, are adopted as soon as they are proven successful because they will increase production with no more labor. Boserup stressed the "population push" type of inventions, such as settled agriculture or irrigated multicropping that require more labor and hence will not be adopted until demand from more mouths to feed warrants them. Diminishing returns for Malthus spelled the doom of hunger, disease, and war because he could not imagine an already crowded landscape producing more when previously unused labor resources were called into service and when known, but previously too costly, techniques and tools were applied. Intensification gives a selective advantage to those who are goaded into using their slack time and inventive capacity.

We are used to thinking of novel agricultural technology as an unquestionable economic good, increasing production while saving labor. For example, if farmers know about the plow and have suitable draft animals, they should universally adopt it. But in fact, of forty-one European and Asian societies meeting these prerequisites, 36 percent did not use plows (Pryor 1985:729). Boserup says that population-mandated short fallows result in grass turf that can be broken effectively over wide areas only with animal-drawn plows. In Pryor's (1985:736) sample of sixty-eight Eurasian and African societies where plows are possible, a population density level of 25 per mi.[2] statistically discriminates plow-users from low-density nonusers. Labor productivity is apparently higher in long-fallow systems where investment in the implement and in the purchase, care, feeding, and training of draft animals is unnecessary. The ox that draws the plow for ten weeks must be herded, fenced, or tethered for fifty-two, and if it is likely to snow, barns must be built and hay stored for the winter. Appropriate technology is defined in part by costs and benefits that may not be obvious.

An objection to the positions of both Malthus and Boserup has been their lack of ecological sophistication. The qualities of the environment set constraints that can only be overcome at great cost. Geographers and development economists were quick to point out that local climate, water, soil, and domesticates necessarily conditioned the type and degree of intensification possible (Brookfield 1968; Grigg 1979; Matlon and Spencer 1984), though the limits were by no means as fixed as previous environmental determinists had thought (Meggers 1954). If technology is held constant, Malthus would postulate a relatively inflexible environmental ceiling on population. Demographic density

33

or growth would be governed by the relative richness of the environment (Pryor 1986:883). Agricultural intensity that is closely linked to population density should therefore be most frequent in those areas with the greatest environmental potential for agriculture. Pryor (1986) has coded worldwide geographic surveys for the relative favorability of soil, weather, and topography for agriculture. Eliminating the cases where cultivation is impossible, he finds that agricultural potential accounts for only 10 percent of the variation in the importance of agriculture and only 4–5 percent of the variation in population density (Pryor 1986:883–84). In sharp contrast, population density explains 40 percent of the variation in importance of agriculture and 30 percent of variance in cropping index, which measures the percentage of total agricultural land under cultivation at one time (Pryor 1986:884–85). Although the correlation does not account for all the observed variation, and does not imply the direction of causality, it does cast doubt on the Malthusian proposition that environmental potential and fixed carrying capacity are major determinants of populations density. Malthusian limits to growth are relatively clear in dry or cold regions where hunter-gatherers have survived, but even in these situations, the positive checks of mortality are less in evidence than the biological regulatory mechanisms relating nutrition, work effort, seasonality, lactation, ovulation, and birth spacing (Howell 1979; Konner and Worthman 1980).

Boserup is often faulted for espousing the view that human populations display an inherent tendency to grow, necessarily exceeding their resources and encountering the declining returns that lead to intensification. That humans seldom approach their biologic potential for reproduction, and that high rates of natural increase are brief and local in the prehistoric record are not in dispute (Cowgill 1975). Boserup's proposition originally ignored the sources of population growth and avoided assigning this exogenous factor any constant rate. Indeed she had no theory of population growth (Lee 1986b:6). She merely postulated that *if* population density increased, a likely (though not the only) recourse was to increase the food supply by intensification. That more food could in turn contribute to further demographic expansion is not ruled out, and Boserup (1981:15) now refers to a "process of mutual adaptation."

Intensification, though requiring longer hours and more laborious agricultural techniques, does not merely keep up with subsistence demands but may potentially exceed them. It may, in fact, be more

34

useful to think of farmers having a "reference income" of goods they seek; these are seldom confined to immediate subsistence needs. Like workers everywhere, if current income falls, farmers will vary their level of production according to whether they are above or below their reference income level (Pryor and Maurer 1982:328). Efforts to maintain a desired income by means of diversified agriculture with better storage, more local specialization and exchange, and more control of environmental risks increase the possibility that a surplus will be regularly produced. Even if former shifting cultivators do not increase previous individual levels of ordinary insurance and surplus production, their larger numbers may allow concentration and circulation of more goods (Orans 1966), lowering the per capita costs of risk management (Johnson and Earle 1987:209), and promoting a higher standard of living (in at least a part of the population) as well as stimulating further technological development (Boserup 1981; Lee 1986a). Material well-being does in fact increase fecundity and child survival and decrease mortality, as Malthus implies. It is possible that people who are intensifying can be working more and, at the same time, can be enjoying it more and reproducing more, especially as children contribute their labor to family subsistence, security, and wealth.[1]

Endogenous population growth and an exogenous technological change were given very different weights by Marx and his followers. The specter of starvation for the masses was powerfully evoked by both Malthus and Marx, but they differed in fundamental ways as to its causes, and neither could measure statistically the secular variations of rural population, land-use, labor expenditure, average diet, and mortality. Marx's view of the primacy of technological and scientific progress in raising human welfare places him with the more optimistic evolutionists. Scarcity for him was a creation of an external and dysfunctional political economy.

Engels, in his *Outlines of a Critique of Political Economy*, critically summarized Malthus as contending "that the earth is perennially overpopulated, when poverty, misery, distress, and immorality must prevail, that it is the lot, the eternal destiny of mankind, to exist in too great numbers, and therefore in diverse classes . . ." Engels said that Malthus, seeing the tendency to overpopulation in both civilized and natural man, explained human misery as caused by an eternal law of nature, thus diverting attention from the misery created by class exploitation and, more particularly, capitalism (Meek 1953:25). Marx

35

and Engels pointed out that labor power increases with population, and that even if returns to labor in agriculture diminished, the progress of science and technology would more than compensate for this decline (Meek 1953:30). Individual labor could in fact be reduced. Engels insisted that every adult can produce more than he can consume, and that children will return abundantly the expenditure laid out on them. The degradation of humanity inherent in the Malthusian myth can be eliminated "by doing away with private property, competition and conflicting interests" (Engels 1972 [1844]).

There is now evidence from the past that growing populations experienced the physical costs of intensification and that the deteriorating per capita food supply cannot be credited solely to social factors. Agricultural systems focused on a few highly calorific plant species may support more people per ha. but be less stable and less favorable nutritionally than more broadly based ones (Roosevelt 1984). Osteological evidence from Nubia indicates that the groups that raised the productivity of the Nile Valley experienced malnutrition and developmental stress (Martin et al. 1984).[2] Higher population densities could result in increasing morbidity and mortality, but even these chronic conditions may not have been sufficient to restrain or reverse demographic growth.

The fact that Boserupian rapid growth of population *and* technology over the short run exists does not deny the presence of Malthusian resistances and upper limits. Even among land-short intensifiers, some preventive population responses might be taking effect (Pryor and Maurer 1982:347). At some point, diminishing returns to fixed resources and the growing cost of technology and labor outweigh the stimulus to intensification, and population increase can no longer be sustained (Lee 1986a). The system, after first accelerating, then decelerating, comes to rest at a higher technology/higher population equilibrium. At this new, stable node, Malthusian forces prevail over Boserupian (Lee 1986a:120). "Boserupian technological change eventually reaches a dead end . . ." (Robinson and Schutjer 1984:364). Further growth in population or decline in technology may send the system into decline, tracing a downward path around the Boserup space. Boserup and Malthus agree that a population that is *too* dense cannot generate sufficient surplus to support further collective investments (Lee 1986a:122). Where no further increase in output is possible, additional workers may work fewer average hours per capita (Robinson and

Schutjer 1984). At low-density and ultra-high-density levels, Malthusian limiting forces are of primary significance, but in the Boserup space, the dynamics of population and agriculture are mutually reinforcing, and either factor can take a leading role. An exogenous shock, such as climatic amelioration, military concentration of population, or the diffusion of a new food crop from another society, may be necessary to move a local group from a Malthusian stasis to the next Boserup space (figure 2.1). Because each theory offers an explanation for a variable (Malthus's change in population, Boserup's development of technology) that the other treats as exogenous, the theories are, in fact, consistent and form a closed system (Lee 1986b:6). Technical change for Malthus may only be futile in the long run, and Boserup does not

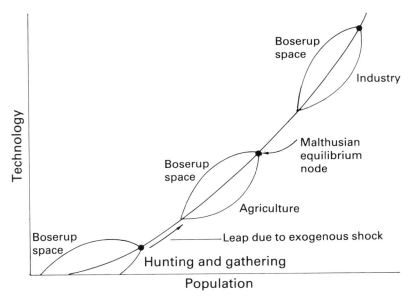

Figure 2.1   The diagram redrawn from Lee (1986: 122) shows a sequence of elliptical Boserup spaces representing technological regimes. Within each there is a self-reinforcing growth of population and technology. But as the upper node of Malthusian equilibrium is approached, there are diminishing returns and growing costs of technology, and population growth cannot be sustained. Demographic overshooting of this point brings Malthusian positive checks into play, leading to both population and technological decline. An exogenous shock is required for the leap from one Boserup space to another.

37

insist that technical amelioration be permanent (Hammel and Howell 1987).

There is now a consistent body of evidence from ethnographic case studies, cross-cultural comparisons, and formal economic models that lend support to the following propositions:

1. Population density and agricultural intensity are directly and regularly associated.

2. Agriculture can be intensified, increasing production per unit area and frequency of land-use, by a variety of techniques present in prehistory.

3. Extreme environmental conditions may prevent or seriously curtail permanent sedentary agriculture, but elsewhere local population density and intensity of farming systems are not determined by the agricultural potential of particular geographic areas.

4. Measures of agricultural intensity such as average farm size, land per person, yields per unit area, and frequency of fallowing vary with population density within local regions where climate, precipitation, soils, topography, crops, tool types, and ethnic groups are held constant.

5. Intensification linked to scarce resources generally requires more labor and capital per unit produced, and these costs (in diminishing returns) make it unlikely (and economically irrational) that low-density populations of foragers, pastoralists, and shifting cultivators will adopt such techniques. The technology of preindustrial intensification demands the expenditure of more rather than fewer work days annually, though the efficiency of particular labor processes may be variable.

6. Seeming contradictions in Malthusian restrictive and Boserupian expansive models relating population and technological change are resolved in more inclusive systems with long-run and reversible trajectories and cyclical processes of mutual adaptation by functionally interacting variables.

WHO DOES THE WORK? THE HOUSEHOLD AS PRODUCER/CONSUMER

The anthropologist's reaction to the proposal of any such universalistic, generalizing formulation of "demo-techno-econo-environmental" evolution is almost reflexive: it doesn't fit particular cases (especially the way *my* Bongo-Bongo do it). Its mechanistic determinism is simplistic and naive, and its isolation from social, institutional, and cultural factors is arbitrary, reductionist, and scientistic. One way to make such admittedly abstract paradigms worth something more than four nickels is to investigate their implications for a series of limited problems in labor organization, land tenure, and inequality, which in turn may or may not be related to questions of political centralization and hierarchy.

The kind, amount, and especially quality of labor that intensive cultivation demands are provided most effectively by the independent family household that derives most of its own subsistence from its agricultural efforts. Certainly not every society has the spatially neat and economically direct fit of the Kofyar family household occupying a physically distinct homestead cluster of round huts situated on (and often surrounded by) the intensively tilled field from which it derives its subsistence. Even so, the pattern of a resident family kin group who cooperate in (a) growing food, (b) tending domestic animals, (c) processing, storing, and consuming agricultural produce, (d) maintaining and transmitting intergenerationally their rights in resources, and (e) reproducing and training the work force is practically ubiquitous. Common features of household activity or function such as production, distribution, transmission, reproduction, and residence (Wilk and Netting 1984) are not limited to intensive cultivators, but I would argue that the particular ecological and economic stresses they confront increase the salience of the household as compared with such alternate social groupings as the lineage, the age set, the village, the manor, the plantation, or the business enterprise.

The permanence of land-use and the necessity to squeeze more production from limited resources under intensive cultivation confer benefits on farmers who till the same fields over the long term and invest in improvements. Small, diversified, labor-intensive farms oriented to minimize risk rather than to maximize production of any single crop are ecologically sustainable for generations. What Salamon (1985) calls a "yeoman strategy" contrasts with an expansive, labor-efficient but often resource-depleting agricultural style characteristic of both swidden frontiers and modern entrepreneurial agribusiness (Barlett 1987).

Intensive cultivators need detailed knowledge of the micro-environmental resources at their disposal. The size and soil of a plot, its exposure to sun or to frost damage, its special qualities of moisture retention and drainage, its distance from home and the ease of travel and transport to it, and the similar or complementary characteristics of other arable lands to which the farmer has access create options. But experience with various crop mixes and the timing of agricultural operations under different climatic conditions permits the farmer to make informed decisions and practice ecological fine-tuning (Richards 1985). Each household's unique blend of resources and labor may require a higher order of individual ethnoscientific knowledge and careful management for sustained and secure production (Leaf 1973). Smallholders cannot hew to a single conventional agricultural pattern. They differ from each other, vary their practice from year to year, and experiment (Johnson 1972; Richards 1985), exhibiting ranges of utilitarian behavior far from the stolid homogeneity of Marx's peasants, as alike as potatoes in a sack.

Members of a household share what may be a lifelong attachment to specific resources. The fund of ecological information so vital to the farming endeavor is transmitted through daily socialization and training within the family. The interdependence and long, intimate association of close kin mean that activities can be coordinated with a minimum of overt authority and direct supervision and that household labor will generally cost less than hired wage workers (Binswanger and Rosenzweig 1982). The group is small enough to enable members to monitor each other and prevent laziness or carelessness (Becker 1981:238). The division of labor allows a variety of tasks to proceed simultaneously (Sahlins 1957), coordinated by a household head who is also parent, spouse, or sibling of the other members. Altruism within the family assures the pooling and sharing of subsistence. The conscientious hard work and responsibility necessary for intensive agriculture are promoted by the direct incentive of secure consumption and the psychological rewards of respect and affection among interdependent kin.

The household is an especially effective mechanism for mobilizing the labor of children. Without their contributions the high labor demands of intensive agriculture could scarcely be met. Bangladeshi rural children begin economically useful lives around age six, gathering fuel, fetching water, and caring for younger children (Cain 1980). By age thirteen, children are working more than nine hours a day, equivalent to adult men and women (Cain 1980). Children may also be active in home handicrafts or marketing. A household survey in the Philippines showed children contributing 15 percent of market income and putting in 30 percent of the farm family productive time (Folbre 1984). Children in Java and Nepal are producing economic returns equal to the costs of their upkeep by the age of nine, and by age twelve they have, in effect, repaid the total costs to their parents of raising them to this age (Nag, White, and Peet 1978).

Women may be major contributors to the household productive enterprise as well. The most rapid way to increase production among Kofyar households, which raise both food and cash crops by increasingly intensive hoe cultivation on the Benue plains, is to increase the number of wives in a polygynous household. Cross-cultural comparisons show, as we would expect, that the labor time of both men and women rises substantially in intensive agriculture (plow or irrigation) as compared to simple, extensive systems. Total daily work hours for women rise from 6.70 to 10.81, while those of men go up even more sharply from 5.15 to 9.09 (Ember 1983:285). Though female time in direct crop production may decline, the increase in related food processing, animal care, fuel and water collection, cooking, and house maintenance more than compensates for this drop. Men's work, which may be confined to clearing and harvesting in slash-and-burn regimes, jumps by 94 percent, becoming less seasonal and more critical to the household economy.

Unlike the wage laborers on a capitalistic plantation or the members of a collective farm, a family household can respond sensitively to changes in resource availability by altering its labor input and possibly its consumption standards. This change may mean more hours of work on and off the farm with lower rates of return for farmers with less land. The household striving for subsistence can enlist more labor from its members, including women, children, and underemployed men, because it will accept rates of return far below market wages (if any) for these services in the money economy (Cain 1980). It is an enterprise geared to provide food even at the expense of labor that would bankrupt a capitalist enterprise designed to yield a profit. Intensification reflects a response to scarcity on the part of the household that is the greater for being voluntary and internally generated, rather than externally purchased or coerced.

Where land is the factor of production in shortest supply, household

Table 2.4. *Japanese rural household size by landholding*

Year	Small holders (0–4 koku)	Medium holders (4.1–18 koku)	Large holders (over 18 koku)
1716	1.6	2.5	4.1
1738	2.7	3.8	5.1
1780	3.0	4.3	5.6
1802	4.0	4.5	5.8
1823	4.9	5.1	5.4
Average 1716–1823	3.7	4.2	5.3

Source: Smith 1959:123.

numbers must be adjusted to the resource base. Households grow and fission or diminish through mortality or loss of members in conformance with their access to resources, as demonstrated by agricultural censuses for the Japanese village of Nakahara (table 2.4). Families with growing holdings kept or increased their membership; those whose holdings shrank lost people. Causation worked in both directions, but in this region of intensive rice agriculture, it ran powerfully from land to household (Smith 1959:126).

Any measure of the size of agricultural operation in a sampled community (land area used, land ownership, taxable value of land, wealth in domestic animals, or market value of crops) correlates with household size (Netting 1982b). In some societies, such as seventeenth-century England (Laslett 1965) and nineteenth-century Sweden (Löfgren 1974) and Austria (Mitterauer and Sieder 1979), adolescents were moved from land-poor households to be servants on the farms of more prosperous peasants. Kofyar adjust household size to labor opportunities and subsistence possibilities by adding polygynous wives, and subsequently their offspring, and by retaining married sons, siblings, and other relatives in the paternal household (Netting 1965b, 1968; Stone et al. 1984). Those families who were restricted to fixed, intensive, homestead farms in the hills averaged 4.5 members, but those who migrated to the plains frontier, where there were abundant lands, had steadily enlarging households, averaging 6.31 in 1966 and 7.60 in 1984. Additional household members produced increasing subsistence and cash crops. Money income went for consumer goods such as motorcycles and metal roofs as well as for medical and educational services. Because the Kofyar have occupied much of the available virgin

Benue valley land in the last thirty years, passing from pioneer shifting cultivation to an intensified annual cropping with shortened fallow, it appears that household size has stabilized and may even decline as multiple or extended family household farms are divided. The point worth emphasizing is that intensive agriculture on smallholdings is carried on by households, and that there is necessarily a close mutual adaptation of land and labor achieved by transfer of land or social adjustment of household membership.

CRAFTS, TRADE, AND WAGE WORK: WHEN YOU CAN'T KEEP THEM DOWN ON THE FARM

It is perhaps obvious that rural landless laborers or *minifundistas* who lack the resources to provide their own minimal subsistence will be poorer than their better-endowed neighbors. In practice, they must work longer for equivalent returns, in effect an intensification of labor without the opportunity to derive income directly from land or from capital goods. The same economic bind results in the appearance of craftworkers, artisans, and traders who may also be forced to accept lower returns on their labor. Such specializations may supplement home farm work during the off-season or employ family members whose labor cannot be used on the household's limited landholding. It reflects a growth of the local population beyond the capacity of even intensified use of available agricultural resources, and it also requires the presence of a market or other effective means of exchange.

For farmers, wage work or handicrafts seem to be a second choice, a less desirable economic option than agricultural intensification. The Maya potters described by Manning Nash (1961) left their cottage industry if they acquired sufficient *milpa* land to support themselves, and richer farmers never became potters. Guatemalan lakeside villagers without good corn land may have made rope, but the tasks of decorticating maguey and twisting fibers involved a higher percentage of active workers (58.2 percent of household members over age seven vs. 41.9 percent in villages with irrigated maize), more continuous year-round work than the seasonal cycle of farming, and a larger household labor force (Loucky 1979). In Java (Nag, White, and Peet 1978), returns in rupees per hour to rice cultivators and gardeners, though they declined with smaller field areas and sharecropping, still exceeded the average

43

Table 2.5. *Returns per hour in various occupations – rural Java (rupees)*

Rice cultivation	
Owner-cultivator (0.5 ha.)	50.0
Owner-cultivator (0.2 ha.)	25.0
Sharecropper (0.2 ha.)	12.5
Garden cultivation	25.0
Agricultural wage labor	
Plowing (own draft animals)	70–90
Hoeing	9–11
Transplanting	6–7
Weeding	9–11
Harvesting	16–20
Nonagricultural wage labor	
Carrying/construction	10.0
Crafts (carpentry)	15.0
Weaving	7.0
Trade	
Women on foot (rp. 1,000 capital)	5–10
Men on foot (rp. 1,000 capital)	15.0
Men on bicycles (rp. 15,000 capital)	20.0
Preparation of food for sale	
Coconut sugar (own trees)	5–6
Coconut sugar (sharecrop)	2.5–3.0
Fried cassava	3.5
Fermented soybeans	5.0
Animal husbandry	
Ducks	5–12
Goats	1–2
Cattle	4–6
Goats/cattle (sharecrop)	2–3
Handicrafts	
Pandanus leaf hats	1.5
Bamboo mats	3.0

Source: Nag, White, and Peet 1978:298.

hourly incomes from most crafts and trades by a significant margin (table 2.5). Contract plowing, because of the capital invested in the implement and draft animals, gave a better return than plowing by an owner/cultivator, but it and the various paid agricultural jobs were seasonally defined and limited in duration. Extremely high population densities resulted not in rural unemployment or underemployment but in very low economic returns to labor (Nag, White, and Peet 1978).

In a Javanese community relying on wet rice and fish ponds, a household of five must control at least 0.5 ha. of double-cropped fields to attain an adequate level of income and 0.2 ha. to meet family rice consumption alone (Hart 1980). Fifty percent of the population do not own any productive assets at all. Richer households in Class I can

Table 2.6. *Household patterns of labor allocation in a Javanese village*

	Average annual hours and percentages per "worker unit"[a]					
	Class I (+0.5 ha. rice or fishpond)		Class II (0.2–0.5 ha. rice)		Class III (<0.2 ha. rice or landless)	
Own production (rice, fishponds, gardens, livestock)	1,048.4	(55.4%)	431.9	(21.4%)	92.9	(4.3%)
Wage labor	151.9	(8.0%)	770.9	(38.2%)	1,289.0	(59.7%)
Trading	169.6	(9.0%)	123.1	(6.1%)	73.7	(3.4%)
Fishing and gathering	26.0	(1.4%)	252.7	(12.5%)	314.6	(14.6%)
Housework[b]	497.5	(26.3%)	437.4	(21.7%)	389.7	(18.0%)
Total work	1,893.4	(100%)	2.016.0	(100%)	2.159.9	(100%)

[a]Persons aged ten and over.
[b]Excluding child care.

therefore devote a high proportion of their time to farming their own land, which brings higher returns (table 2.6). The poor in Class III must settle for the lower returns of wage labor and the marginal payoff of fishing and gathering. Richer women can devote more time to housework than can the poor (Hart 1980:204). In a society where intensive cultivation and aquaculture mean high labor demands for all landholders, those with inadequate land must put in even more hours per year for smaller and less reliable returns, and they are more dependent on market relations with others. Despite an amazing degree of intensification and the famous ethic of shared poverty (Geertz 1963), a significant portion of the population are forced to accept more arduous labor and definitively lower standards of living (Alexander and Alexander 1982).

Wage labor may also vary inversely with the opportunity to sell intensively produced agricultural goods. Hausa rural communities close to urban markets can concentrate on irrigated vegetable production during the five-month dry season, while two-thirds of all men from more remote villages must accept the lower returns of migrant labor (Goddard et al. 1975; Goddard 1972; Norman 1977).

Cottage industry in Europe sprang up in communities with relatively dense population, and its low investment needs (for spinning wheels, looms, knitting frames) and potential for absorbing the year-round labor of men, women, and children further stimulated demographic growth

(Hoskins 1957; Thompson 1963; Levine 1977). Swiss village weavers were enabled to marry early, build houses, and contribute to a population explosion, but farmers delayed marriage or remained celibate to keep the peasant holding intact (Braun 1978; Netting 1981). Agricultural intensification and specialized occupations are not necessarily alternatives; both can be simultaneously evident as "high pressure solutions to ecological difficulties" (Wrigley, cited in Skipp 1978) in a single region.

What we see (if we can tolerate, for the moment, a heretical oversimplification) in the market economies of premodern Europe and contemporary peasant Asia is less a qualitative, market-dominated break from a past of self-sufficient little communities than a larger arena in which population growth, technological change, and declining returns to labor (as reflected in the prices of food and land, and in wages) form systems of exchange involving wider geographic areas and implicating a great variety of nonagricultural economic activities.

LAND TENURE AND OTHER PROPERTIES (PRIVATE) OF INTENSIVE AGRICULTURE

Our preoccupation with the market economy and the state, added to an ingrained, unilinear, and categorical model of evolutionary origins, persistently connects private property with civilization and ill-defined communal rights with everything that was earlier and more primitive (see also Lee, this volume). It is here that the logic of intensification – permanent use of scarce land, higher labor input by a resident household, the achievement of reliable sustained yields by investment in improvements, and competition to acquire, keep, and transmit such valuable resources – collides with a classification that lumps simple tools, kin-based polities, and small communities with presumed free access to resources and economic equality of members.

Shifting cultivators with larger reserves of virgin or fallow land may exercise only rights of household usufruct over currently growing crops, but it is now abundantly clear that intensive agriculturalists claim well-defined, heritable property rights in land, water, trees, domestic animals, fences, barns, in short, in an entire agricultural enterprise. The property complex occurs at every political level from autonomous village through chiefdom, state, and empire. Ownership is present, and defended, even when market sale is not possible and permanent

46

alienation of land outside the group of rightful claimants is unimaginable. The institution grows gradually as an integral social aspect of intensification and the population increase that makes resources scarce. "The attachment of individual families to particular plots becomes more and more important, with the gradual shortening of fallow and the reduction of the part of the territory . . . not used in rotation" (Boserup 1965:81). Individual occupation of forest land on the frontier, easy movement (as among Iban shifting cultivators of Sarawak) to a new longhouse community where land is available for the asking (Freeman 1955), or periodic reallocation of the arable land among Russian village peasants (Robinson 1932) is rapidly ruled out when vacant land fills up. And this process of possession does not require a legal revolution or governmental fiat.

Land tenure in stateless societies of intensive cultivators is important and well defined. Fields have permanent, marked boundaries, and trespass or use without the owner's consent can occasion fights and litigation. There must be legitimate ways of gaining access to land, either temporarily by loan, lease, or pawn, or permanently through inheritance, transfer between kin, or sale. Whenever land is brought into regular annual use by invested labor (as in heavy, specialized fertilization, terracing, leveling, or irrigation), or when it can produce consistent crops of grain, fruit, nuts, or hay because of special conditions of soil or moisture, there will be a system of enduring claims by households or individuals (Netting 1976).

A controlled cross-cultural comparison of fifteen ethnic groups in the New Guinea highlands supports the association of higher population density with greater agricultural intensity and more individual land tenure (Brown and Podolefsky 1976). Intensive cultivation of sweet potatoes in this area makes use of fencing, drainage ditches, erosion control, and fertilizing. The closest correlation is between land tenure and the length of the fallow period. "All cases of . . . individual tenure are in societies where agriculture is permanent or fallow is less than six years; group tenure . . . is found with longer fallow periods. While group territory is recognized nearly everywhere, individual plots are held and inherited mainly where the fallow period is short and trees or shrubs are planted by the owner" (Brown and Podolefsky 1976:221). Indeed, if land-use is a major factor in determining land tenure (Netting 1976; 1982a), then we would expect to find contrasting bundles of rights within the same community, according to whether the land is unused wasteland, used extensively for rough grazing or at long intervals for shifting cultivation, or farmed under a permanent, intensive regime. For the Bontoc Igorot of Northern Luzon, village members claim only usufruct rights in long-fallow sweet potato lands, but irrigated rice terraces are individually owned by men and women, and inherited along with heirloom wealth objects under strict rules of bilateral primogeniture (Drucker 1977).

Even without an open market in land, differences in size and productivity of landholdings, in the value of surplus crops that can be exchanged, and in the domestic animals will necessarily differentiate households. As Flannery et al. (1967) pointed out for Oaxacan cultivators, the most fertile alluvial lands with the high water table allowing pot irrigation are more equitably distributed than the higher, drier land requiring investment in extensive canals. Uneven rates of reproduction may mean that one family has to divide its plots among several children, but another with fewer offspring can keep a holding intact. Where energy, skill, household labor, and good luck can be translated into leased or purchased land, it is possible for a family to add to its property over the developmental cycle, going from the small farm of a young couple to a large holding worked by the married sons of a patriarch (Chayanov 1966; Bennett 1969; Greenhalgh 1985; Eder 1982).

The possession of valued property under intensive use, the chance demographic fluctuations leading to differential inheritance, and the rewards for effective management and labor mean that communities practicing intensive agriculture will have inherent, internal inequality of resources and wealth. Kofyar traditional subsistence cultivator households differed substantially on an index of staple crops produced and domestic livestock owned. The Gini index of inequality (0 = all households equal, 1 = one household monopolized total wealth) shows village regions with the highest levels of inequality (0.414 as compared to 0.217) coincide with the most densely populated areas, suggesting that scarcer farm land is less equitably distributed, even when there are no landless households and little market exchange (Stone et al. 1984). Gini indices calculated on taxable real estate for an "egalitarian" Swiss alpine peasant community in the nineteenth and early twentieth century range from 0.340 to 0.487, reflecting appreciable wealth inequality, though less than in a medieval French community (0.619) or the United States in 1962 (0.660 [McGuire and Netting 1982]). It is inappropriate to regard stateless societies of cultivators or relatively

48

autonomous corporate communities of peasant proprietors as having fixed class division. There is in both cases considerable mobility up and down the ladder of relative wealth in the course of individual household life cycles, and from one generation to the next. But the nature of intensive agriculture is to differentiate and crystallize property rights, and to promote continuity in land use and labor investment over a period of time. Critical resources cannot help but be objects of competition, and at any point in time they are likely to be unequally distributed.

Ifugao intensive cultivators in the mountains of Luzon exercise private property rights in rice terraces and woodlots, although their legal system of inheritance, mortgage, and sale is not enforced by any centralized polity. The Ifugao assume that resources, goods, and services are distributed unequally, that individuals occupy ranked statuses, and that modifications in wealth and property control can be achieved by skilled long-range calculation and competitive action (Conklin 1980:36).

The portrayal of the individual farmer as making independent agricultural decisions, coping with scarcity and inequality, and strategizing to raise his rank sounds suspiciously like Economic Man with a bourgeois capitalist view of reality. But private property, inequality, and competition are too pervasive and structurally intrinsic among intensive cultivators to be credited solely to the external influences of the state, the market, or the dominant class. As long, however, as the community maintains a relative autonomy from more inclusive political organizations, and continues to be responsible for its own basic subsistence, inequality will be expressed as ranking with the possibility of internal mobility, as opposed to the polarization that decisively divides landless from landed, or farming commoners from specialized nonfarmer chiefs or aristocrats.

The clouds of confusion and mystification that still swirl through our discussions of the evolutionary significance of communal versus private property and equality versus stratification or polarization arise from speculative assumptions that long ago condensed into an ideological fog. The philosophers of the Enlightenment and the classical evolutionists were concerned both to postulate origins for modern civilization and to set up simple dichotomies with moral overtones. Thus, stone–bronze–iron showed technological progress; communally shared resources followed by individual property rights showed the achievement of political order and law, or the triumph of greed and exploitation over noble savagery; egalitarian communities preceding stratified hierarchical states showed the development of complexity, the division of labor, and the state, or they revealed the course of tyranny, unequal accumulation, and exploitation. Such issues were more stimulating than ethnographic cases and less mundane than the barely discerned facts of land-use, the social organization of production, and demography.

I would argue that the rudimentary contents of Morgan's ethnical periods still flavor our notions of land tenure conceived as a set of evolving ideas. Marx believed that "in the most primitive communities work is carried out in common, and the common product, apart from that portion set aside for reproduction, is shared out according to current need" (Engels 1884, quoting Marx's letter to Vera Zasulich, as cited in Meillassoux 1972:145). Though the statements might loosely fit hunter-gatherers, they seem to be based not on anthropological evidence but on an *a priori* formulation of an original human condition. For Morgan, the more intensive cultivation of plants in the period of Barbarism created a new species of property in family gardens, with "possessory right" in a portion of tribal land belonging to the individual or family, and the first inheritance rule enjoining the transmission of this right within the *gens* or unilineal kin group (Service 1985:204). Neither Marx nor Engels devoted much concern to the postulated primitive communal societies, and Marx knew little about prehistory, pre-Colombian America, or Africa (Hobsbawm 1964:26). Their discussions of land tenure were grounded more firmly on Greek and Latin sources, histories of the Orient, and materials of Germanic law and politics.

None of the precapitalist economic formations that Marx (1964 [1857–58]) treated in detail were strictly communal. The Oriental form involved only communal property, but it included private possession that might be hereditary. Marx learned from Maine's lectures of 1875 that the Oriental village remained a collectivity though under the dominance of the state (Krader 1979). The Germanic form distinguished between community and private land. Engels traced this change in communistic household communities to the increasing pressure of population on land resources and the lack of sufficient territory to sustain shifting cultivation. Disputes over land interfered with the common economy. But only certain resources became private. "The arable and meadowlands which had hitherto been common were

50

divided in the manner familiar to us, first temporarily and then permanently among the single households that were now coming into being, while forest, pasture land, and water remained common" (Engels 1972 [1884]:202). The pattern of grazing and forest commons side by side with individualized, continuing rights in grainfields, gardens, meadows, vineyards, and orchards has indeed been widespread in rural Europe, but it reflects the different functions of intensive and extensive land-use (Netting 1976), a contrast that Engels suggests, but does not analyze. Marx's (1964 [1857–58]:75) Ancient form was that of the city state where all land was held as the private property of citizens. The city's kinship groups are organized along military lines, and war is "the great communal labor" (Marx 1964 [1857–58]:72).

The approach to land tenure taken by Marx and Engels represents an attempt to establish valid social scientific comparisons using evolutionary (though not unilineal) categories, historical evidence, and a functional, systemic orientation. It rightly points up the variety of tenure types and relates them to conditions of social group membership, political structure, citizenship, labor organization, and war. Except for Engels's passing comments, landholding is not related to agriculture or population. But Marx's analysis is considerably more sophisticated than Morgan's concept of the controlling idea of property that led mankind "to establish political society on the basis of territory and of property" (Morgan 1963 [1877]:6). The unfortunate legacy of Morgan, Maine, and Marx has been a persisting focus on the corporate aspects of the lineage, the clan, and the community that are assumed to imply collective work in agricultural production, communal rights in resources, and the consequent equality or economic leveling of group members.

Paradoxically, it has been social anthropology's success in taking the "native's point of view" and shaping models that are culturally acceptable to the subjects that has obscured the difference between these generic, ideal statements and behavior. Radcliffe-Brown's generalization that descent group corporateness rested in joint control of an estate – persons, things, territory – has persuaded anthropologists to expect that the lineages their informants describe will control and inherit property. (The kernel of the idea is Morgan's, though wrapped in the husk of Radcliffe-Brown's legalistic terminology.) Furthermore, in acephalous sedentary societies, it is assumed that the kin group will be the dominant social institution, exemplifying a kinship mode of produc-

51

tion (Wolf 1982b). I have suggested that descent groups are seldom cooperative labor units, and that, as agriculture intensifies, they may diminish in economic importance as compared to households, exchange groups, and neighborhood work parties. It may also be misleading to conceive of a unilineal descent group as always corporately based on a joint estate of productive property (Whiteley 1985).

Hopi terraced gardens, vegetable plots, fruit tree orchards, and livestock were personal and not matrilineal clan or lineage property. Clans did, however, control blocks of alluvial corn lands, some of which could be more regularly flooded and produce more dependable yields than others (Bradfield 1971). Annual variations in rainfall promoted the utility of reallocating land among members of the same clan, but good, easily accessible land was sufficiently scarce that well-defined clan property rights reflected major inequality among clans in productive resources. Farming continued to be carried on by individual households while the corporate kin group remained an effective means for both defending and internally sharing rights to important but less predictable resources. While scarce, intensively cultivated resources were held and inherited by individuals, rights to more extensively farmed corn lands were protected by the corporate unilineal descent group as part of its key role in social, religious, and political life (cf. Whiteley 1985). What we see is an incongruence between the individualized ownership and inheritance of rights to scarce, intensively farmed resources, and the central ideological role of the corporate unilineal descent group in social, religious, and political life.

Does the relative uninvolvement of the Hopi clan in direct production mean that, as Fortes (1969) asserted so vehemently, descent group organization is always *sui generis* and cannot be "reduced" to economics or ecology or property? In fact, corporate groups of kin do allocate, protect, and appropriate land and other agricultural resources, but they do so most effectively under conditions of middle-range population density and local competition for land. Unilineal descent group membership is exclusive, lifelong, and unambiguous, and it carries specified rights and duties. Where rights to resources must be claimed and defended, especially where new land must be occupied or fallow reserves defended and periodically redivided, the descent group can effectively mobilize relations beyond the household. Expanding shifting cultivators can use acephalous segmentary lineage organization in just this manner (Sahlins 1961).

Population, permanent agriculture, and polities

Critics of Boserup have often pointed out that intensification may be a secondary response to population pressure. They claim that she ignores the frequency of constant extension of cultivation into unsettled areas in periods of demographic growth and the abandonment of agricultural land when population declines (Grigg 1979:73). She does admit that "the first spontaneous reaction of tribal or peasant families to population growth within their community is to look for additional land to cultivate by the traditional methods" (Boserup 1970:101). Environmental or social circumscription (Carniero 1970) may prevent free access to more such open territory, and under these circumstances, a corporate group of kin with a geographical base and shared interests in agricultural resources would be a ready-made support system for arguing claims, engaging in legal disputes, and resorting to force, either within or outside of the society.

The localized lineage segments of the Nigerian Tiv have chronic border arguments in which individuals extend their swidden farms, then call out their patrikin for acrimonious and lengthy debates on where the boundary should be. Because the outward push is characteristically directed against the most distantly related lineage or against a foreign ethnic group, a direction of massed movement is established, with each lineage losing land to its neighbors in the rear and gaining ground in front (Bohannan 1954; Sahlins 1961). Lacking the permanent political centralization of a paramount chief, the Tiv may rearrange their genealogies to bring the idealized segmentary structure of kinship reflecting proximity in line with the less regular movements of lineages over the land (Bohannan 1952). Fighting for forest fallow as an alternative to the demanding intensification of agriculture may require more coordination and central direction than segmentary, fissiparous lineages can give. This may have been the case when the Maori chiefdoms carried on a vigorous internecine warfare of conquest and expulsion (Vayda 1961).

Solidifying unilineal descent group protection of property may remain a significant social strategy as groups settle more permanently and build up collective rights in land or other durable goods (Forde 1947:70). Meggitt (1965) found that areas of land shortage among the Mae-Enga of highland Papua New Guinea positively correlated with patrilineal organization or patrilocality. As a single Tsembaga Maring kin group of shifting cultivators went from low to higher population density, it first granted land rights in the abundant resource to a wide

53

variety of bilateral relatives, and then narrowed land-use and inheritance to the more rigidly defined patrilineage as the supply of open land declined and conflicts over farms and pigs increased (Rappaport 1968:27–28). As resource competition escalates, a corporate descent group can both reduce conflict for land among its members and secure cooperation beyond the household and the settlement for defensive and predatory operations (Harner 1970). Whereas Mae Enga household and local groups of patrikin respond to subsistence problems and food procurement needs, the larger subclan and clan units cope with external relationships of warfare, defense, alliance, and exchange (Johnson and Earle 1987:177–83). Both corporate kin groups and larger, labor-mobilizing family households may be most prevalent at intermediate population levels. When virgin land is plentiful, Kekchi shifting cultivators in the tropical forest of Belize gather as neolocal nuclear families in small villages (Wilk 1984). Adult males form a communal labor group to clear, fence, and plant a single cornfield near the settlement. At higher human/land ratios, multiple family patrilocal household clusters intensify their agriculture with dry season river-levee corn, more complex labor schedules, and pigs for market. Household-based organization of labor, authority, economic pooling, and solidarity in village politics respond to a situation of declining local resources (Wilk 1984).

PRODUCTION OR PROTECTION? POPULATION DENSITY AND THE PURPOSES OF POLITY

As a purported contribution to a book on the development of political systems, this chapter has so far had almost nothing to say about political institutions. It is not that the topic has slipped my mind. Rather it now seems to me vital to break the evolutionary lock-step and to disengage the elements that *are* firmly linked in systems of change – population density, agricultural intensification, returns to labor, household and work group organization, land tenure, and intra-community economic inequality – from those that are less or *not at all* functionally related to the local human/land complex. I refer to supra-community political organization, centralized authority, specialized political roles, and hierarchies of power, wealth, and status.

I once believed (and still do not completely disown) the idea that in every priest-chief or big-man of a stateless society, there was the germ of chieftainship, needing only the population-generated pressures for dispute settlement, trade extension, and psychological reassurance in environmental crisis to bring it to political flower (Netting 1972). I am now ready to contend with equal fervor that the problems of demographic density and technological change in cultivation can be ameliorated, if not solved, by actions of individual farm households in autonomous little communities. Political leadership of more than ad hoc, transitory character could neither initiate nor compel intensification, and conversely, chiefdoms could emerge where populations were low and resources were not in short supply (Fortes and Evans-Pritchard 1940; Goody 1977; Shipton 1984).

The political level that is salient for my purposes is that of the chiefdom, "an autonomous political unit comprising a number of villages or communities under the permanent control of a paramount chief" (Carniero 1981:45). I accept Carniero's qualitative distinction between single, relatively small, independent tribal communities, and the chiefdoms and states with markedly higher institutional complexity and two or more levels of political organization.

Impressive irrigation systems, once seen from the perspective of Wittfogel as proof presumptive of the connection between intensive agriculture and governmental control of labor and livelihood, are now perceived to begin as cellular local growths (Gray 1963), and they may remain encysted in the state but independent of it (Geertz 1972; Netting 1974a). Allocation of water and routine maintenance continue in the hands of local social organization, even when massive construction and conflict resolution are taken over by centralized government (Hunt and Hunt 1976). Intervillage cooperation in irrigation does not presuppose central administration, and systems involving high capital investment or large-scale engineering seem to have followed from the prior existence of a state rather than contributing to its formation (Spooner 1974; Wolf and Palerm 1955). On the other hand, there is no evidence that some high population density threshold must be passed to enable a chiefdom to exist (cf. Stevenson 1968). Chiefdoms occur in conjunction with intensive agriculture, with shifting cultivation, and even occasionally with locally abundant and reliable wild foods (Carniero 1981:49). An economic ranking "in which members of the same sex and equivalent age status do not have equal access to the basic resources that sustain life" (Fried 1967:186) is usually attributed to chiefdoms, but

55

such differentiation is also present among acephalous-community intensive cultivators, as I have previously indicated.

The distribution of traditional polities in East Africa gives some support to the concept that chiefdoms with territorially defined political and landholding groups were commonly found in areas of low population density and that descent-based lineage systems occupied regions of higher population pressure (Shipton 1984). All these peoples cultivated cereals and herded cattle in similar environments. In areas where chiefs were dominant, they claimed ownership of plentiful land resources and competed with each other to attract as subjects shifting cultivators who moved frequently and did not ordinarily establish heritable property rights. In descent-group societies, on the other hand, land was inherited from agnates, and there were elaborate systems of land clientage for those who could not obtain adequate holdings. Land shortage encouraged sons to stay, after marriage, on or near the land of their fathers and paternal kin. European colonial appropriation of land in Kenya and the territorial confinement of Gusii and Luo peoples has fostered local crowding and the tightening of segmentary lineage control over land (Shipton 1984:621). Similarly, in Nyakyusa chiefdoms with residential mobility, growing population density forced families to sit tight on their lands, defend their inherited titles on the basis of descent, and resist reallocation by village headmen. Political *de*-centralization took place under population pressure.

Shipton (1984:626) extended his model to the whole of Africa, claiming that the vast majority of societies with kingdom or chiefdom organization had low densities (averaging below about 40 per mi.[2] in the mid twentieth century) and that the highest mean densities (200 to over 1,000 per mi.[2]) were found in societies with no important permanent hierarchical offices. He qualified this simple opposition by pointing to a high-density threshold that may induce "the hardening of individual rights of ownership and transfer" as against lineage control, raising the question of the declining corporate functions of the descent group. Dense populations may undermine the ability of the unilineal descent group to provide adequate land to all its members. In the most crowded Igbo regions of Nigeria, corporate lineages no longer allocate usufruct rights in land, large compound households disintegrate, and individual families take up residence on dispersed, intensively tilled, heritable plots (Udo 1965; Netting 1969).

If a chiefly political organization does not contribute positively to the

56

maintenance, productivity, or technology of an agricultural system, how then does it benefit cultivators? Is centralization an adventitious or a parasitic growth of the body politic? There are some suggestions that multi-village political aggregates are superior instruments of military defense and expansionist warfare. A permanent alliance of villages under unified authority provides protection, and community units may sacrifice local sovereignty and a degree of economic independence for this immediate, possibly crucial, goal. "In agricultural groups the primary cause of organizational elaboration appears to be defensive needs" (Johnson and Earle 1987:158).

Steward's (1948:2–3) original description of the Circum-Caribbean tribes' chiefly organization mentioned large villages surrounded by palisades, and Oberg (1955:484) discussed the paramount chief's power to requisition men and supplies for war (cited by Carniero 1981). It is possible that widely dispersed shifting cultivators are especially vulnerable to outside attack, especially by a military force with leadership more inclusive than one based on ties of kinship or locality. But any effort to concentrate population and build defenses would demand the investment of farmers' time and increased travel and transport to distant farms. Physical relocation, military service, and tribute payments would all *decrease* agricultural efficiency, especially for intensive cultivators with high-value fixed property. Thus, the economic costs of voluntary incorporation into a chiefdom would be considerable. Perhaps only the threat of warfare and destruction would justify the economic advantages foregone.

We should not assume that warfare is absent or infrequent among dense populations of intensive cultivators. Indeed the competition for space and the potential for trespass, theft, and interpersonal conflict might well increase with pressure on resources. In autonomous, roughly equivalent communities, however, fighting may well be episodic and fitful, directed at a variety of neighboring villages and without permanent coalitions or effective conquest (Netting 1973, 1974b).

It is apparent that effective military mobilization of multi-village forces with permanent leadership and at least a rudimentary command hierarchy can usually defeat localized villages or massed segmentary lineages (Sahlins 1961; Gluckman 1960). The benefits of voluntarily joining a new political order that was successful in war and impressive in ritual, regalia, and accumulated wealth must have been obvious. Natural disasters may have further precipitated such decisions. Lineage traditions of groups joining East African chiefdoms often refer to a time of severe dislocation when they were forced to leave their homes following a major drought or famine, or after fighting with an enemy against whom they needed assistance or protection (Atkinson 1976). The decisions involved security considerations, and they may have been neutral or even detrimental to local agricultural production.

There is no reason why centralization could not in some cases have grown spontaneously from within a densely settled region of sedentary intensive agriculturalists, as feuding took on a more severe and predatory aspect or as unequal rights to local resources and trade goods differentiated a self-perpetuating elite. Fertile, well-watered plains or alluvial valleys may have fostered such development, allowing warfare to spread rapidly with no natural barriers. Evenly dispersed intensive agri-cultural homesteads would be deserted under such circumstances, and refugee populations might retreat to nucleated settlements that could be fortified. There are hints of such defensive coagulation in Madagascar (Kottak 1980) and ancient Uruk (Adams and Nissen 1972:21), as well as in Hastorf's Mantaro Valley (this volume). Mountainous habitats, on the other hand, supply natural defenses against easy invasion and protection from extortionate demands for tribute. Steep and sterile rocky areas or forests limit surplus production at the same time they make extraction of this surplus by outsiders difficult and expensive. It is no wonder that our contemporary examples of dense, intensive cultivators in acephalous polities are usually hill-dwellers. Mountains may not determine freedom, but they make it easier to maintain.

There are indeed ethnographic cases where the logic of permanent intensive agriculture in the context of dense sedentary populations has seemingly militated against the emergence of the state. The Gamo of the south-central Ethiopian highlands achieve densities of 550 to 2,600 per mi.[2] with the cultivation of *ensete* gardens, barley, cabbage, chickpeas, and potatoes on manured terraces around their dispersed homesteads (Abeles 1981). Citizen farmers own and will land to specific heirs (Olmstead 1975); non-citizen dependent artisan castes are present, and there is an active regional market network. Endemic warfare did not result in conquest and expulsion of resident farmers. Political power in the past was divided among local assemblies, elected dignitaries, and hereditary priests. As Abeles (1981:38) points out, the implicit assump-tions of Marxists, as well as many others, of inevitable movement from segmentary society to a chieftaincy or kingly state are not supported by the evidence.

58

Political centralization, valuable as it may be for organizing territorial defense and promoting regional exchange, does not appear to be directly implicated in the efficient functioning of intensive agriculture under conditions of rural demographic pressure. In fact, attempts to control and standardize the type of agricultural regime, the specific crops planted, the timing of agricultural activities, and the amount of labor applied can directly interfere with the individual cultivator's need to deal flexibly with a particular micro-environmental situation and a distinctive changing mix of resources. The adaptive variability of smallholder ecological and economic decision-making is threatened by close bureaucratic supervision or rigid norms imposed by nonfarmers (Bayliss-Smith 1982). Heavy tribute or taxes may reduce the farmer's incentive to invest the extra labor and develop the expertise that brings higher production from a limited land base. Under such circumstances peasants can and do cut back surpluses. Governmental interference in markets or restraints on producer prices may also cause farmers to retreat to subsistence. Demands for corvee labor or military service can disrupt agricultural scheduling. Nucleated settlement patterns that promote group defense and efficient political administration increase travel time to intensively tilled land and make the careful, integrated management and guarding of mixed crops, orchards, and irrigated gardens more difficult. Population pressure and its associated intensive agricultural regime increases the probability that effective economic control of the land and labor will remain in the hands of the cultivator, and that the local community of farmers will retain some autonomy in the management of resources. Political centralization is not a functional necessity of such an agro-ecosystem.

INTENTIONALLY GROUNDING PREHISTORY

A mixed bag (or a midden) of ethnographic observations does not necessarily an evolutionary paradigm make. What does it mean for archaeology? How does the rearranged portmanteau look? We may have grounds for a few, albeit provisional, suggestions:

1. Firm indications of sustained rural population densities above approximately 150 to 250 per mi.[2] suggest the likelihood of intensive agricultural systems.

2. Similarly, the widespread appearance of pre-industrial techniques

such as terracing, specialized tillage (soil turned, elaborately mounded, ridged, or leveled), multicropping, fertilization, drainage, or irrigation points to the presence of a dense, permanent, sedentary population.

3.   Direct and indirect labor requirements of intensive farming systems are likely to be consistently higher than those of shifting cultivation, pastoralism, or foraging. More person-days per year and a more regular application of labor are directly correlated with intensification, even when efficiency (returns per person-hour) is stable or even rising slightly.

4.   The major social unit of production and consumption in intensive agriculture is the family household, including children, women, and men, in which work effort, disciplined cooperation, and effective management receive the direct incentive of higher and more sustained material production. Corporate unilineal descent groups are not usually production or shared communal consumption groups, though they may function to secure and defend resources.

5.   Rights in intensively utilized agricultural resources reside largely in the individual and household, where they are treated as jurally recognized and inherited property. These rights in the means of production are jealously guarded, and, in a market economy, they may take on high economic value. Differential inheritance, farming skills, stage in the life cycle, demographic chance factors, and external sociopolitical demands contribute to local inequality in the distribution of productive resources.

6.   Those with inadequate access to agricultural resources may derive income from cottage industry, crafts, trade, or wage work, but these full-time or part-time rural specializations provide a poorer and less secure livelihood than that of a farmer/owner.

7.   Intensive agriculture with conditions of dense population exists under a variety of different polities. Political centralization under a chiefdom or state regime contributes little directly to the organization of production, though government's roles in military and defensive activities, enforcing tributary obligations, and promoting regional market exchange affect the farm household. Population density and centralization do not vary dependently in a uniform manner, and chiefdoms may occur with sparser populations than those of lineage-based societies.

60

Evidence of intensive agriculture is therefore not diagnostic of the presence of supra-local polities.

NOTES

An earlier version of this chapter under the title "Population Pressure and Intensification: Some Anthropological Reflections on Malthus, Marx, and Boserup" was prepared for the symposium *Anthropological Demography* convened by Nancy Howell and Eugene Hammel at the 1985 annual meetings of the American Anthropological Association. I was able to rewrite and expand the draft during a year as a Fellow at the Center for Advanced Study in Behavioral Sciences, Stanford, California. I gratefully acknowledge the assistance of the Center staff, especially the valuable editorial advice of Kathleen Much. Financial support came from a University of Arizona sabbatical leave and National Science Foundation grant BNS 84–11738 to the Center. The helpful comments of Michael Mortimore and Jerrold Levy enabled me to eliminate some errors of interpretation and fact in the text. The necessary pruning of an overlong manuscript was done by the volume editor with a deftness and tact that I appreciate.
1. If the intensification process starts food production increasing at a higher rate than population growth, nutritional stress may be at least temporarily ameliorated. This process may, in turn, promote lower incidence of infectious disease in childhood, more individuals reaching reproductive age, and rapid demographic growth, such as that observed in the Guatemalan highlands (Scholl et al. 1976).
2. Following the nonintensive agriculture of the Nubian A and C Groups, Meroe and the following cultures intensified the use of the Nile Valley with three annual growing seasons, water wheel irrigation, and tree crops. Skeletal remains from this period show a pattern of nutritional deficiency in long bone growth indicating developmental stress in subadults. There is also evidence of porotic hyperostosis, dental caries and enamel microdefects, and premature osteoporosis in response to protein–calorie malnutrition (Martin et al. 1984).

Selection and evolution in nonhierarchical organization

DAVID P. BRAUN

Northern Arizona University

This chapter addresses several issues in the study of nonhierarchical communities. In particular, what is the nature of causality and constraint in shaping the social history of such communities? Are there cross-cultural limits or central tendencies evident in nonhierarchical organization? How do people living in nonhierarchically organized communities experience and generate or resist change in their ways of life?

The first part of this chapter introduces my central themes and presents some background information. The second summarizes "adaptationist" perspectives on the nature of nonhierarchical organization. The third discusses critiques of adaptationist anthropology, including so-called "epigenetic" (e.g., Friedman and Rowlands 1978) or "generative" (e.g., Ellen 1982) critiques arising in a Marxist tradition of anthropology. The fourth outlines a "selectionist" approach to the questions raised in my opening remarks, which subsumes the strong points of both the adaptationist and generative perspectives.

Two interpretive programs presently dominate anthropological discussions of nonhierarchical social variation. On the one hand, we have a functional-holistic and adaptationist program. This position emphasizes the role of social practices in promoting and maintaining group survival in the face of ecosystemic risks and opportunities, and in the face of competition from other groups (e.g., Braun and Plog 1982). On the other hand, we have a program focusing more on social dialectics. This alternative emphasizes the role of strategies pursued by individuals, households, and descent groups to establish or maintain themselves socially in their mutual interactions. We then view the patterns of social practices in a region as consequences of the interplay of such strategies, not necessarily as manifestations of any group adaptation (e.g., Kristiansen 1984; Bender 1985a, 1985b). I have come to question both of these interpretive programs (see also Braun 1989).

My challenge here follows recent critiques of interpretive paradigms in evolutionary science (see reviews in Gould and Lewontin 1978; Gould 1982, 1986; Sober 1984); in ecological anthropology (e.g., Vayda and McKay 1975; Alland 1975; Winterhalder 1980; Kirch 1980; Ellen 1982; Moran 1984; Rindos 1984, 1985, 1986; Bargatsky 1984; Boyd and Richerson 1985); and in archaeology (e.g., Rowlands 1982; Dunnell 1986; Leonard and Jones 1987). Many of the contributors to the present volume have also influenced me. By "evolutionary science" I mean not the progressive evolutionism of much of American archaeology, but the historical science of, for example, neo-Darwinian paleobiology. It is the structure of historical science that interests me here, however, not the relationships between biological and cultural evolution. As Dunnell has most critically noted (1980, 1982, 1986), archaeology (and, by extension, all of cultural anthropology) presently lacks the structure and content of an evolutionary science. The influences of the works cited in this paragraph pervade my entire chapter, and I do not cite them further except to draw specific points.

We should approach social evolution as a matter of "descent with modification," to use Darwin's phrase. But by "descent" here I refer to sociocultural rather than biological descent. That is, we should analyze social evolution as a matter of continuity and change in the statistical popularity of different social practices over time among individual human communities. Social practices, broadly defined, are any actions that affect the flow of materials and information among people, that affect the extent of their competition or cooperation, that affect the ways in which decision-making takes place within groups, or that affect the persistence of groups. In this sense, a social practice is any action by one person or group that affects action on the part of others.

We can describe continuity and change in the popularity of different social practices in terms of two phenomena (e.g., Alland 1975; Kirch 1980). First, there always exists variation in the statistical popularity of different social practices at any given time among different interacting sets of people. These sets may be individuals, households, descent groups, villages, or larger arrangements. Second, there always exists a pattern of differential transmission of that variation over time. In some cases, a limited set of practices may prevail for a long period; in other cases, greatest popularity may shift from one set to another; in still others, the breadth of variation in practices may itself change. People may also adopt new practices or abandon old ones.

To understand social evolution, then, we must answer two questions: What generates the variation in social practices among interacting people? And what shapes the differential transmission of this variation? My critique of the dominant perspectives in anthropology rests upon their inadequacies for handling these two questions.

Framing our inquiry with these last questions has two important implications for how we study social variation and change. First, we do not have to think in terms of "societies" or other superorganic wholes, but only in terms of concrete, active entities we can define empirically at any one time, such as specific communities, groups, or individual people. The number and character of these entities also may change over time.

Second, we have to distinguish the processes that may generate variation from those that may shape change. Unfortunately, this also introduces the question of the time scale at which we can appropriately draw this distinction. Some variation comes in the form of fluctuations over time about some stable mean, either random or cyclical. The tribal ethnographic literature is rich with descriptions of household cycles, ritual cycles, big-man schemes, exchange cycles, and many political phenomena that all exhibit such fluctuation (e.g., Gearing 1962). Change, I would argue, is any difference in conditions between successive increments of time that persists in succeeding increments, that does not appear to reverse itself during the timespan studied. Change is nonreversible variation over time (see also Slobodkin and Rapoport 1974). Social evolution is transgenerational social change.

NONHIERARCHICAL SOCIAL ADAPTATION

Lewontin summarizes the basic elements of adaptationism as follows (1984:236):

> It is the concept that there exist certain "problems" to be "solved" by organisms and by societies and that the actual forms of biological and social organizations that we see in the world are "solutions" to these "problems."

Gould and Lewontin (1984) further identify two basic steps to adaptationist inference. First, the researcher isolates particular traits of form, function, or behavior in the entities being studied, and seeks to explain these as 'structures optimally designed by natural selection for their functions" (1984:256). Second, if a part-by-part interpretation fails to make sense of a given situation,

> interaction is acknowledged via the dictum that an organism [for us, any social entity] cannot optimize each part without imposing expenses on others. The notion of "trade-off" is introduced, and organisms [for us, different groups' social practices] are interpreted as best compromises among competing demands (1984:256).

Much of evolutionary anthropology follows this adaptationist program. The concept of natural selection, however, has not entered much into the modern social anthropological discourse.

Social organization as adaptation

Anthropology has a long history of efforts to interpret social organization as adaptation. Eggan, Evans-Pritchard, Flannery, Fried, Radcliffe-Brown, Rappaport, Sahlins, Service, Steward, and White are among the most familiar contributors to this history in our century. Prior to the 1970s this work was largely functional and holistic. Many recent works additionally treat adaptation as a process of problem-solving carried out by people in response to environmental challenges to their conditions of existence (e.g., Vayda and McKay 1975; Alland 1975; Kirch 1980; Winterhalder 1980; Jochim 1981; Moran 1982; Durham 1982; Moran 1984). Adaptation here is understood as a process in which people in a given historical setting encounter greater advantages or disadvantages from some courses of action than from others, and arrange their social strategies accordingly. I emphasize this more recent understanding in my summary here.

Adaptation presumably can occur in the cultural practices of any aggregate of people who consistently act together under particular kinds of circumstances. These aggregates may consist of households, various kin-based or nonkin-based associations, villages, or entire local communities according to historical circumstances. The cultural practices of interest to us are those that may affect the persistence, internal organization, or external patterns of interaction of the aggregates under study.

Adaptation and resource exploitation

All humans face problems of establishing and at least maintaining access to material resources for their biological survival and reproduction. Risks for individuals and groups arise in all physical environments, however. Resources can vary unpredictably in their availability over space and time as a result of geophysical and ecological conditions, and as a result of the actions of other humans on the landscape. Social adaptations, then, can be interpreted as parts of people's solutions to the problems of maintaining satisfactory levels of predictability in their efforts to obtain necessary resources.

We can view social relations in nonhierarchical communities in particular as networks of material transactions of varying intensity among individuals, households, and larger aggregates. The transactions also entail obligations, for example to cooperate in the acquisition of material needs or in the physical safeguarding of people's lives in general. We may then define a community's social organization as the organization of who has access to what resources (and who does not), who acts together to procure, process, or consume these resources (and who does not), and who comes to whose aid when resources are endangered or uncertain, or when conflicts arise (and who does not).

The resources handled foremost in such community organization are those of time, labor, matter/energy, and space – the standard topics of ecological anthropology (e.g., Jochim 1981). Recent work emphasizes that we should also include knowledge in this list of resources (Alland 1975; Moore 1981, 1983; Moran 1982). Not only do different individuals and groups continually accumulate differential knowledge about conditions on their immediate landscapes, but they may also come to hold diverse specialized knowledge of a more enduring or traditional form. The various kinds of knowledge held by different members of a community constitute potential resources for themselves and for others.

In the adaptationist view, people respond to resource problems by developing and maintaining beneficial relationships with each other. These relationships make it possible for people to look to each other for help when they are unable to help themselves. This is the concept of the social "safety net," or of "generalized reciprocity," that pervades the adaptationist literature on nonhierarchical communities. It boils down to the notion that people in such communities treat *each other* as resources to help themselves get by.

Resources, of course, can be overexploited, and all social relationships are susceptible to inequality. Someone can always try to take too much and/or give too little.

As others in this volume discuss in greater detail, however, nonhierarchical communities are, precisely, communities in which there are limits to just how unequal people can be. These limits come in two main forms. First, exchanges of material, labor, or knowledge entail obligations to reciprocate, even if the time of this reciprocation is left open. This notion of mutual indebtedness pervades community moral codes, and violators lose prestige and the support of their neighbors (e.g., Sahlins 1972:149–83). Second, people do not allow prestige acquired in one sphere of activities to carry over into any other sphere. For example, prestige acquired through generous gift-giving may not increase a person's political authority. Yet to sustain a leadership role, a person must be more generous than others (e.g., Douglas 1967, cited in Rowlands 1982; Netting this volume; Trigger this volume). These limits are people's solutions to the problems of needing each other as resources, but not wanting anyone to overexploit anyone else.

Competition, cooperation, and adaptation

People may be potential resources for each other in nonhierarchical communities, but they may also be potential competitors. People may find it more advantageous to seek exclusive control over a resource, rather than to share it, if that resource is both concentrated on the landscape and highly predictable in its availability over space and time (Dyson-Hudson and Smith 1978). Control and/or exclusion of others' access to material resources is, in fact, widely recorded in the tribal historic record, particularly under conditions of extreme variation in resource distribution or availability (e.g., Meggitt 1965; Kelly 1968; Minnis 1985:25–32).

Similarly, predatory behavior, which seeks out concentrations of resources created or held by others, can also be understood as a form of competition. Under specific conditions, such predation can confer at least short-term advantages for the predator in comparison to a strategy of sharing (e.g., Vayda 1961; see also Axelrod 1984). Even violent attacks on neighboring people are not uncommon among nonhierarchical communities. As Sahlins (1972:185–230) emphasizes, negative reciprocity is the outward face of many such communities.

In the adaptationist view, people in nonhierarchical communities treat cooperation and competition as social alternatives, weighing their possibilities against each other when deciding how best to exploit different resources at different times. Around core groups of people holding close solidarity with each other, the different social entities in any community thereby come to maintain varying degrees of cooperative and competitive adaptive relations with their neighbors. Additionally, cooperation (or competition) in one set of activities need not always entail cooperation (or competition) in all activities or at all times. Ethnographies regularly record such variation (e.g., Sahlins 1961, 1968; Suttles 1968; Rappaport 1968). We then recognize that the people of different communities at different times may achieve different balances between the extremes of "everyone for him/herself" and "everyone pulls together."

The sizes of social entities appear to figure importantly in this adaptive balancing. Households, clans, villages, and larger entities can change in size not only as a result of biological cycles, but also through social processes of fission and fusion, antagonism and alliance. From an adaptationist perspective, these changes presumably arise as people work out the opposing advantages versus disadvantages of inclusion versus exclusion in their given circumstances. (Netting, Plog, and Trigger, this volume, discuss this phenomenon more fully; see also Johnson 1978, 1982, 1983; and various papers in Lee and DeVore 1968; Wilk and Rathje 1982; Ember and Ember 1983; Netting, Wilk, and Arnould 1984.) The specific size modalities that evolve, and the specific factors taken into account in the balancing, differ from one case of presumed adaptation to the next.

Adaptation and consensus

Nonhierarchical organization is more than just a matter of resource transactions, however broadly defined. It is also a matter of how decisions about these transactions get made and coordinated among individuals, households, and other groupings (e.g., Moore 1981; Johnson 1982). And here, again, inferred adaptation appears to be a matter of balance. Effective cooperation in the use of resources brings with it a need to coordinate decision-making, so that the right information is brought to bear in the right place at the right time for the right people. Yet, as Johnson (1978, 1982) in particular shows, the efficiency and accuracy of decision-making always goes down, and the potentials for uncertainty and conflicts of interest always go up, the greater the number of people involved.

How, then, do people in nonhierarchical communities keep the potentials for uncertainty and conflicts of interest in check, and adjudicate conflicts when they arise? Johnson finds that the solutions to these problems largely involve the organization of people into groups of efficient sizes for decision-making purposes, which are themselves grouped into larger segments, and so forth. People can then arrive at consensus decisions in a stepwise manner, as needs arise, among successively larger groupings.

Households form the most basic level in this kind of nested social arrangement. For wider purposes, households can arrange themselves according to kinship, geography, or other criteria of association into larger entities, which in turn may ally themselves with each other in larger arrangements, and so forth. Such nested arrangements provide a structure of allegiance and interests within which people can develop consensus more efficiently, and within which conflicts of interest can be identified and resolved more easily (see also Sahlins 1961).

Johnson (1982) suggests calling the stepwise coordination of consensus "sequential hierarchy." This label draws a contrast to what he suggests calling "simultaneous hierarchy," the delegation of authority to some individuals to make decisions for others without waiting for their consensus. When we refer to some human communities as nonhierarchical, we have in mind the absence of this latter form of hierarchy. Yet some delegation of authority does occur in nonhierarchical communities. What, then, do we mean by "nonhierarchical"?

Adaptation and authority structures

In the adaptationist view, we can interpret the delegation of authority as a solution to a particular range of problems (Leeds 1969; Adams 1975;

Peebles and Kus 1977; Johnson 1978; Miller 1978). Delegating authority appears to increase the efficiency and speed with which people can make decisions, especially in situations in which they must sort quickly through a great quantity and diversity of information. Having someone responsible for holding all the lines together and reacting quickly is useful for such diverse tasks as conflict adjudication, task coordination, and negotiation with other parties. The leader fills a simplifying managerial office for everyone else. Also, the greater the number of people looking for a decision, the more effective delegated authority can be.

Delegating authority can bring mixed blessings, however. Accepting other people's decisions that affect one's own interests entails a loss of freedom of action. The "other people" comprise a minority whose interests may not coincide with a majority's in all situations. Thus, both consensual and authoritative decision-making can exacerbate conflicts of interest. The potential, perhaps, is even greater with delegated authority, for the conflicts would arise between a minority and a subordinate majority, rather than between a collective and some of its constituents.

We can characterize a community as nonhierarchical or not depending upon the manner in which the people "solve" this "problem" of potentials for conflict in decision-making. As noted earlier, and as others in this volume discuss more fully, nonhierarchical communities are ones in which people's actions and moral codes work against unequalness in any one sphere of life carrying over into any other. In our present discussion, this resistance means that authority in some sphere of activities does not give a person the right also to hoard the resources generated by those activities. Nor does authority in some sphere of activities give a person any command of resources with which to coerce action from others. Indeed, such links are resisted.

Social relations in nonhierarchical communities clearly do change, however, and in some instances have evolved into hierarchy and inequality. An adaptationist approach admits two basic models for how this latter transformation might initially occur, that is, for how inequality in authority and in access to resources could become linked. A group could solve problems of competition with its neighbors through conquest and dominance, thereby imposing hierarchy on a larger population (e.g., Carneiro 1970). Or, a group might voluntarily accept inequality as the cost of maintaining a subgroup of managerial special-

70

ists in return for the adaptive benefits of managerial organization (e.g., Peebles and Kus 1977; Johnson 1978). Johnson's work (see above) seems to suggest that group size will crucially affect the probability that people will attempt or sustain such managerial reorganization. I will return to this point.

Ideology, ritual, and adaptation

I have noted the interpretation that codes of morality and systems of knowledge contribute to adaptation in nonhierarchical communities. They are said to do so by reinforcing social conventions and by providing a continuity of traditional knowledge and belief that summarizes previous generations' experiences and wisdom. A broader view places belief, ritual, ritualized behavior, and patterns of communication and socialization together as crucial elements in the ways communities perpetuate themselves over time (e.g., Gluckman 1962; Rappaport 1979).

People react to each other on the basis, in part, of the systems of knowledge and belief to which they are conditioned throughout their lives. These systems of knowledge and belief exist in people's minds as expectations about how the world works, at two different levels. At one level, various schemata define social categories and criteria for membership in these categories, allowing people to treat each other not as individuals but as members of particular sets (e.g., Nadel 1957; Goodenough 1965; Blau 1977). The criteria of membership among peoples of noncapitalist communities are mostly those of residence, descent (real or fictive), age, gender, and marital relationships.

At a more general level, various schemata define broad principles for what constitutes appropriate interpersonal behavior. These principles cover such matters as the ranges of relationships appropriate between members of different social sets, the ranges of social roles appropriate to members of any one particular set, and a general moral code. At its broadest, this general level defines what we might call people's social self-image. The principles involved find expression and reinforcement not only in people's actions (e.g., as discussed in Gluckman 1962), but in ritual, iconography, language, myth, and oral tradition. Together, these schemata constitute what Sahlins (1972:137) has called "the anonymous and silent government of structure."

Generations of social anthropologists have noted the importance of social-symbolic structures for the continuity of communities over time. In the adaptationist view, this continuity exists for two reasons. First, the need for mutual intelligibility leads people to interact more with those with whom they can more readily communicate, and also who respond in mutually appropriate ways to nonsemantic cues (Krippendorf 1971; Leach 1976). Second, people avoid uncertainty in their social interactions, and so interact more often with others who operate under similar expectations about proper social conduct. People's actions thus tend to perpetuate social expectations and the patterns of conduct they entail.

Finally, not only have anthropologists interpreted as adaptive the simple existence of ritual and symbolic systems; they have so interpreted specific ritual practices as well. Because public ritual events bring together people who have interests in participating, for example, such rituals have been interpreted as occasions when people publicly express (through action or failure to act) their acceptance or rejection of the social status quo. By invoking underlying moral codes represented in particular beliefs, public rituals also reinforce the importance of such social expressions. Further, as occasions when people can exchange material resources and information, public ritual events also help directly in adjusting ecological relations (e.g., Rappaport 1968, 1979).

CHALLENGING ADAPTATIONISM

Adaptationist interpretations of nonhierarchical organization face several difficulties. These ultimately stem from the functional and holistic interpretations upon which adaptationism rests. Few people have studied a specific nonhierarchical community sufficiently to be able to analyze its adaptation *as a process through time*. What we have instead are impressive synchronic studies of how specific people's lifeways are adapted to their conditions of existence. Anthropological adaptationism is a way to try to rephrase functional pictures into historical terms.

But this "way" contains no method for understanding how social change happens, how specific historical adaptations *come to be*. Where researchers have attempted to breach this difficulty, they have given us only vague concepts of how complex "systems" seeking homeostasis can change incrementally in order to persist (e.g., Flannery 1972b, 1973; Hill 1977; Rappaport 1979:148–49; Diener, Nonini, and Robkin 1980). These attempts have not specified either the kinds of concrete entities or kinds of physical events that might be involved in the process of adaptation. They offer a language for telling interpretive stories, but no procedures or criteria for their evaluation.

By comparison, adaptationist inference in the more developed evolutionary field of paleobiology can invoke the concept of natural selection to cover the issue of how change physically occurs. Yet even here,

the criteria for acceptance of a[n adaptationist] story are so loose that many pass without proper confirmation. Often, evolutionists use *consistency* with natural selection as the sole criterion and consider their work done when they concoct a plausible story. But plausible stories can always be told. The key to historical research lies in devising criteria to identify proper explanations among the substantial set of plausible pathways to any . . . result (Gould and Lewontin 1984:259; italics in original).

Anthropologists, as we have seen, build "plausible stories" of cultural adaptation-as-process on the assumption that people consciously and successfully adapt themselves to perceived problems. In particular, our stories privilege the people of nonhierarchical communities with the ability always to solve their problems well, and in enduring ways. Yet few of us would accept the assertion that people always get things right when they attempt to solve their problems.

Specific criticisms of adaptationism

Adaptationist interpretations of social variation and change do not adequately address either the question of what generates social variation within a community, or the question of what shapes the differential transmission of that variation over time. Adaptationist interpretations treat continuity and adaptation as properties of a "system" participated in by a community. System persistence results from the adjustment of individuals' and groups' actions toward the collective benefit of the community. While conflicts over specific transactions are recognized, it is assumed that everyone accepts and plays by the same set of rules and for the same kinds of goals. The community comes to be portrayed to us in a highly normative fashion, with the collective norms themselves viewed as parts of the adaptation (see also Wobst 1978).

Such holism allows us no insight into how change can come about, into proximate causality. It allows us no insight into how people generate or adopt alternative social practices, let alone insight into how these alternatives can come to vary in popularity over time or space. It addresses neither the presence of variation in social practices among the members of a community, nor the presence of interpersonal social tensions universally documented in living communities. These microsocial processes are somehow dissociated from the presumably broader processes of adaptation and change.

Further, if social change arises only through adaptive problem-solving, then change in adaptive problems must be the cause of social change (e.g., Hill 1977). This idea underlies the emphasis on environmental and demographic change in most adaptationist inter-pretations of cultural change. Additionally, the process of adaptation must be inherently passive and conservative (Slobodkin and Rapoport 1974). We express this latter notion in the assumption that people solve problems by the easiest means at their disposal, as much as possible, to avoid disturbing the rest of their conditions of existence (e.g., Rappaport 1979:148–49).

In some instances, however, social change may not be conservative, or reactive only to external events (e.g., Friedman and Rowlands 1978; Rowlands 1982; Rindos 1984). People may conceivably change or attempt to change their practices without any change in external circumstances, some social practices may have no adaptive conse-quences at all, and people's actions may even change their external circumstances, albeit perhaps not intentionally.

In addition, if we emphasize adaptive problem-solving in our scenarios of social change, we must view social organization as a by-product of voluntary decisions and interactions among individuals and households. This view invokes an image of individual calculation and rational choice as the basis of social conduct and of conventional belief (e.g., Harris 1977). But culture and social organization are not at all matters of "practical reason," to use Sahlins's (1976) apt phrase.

It is more appropriate to view individual social conduct as a matter of "bounded rationality," to use Simon's (1957) equally apt phrase. This bounding occurs through people's enculturation to various ways of cognition and symbolism, which define (among other things) the ranges of conduct appropriate to people in their mutual interactions (see above). People's perceptions and expectations are not rigidly confined in this way, but are nevertheless biased toward particular patterns of thought and expression. The fact of this biasing means that adapta-tion cannot possibly arise consistently as products of rational problem-solving.

74

Even without this bounding of rationality, people can react to new situations by comparing them only to past conditions, their perceptions of which are filtered through personal memory and community tradition. The ways people live at any given time and place thus constitute their adaptations to the past as they attempt to apply it to the present. To be sure, people always have some knowledge of what has worked for them or for others in the past. People can apply this knowledge to the present, but they cannot know in advance what will continue to work today or in the future (e.g., Slobodkin and Rapoport 1974; Alland 1975; Lewontin 1978; Kirch 1980).

To the extent that new situations may pose different problems from those that existed in the past, people may respond in ways that will not work or will have unanticipated consequences demanding still further action. The actions and reactions of other people, for example, comprise a major source of such unanticipated consequences, as these actions clash or combine to produce new situations ever onward (e.g., Schelling 1978; Barry and Hardin 1982; Corning 1983).

Without perfect foreknowledge of the world around them, then, people must live by trial and error. Yet cultural adaptationism by itself contains no theory of how this process of trial and error produces the patterns of functional adaptation our ethnographies so commonly describe (e.g., Dunnell 1980; Diener, Nonini, and Robkin 1980).

An alternative approach?

Several researchers have countered adaptationism in social anthropology with an alternative in the tradition of historical materialism. I draw here from works that specifically discuss the study of change in nonhierarchical communities (Friedman 1974, 1975, 1979, 1982; Rowlands 1982; Ellen 1982; Kristiansen 1982; Bender 1978, 1985a, 1985b, this volume; Kohl 1981; Gledhill 1981; Hodder 1982, 1985; Trigger 1982, 1984b; and various chapters in Friedman and Rowlands 1978; Spriggs 1984; Miller and Tilley 1984).

Although differing in many respects, these works share a four-part central theme. First, people act not only to maintain but to extend their conditions of existence. That is, people act to increase their control over, flexibility of opportunity in, or security in, their natural and social settings. People exploit nature through their labor and technology, and through the organization of these in systems of production. They try to

75

maintain and extend their conditions of existence through efforts to control these means for exploiting nature. From this perspective, innovation and experimentation with others' innovations are expected as the rule rather than the exception in all communities.

Second, people's actions and expectations are bounded or structured through their enculturation to particular ways of cognition, symbolism, and knowledge, as also discussed earlier in this chapter (see also Bourdieu 1977; Giddens 1979).

Third, social conflicts of interest are expected as the rule rather than the exception in all communities. Social conventions in all communities mediate the possibility of conflicts of interest, but they can never do this perfectly. There is simply too much diversity of interests (even in small communities) for social practices ever to maintain a balance among the demands placed on them.

Fourth, social change results from people's efforts variously to resolve or exploit the conflicts of interest that continually evolve in communities. That is, people generate change through their efforts to retain or gain control of their material or social circumstances. These efforts involve the manipulation of technology, the physical environment, social relations, and beliefs.

Three authors have offered programmatic statements of this perspective and its application to the study of variation and change in small-scale communities: Friedman and Rowlands (1978) and Ellen (1982). These works provide the focus for my critique of the proposed alternative view of social causality and change, a view labeled "epigenetic" by Friedman and Rowlands and "generative" by Ellen.

Ellen (1982) notes that people's patterns of social relations in any given ecosystem will be constrained by the interaction of many different kinds of what he terms "cycles." These will consist of:

annual and longer-term cultivation cycles, the reproductive and growth cycles of animal populations; the developmental cycles of domestic groups, village cycles, kin-group fission and fusion; microclimatic cycles, exchange, ritual and other structurally determined production cycles, as well as non-reversible ecological successions. Depending on the conjunction of different phases in these cycles and trends, there will be different generative possibilities (1982:257).

Ellen then notes that

The notion of cycle implies repetition, but social and ecological systems are accumulative and constantly undergoing change, change which may arise from intrinsic factors, the working out of contradictions within the social formation and between the dynamics of an ecological system and that of a social system. It may, for example, arise from the articulation of contradictory cycles. These processes, whose overall dynamic is located in long-term productive and ecological forces, lead to system transformation (1982:258).

Friedman and Rowlands (1978) explain what is meant by "transformation," on the basis of the idea that social practices are shaped by a hierarchy of constraints. These constraints consist of limitations of the ecosystem, limitations of the productive forces (e.g., technology, labor supply), and limitations of the relations of production

that distribute the total labor input and output of a population and organize immediate work processes and the exploitation of the environment (1978:203).

From the ecosystem up is a hierarchy of constraints which determine the limits of functional compatibility between levels – hence of their internal variation. This is essentially a negative determination since it only determines what cannot occur . . . When these limits are reached, breakdown in the system is imminent . . . functional incompatibilities in the larger totality generate divergent transformations over time (1978:203–204).

In this scenario, specific instances of change involve either: (a) a gradual working out of the possibilities of a particular set of cultural practices and their ecological, demographic, and technological constraints, or (b) an occasional transformation or reorganization of these possibilities when functional limitations have been reached.

Problems with the generative program

The generative program improves on adaptationism in several respects. Most notably, it draws our attention to the microsocial dynamics of communities as sources of instability in social organization. It thereby additionally recognizes that sets of cultural practices in their ecological settings do not constitute homeostatic systems. Further, it notes the importance of innovation and diffusion in contributing to social change.

This program, nevertheless, also is incomplete. Its weaknesses lie in three areas. First, it confuses the processes that generate variation with the processes that shape change. Second, as with the adaptationist program, it leads to arguments couched in vague metaphors of "systems" of constraints. It does not specify any physical mechanisms by which constraints are experienced by any concrete agents of change. It thus also does not offer any procedures or criteria for evaluating specific interpretations. Third, its applications often mix a general method for interpreting social histories with a particular theory of why social change over all human history has followed the particular path it has followed (Dunnell 1980, 1986).

Accumulations of minor changes, cycles, and tensions over social control do comprise processes that generate variation. But they encompass only a limited range of the ways in which people can generate variation in their cultural practices. People can experiment with virtually all aspects of their lives, in all cultural settings. They may do so in their quests for greater social security or for greater security against environmental unpredictability. They may experiment in response to changing demographic conditions or just out of plain curiosity (e.g., Johnson 1972; Lévi-Strauss 1966). To argue that people experiment only (or primarily) in response to social tensions unnecessarily narrows the scope of research.

What motivates people to try out, retain, or avoid different practices in any given setting, in fact, ultimately does not matter. By motivations, I mean such things as intentions to appeal to a supernatural being, or to avoid someone else's control over one's labor, or to reduce the risks experienced with different cropping practices. As I discuss below, what matters only is that (a) variation exists among different people's actions, just as it does in the social, demographic, and ecological contexts in which they act, and (b) these differences among people's practices can entail real differences in material consequences, whether intended so by the actors or not.

Finally, knowing that social-ecological "systems" contain much variation and constantly generate possibilities for new variation does not tell us in what direction change may occur. That is, it does not by itself tell us why the incidences of specific cultural practices in a given setting may increase, decrease, or remain unchanged over time, or why their spatial distributions may expand, contract, or remain stable. In fact, given that people pursue a diversity of interests and practices in any community, it is not clear why any directionality should develop among the many different "accumulations" or impingements on the presumed functional limitations potentially taking place. And to say that the range of possibilities in any given setting is limited by "functional incompatibilities" begs the question: incompatible for what concrete entities, and in what ways?

SELECTIONISM

The concept of "selection" offers an alternative to both adaptationism and generative historical materialism (e.g., Durham 1982; Rindos 1984:37–81, 1986; Boyd and Richerson 1985; Dunnell 1986; see also Plog 1974:49–54). It does so by explicitly recognizing social change as a matter of change in the statistical popularity of different social practices over time. Those changes that accumulate, radiate, or simply persist are caused by a process of selection (e.g., Sober 1984), in our case natural selection acting on culturally transmitted variation.

As an aside, I should note that some authors have labeled this process of selection "cultural selection" (e.g., Durham 1982; Rindos 1986). This is a misnomer. Historically, Darwin coined the term "natural selection" to designate a contrast with "artificial" selection. Natural selection for Darwin referred to the multiplicity of processes that together blindly shape the transmission of heritable characteristics in natural populations without artificial interference (Sober 1984:13–59). Although our interest is in culturally rather than genetically transmitted variation among people's practices, it is still appropriate to talk about natural or blind selection on that variation. The term "cultural selection" may best be reserved for those cognitive processes by which people accept or reject ideas based on their perceived compatibility with existing cultural beliefs and practices (e.g., Alland 1975).

Elements of selection

Variation in individual cultural practices and perceptions exists in every community at all times. This variation constitutes a pool of possibilities for what people will do in the immediate future, and therefore, a pool from which some practices may be carried onward over time. The variation can arise through many processes, as discussed earlier. The range of variation in any historic instance will be limited by a variety of factors, including accidents of history, the bounding of each person's rationality by conventions of belief, people's need to avoid mutual contradictions among beliefs (or cultural selection – e.g., Alland 1975), and scheduling or locational conflicts among different practices.

The differential transmission of social practices over time, in turn, arises from differences in the material consequences of different practices for the people holding to them in particular historical instances.

These consequences pertain to the relative success of the different practices in allowing the continuation of a biological breeding population. It also refers to relative success in allowing the continuation of historically specific social entities in a world of limited resources, limited predictability, and competing populations.

Different, alternative social practices may differ, for example, (a) in the efficiency with which they consume resources (as broadly defined above), space, or time, (b) in where and when they must be carried out, (c) in their potential for allowing interpersonal conflict, or (d) in the social or material risks they may entail for the people carrying them out. No matter how slight the differences in a given historical setting, alternatives that allow less adequate access to or defense of resources or that are less efficient, more prone to scheduling conflicts, more prone to interpersonal conflicts, or less predictable in their consequences; or that leave people more vulnerable to competition or environmental hazards in the long run are less likely to persist.

Selection operates on (or occurs because of) such differences in material consequences among alternative practices. Because of such differences in their material consequences, different social practices will differ in their "replicative success" (Leonard and Jones 1987) in any particular historical instance. People holding to different alternative practices can experience differences in the difficulties they experience with environmental hazards, resource shortfalls, and so forth. Some people will consequently be less successful in recruiting new members to their social groups or in establishing alliances with other groups, and so will pass on their ways of doing things to fewer members of future generations. Over time, these dynamics continuously shape the statistical popularity of different practices. Such selection operates not only on variation in individual and group practices within entire communities at large, but also on variation within individual segments of each community and on variation among different communities simultaneously.

Selection and adaptation

Adaptation can be understood as a consequence of selection, but only a very limited consequence. First, selection does not guarantee that people will not pursue cultural practices that have adverse consequences for their own replicative success. It guarantees only that people who persist in less effective practices will not perpetuate their practices as well as will other people pursuing different practices. Adaptations, then, are sets of cultural practices that simply have allowed people to get by in the past, whose consequences have *so far* proved at least relatively less harmful to the perpetuation of their social groups than any others the people may have tried out.

Second, selection builds cultural adaptations out of only those possibilities that actually exist in a given setting, that is, out of alternative practices that the people may innovate, adopt, or already allow. Adaptations, thus, are strongly shaped by accidents of both innovation and prior history (Winterhalder 1980; Lewontin 1984; Gould and Lewontin 1984). The result follows what Gould has termed a basic principle of all historical science, that adaptations are nothing more (or less) than intricate "contrivances jury-rigged from parts available" (1986:64).

Third, selection has no bearing on whether, faced with an extreme or novel threat to their conditions of existence, people will necessarily respond in ways that allow them to get by. Although humans seek to solve problems through experimentation, trial and error, this does not always guarantee viable, let alone optimal, solutions. Indeed, problem-solving behavior only generates variation and new possibilities for cultural practices, giving a measure of volatility to short-term trends or variation over time, and does not entail omniscience or prior knowledge of the consequence of different practices.

Fourth, the replicative success of alternative cultural practices held by people in a community can change for any of several reasons. They can change as a consequence of shifts in the physical or demographic environment, of course. They can also change as a result of the actions of other people in the larger region, as these may affect the availability of resources (broadly defined). They can change as a consequence of coevolutionary interactions, in which certain cultural practices modify the environment and thereby modify their own selective conditions. And they can change as a consequence of innovations that introduce new alternatives into the picture. It is because of this plurality of causes that, in the long run, social change rather than stability predominates in history. Indeed, long episodes of cultural stability demand explanation in their own right.

Finally, not all cultural practices will necessarily be subject to natural selection (e.g., Dunnell 1978). Beyond serving as potential cues to mutual social identities, for example, it may make no difference at all whether the people in a community use red or blue dyes to mark their hats, believe in one supernatural power or many, make obscene gestures with one finger or many. Only when *alternative* practices appear to *differ* in their replicative success may we analyze their histories as matters of selection (Leonard and Jones 1987).

Selection and epigenesis

The "generation" or "epigenesis" of social change can also be understood as a consequence of selection. First, the concept of selection explicitly separates the two issues of what generates variation and what shapes change. Both stability and change result from selection on variation. For selection to operate, it does not matter how or why people may come up with alternative social practices. What matters is that alternative social practices can have different material *consequences* for the people holding to them. Social change cannot take place without social variation, but that variation does not itself *cause* change.

Second, selection produces both gradual and saltatory or transformational change. Gradual change involves the reworking or reshaping of possibilities. But sets of cultural practices are not always decomposable into independent and separately selected parts. Some practices may not be selected against simply because they are intrinsic to other practices that *together* have successfully allowed people to get by. Conversely, some practices may never find adoption in particular communities simply because they do not fit into already existing ways of perceiving or doing things. The ethnographic literature richly records both phenomena. It is precisely these phenomena that Friedman and Rowlands (1978:203) appear to invoke with their concept of "functional incompatibilities." Selection can operate not only on individual social practices but also on entire sets of interconnected practices, depending on historical circumstances, thereby producing radical instead of gradual social change.

Limits to nonhierarchical organization

We can use the concept of selection to return to a question raised at the start of this chapter: Are there cross-cultural central tendencies or limits to the variation possible in nonhierarchical organization? Our answer to this question does not turn on whether the ethnographic record is historically or methodologically biased (e.g., Wobst 1978; Dunnell 1980). The issue here, instead, concerns possibilities across all human history.

Of course, we should not assume that our ethnographies adequately record the range of possibilities for nonhierarchical social organization. And our evolutionary typologies may tell us more about the historical impacts of colonialism and about typological anthropology than about social evolution. Yet generations of anthropologists have identified constellations of features that nonhierarchical communities appear to share.

Cross-cultural similarities tempt us to explain their existence in terms of analogous function, to assert that people in different historical settings independently solved similar problems in similar ways. Our understanding of selection, however, should lead us to expect few such functional convergences. Rather, we should expect unique historical trajectories colored by unique historical accidents as the rule rather than the exception. Further, even if we were to find a pattern of convergent problem-solving among several historically distinct cases, we should not expect the same kind of convergence in any other historical instances. Nothing about selection guarantees that people will come to solve similar problems in similar, let alone optimal, ways. We can expect only that if people do not arrive at solutions to problems that threaten their conditions of existence, their cultural (and perhaps also genetic) descent will end (e.g., Wagley 1969; Wobst 1974; Durham 1982).

On the other hand, there may well exist limits to the range of variation possible among nonhierarchical communities. Johnson's work (1978, 1982, 1983) shows that the efficiency and accuracy of decision-making goes down, and the potentials for uncertainty and conflicts of interest go up, the greater the number of people involved (see also Winterhalder 1986; Netting, this volume; Plog, this volume; Upham, this volume). This relationship appears to have two causes: limitations of the human brain's ability to process information (in a technical, cybernetic sense), and a positive exponential correlation between the number of individuals present in a group and the number of interactions possible among them. The "group" in this context may be any decision-making aggregate.

Johnson's work demonstrates two consequences of these two constraints. First, for any particular set of decision-making practices in a particular historical setting, increases in group size past certain thresholds will exponentially increase the chances of inaccurate decision-making and inadequate resolution of internal conflicts of interest. Alternatively, when a group's size lies close to one of these thresholds, any increase in the *demands* on existing decision-making practices resulting from events external to the group's control will have similar effects. In either case, groups and communities in any historical setting will usually fission when they exceed some particular consistent size.

Second, the size thresholds past which groups tend to fission should vary among different historical instances because of differences in cultural practices and their environmental contexts. However, in all cultural settings, the sheer numbers of people involved in the activities of any given group constitute the single largest determinant of the size thresholds above which fissioning is most likely. As a result, groups in all nonhierarchical communities should tend to fission when they exceed similar size ranges. Johnson (1982, 1983) notes that, for a variety of reasons, these similar size thresholds are in the range of multiples of six times the average household size in any community.

Yet, clearly, nonhierarchical communities exist in a wide range of demographic sizes, and hierarchical communities do not appear subject to the same size constraints at all. Is there a relationship between these two phenomena? Johnson's work (1978, 1982) identifies two kinds of accidents of social change that, should they occur, might allow a community to persist near or continue to grow past a particular size threshold. If the necessary innovations existed, selection might allow the persistence of an additional layer of sequential hierarchy, or an additional layer of delegated authority. As discussed earlier, these two possibilities have different kinds of consequences for social relations and decision-making. But the possibility of reorganization in a particular circumstance is a matter of historical accident and selection. If none of the people in a particular instance possesses an appropriate possibility, selection will guarantee that no reorganization will take place.

Johnson (1982) uses the term "scalar stress" for the pattern of degeneration of decision-making with increasing group size. The term unfortunately invokes the image of a "problem" for which people may seek adaptive "solutions." That is, an adaptationist would be encouraged to interpret examples of increasing sequential or simultaneous hierarchy as solutions to problems of scalar stress. And any social change that involved the formation of a hierarchy of delegated authority, if it persisted, would of course mark the end of a community's nonhierarchical organization.

However, selection does not operate in this way. We need to think of scalar stress instead as a kind of *potential* selective circumstance closely related to existing demographic conditions and social practices. Events, demographic conditions, or social practices in some historical instances could increase the possibilities of scalar stress. Such instances would provide the kind of selective circumstance under which accidents of social practices involving social inequality might find greater replicative success. But people culturally bound by conventions that limit inequality are not likely to yield up such accidents very often.

CONCLUSIONS

I return, at last, to my first major question: What is the nature of causality and constraint in shaping the histories of nonhierarchical communities? I have reviewed two dominant answers to this question. On the one hand, causality is presented as a matter of external events and group adaptation. On the other, it is presented as a matter of internal and external events, dialectics, and social epigenesis. My conclusion is that neither answer is correct.

Causality instead appears to be a matter of historical accidents and natural selection acting on culturally transmitted variation. Selection takes place because people vary in how they do things. This variation has a variety of causes, including but not limited to people's culturally bounded efforts at problem-solving and their efforts to establish or perpetuate themselves socially in their mutual interactions. Selection acts upon the possibilities for cultural practices that people happen to come up with, upon historical accidents. These accidents will almost always confer differences in material consequences for their practitioners, although these differences may be slight. Selection acts through those differences that affect each practice's likelihood of perpetuating itself.

Such a view of social evolution has many implications for how we study social relations, social variation, and culture change in nonhierarchical communities. First, we should expect variation over time and space *as the rule* rather than the exception. Second, we should expect individual communities to exhibit adaptation but not necessarily stability in their cultural practices; communities may also fail. Third, in any given cultural setting, we should expect to see size thresholds above which groups – households, local kin-based associations, villages, or larger aggregates – will tend either to fall apart or come to exhibit radically different social practices. And fourth, whether or not a community will evolve into hierarchy and inequality is a matter of historical accident, except that the decision-making processes covered by Johnson's concept of scalar stress may figure in many cases. Returning to a quotation from Gould (1986:64), we should not expect nonhierarchical social adaptations to be anything more or less than intricate historical "contrivances jury-rigged from parts available." Any theory of human social evolution, of how inequality and social complexity have come about must accommodate these four facts of evolution.

NOTE

My thanks to Steadman Upham and the Advanced Seminar group for their energetic comments on my original paper. Barbara Bender, Art Keene, Dean Saitta, Jon Haas, Kris Kristiansen, and Steve Plog have also stimulated my rethinking the issues here for many years past; the impact of Robert Dunnell and David Rindos should also be apparent. I owe much of the time for my rethinking to Grant BNS–8311976 from the National Science Foundation, and to an NEH Resident Fellowship at the School of American Research in 1985–86. Finally, Shirley Powell and Kathryn Koldehoff gave editorial advice.

4
Analog or digital?: Toward a generic framework for explaining the development of emergent political systems

STEADMAN UPHAM

New Mexico State University

Most scientific work is guided by predictions derived from comprehensive bodies of theory. As scientists are quick to point out, however, the world is wonderfully unpredictable, especially for a system whose natural laws are invariant. Social scientists, whose many subjects include the evolution of human behavior and culture, are especially aware of just how unpredictable the world can be. Yet there is in the social sciences a constant drive to make the events and processes of the world predictable and understandable. Often, social scientists seek to explain such events and processes using categories that reduce variation and order complex aspects of reality into neat, ideal types. The facility with which humans categorize and bound reality, however, is the double-edged sword that both drives and hinders attempts to formulate a theory of history and explain the evolution of culture and human behavior.

Such is the case with many of the efforts in anthropology to explain the evolution of social and political systems, especially in terms of broader themes like the origin of inequality and the formation of social, political, and economic "elites" in human societies. Many attempts have fallen victim to the classificatory dilemma that places the construction of cultural taxonomies before the explanation of long-term change, and confuses cross-cultural comparisons with history and cultural evolution. This classificatory dilemma is faced in different ways by all scientists. Yet social scientists, who have no mathematical shorthand to provide proofs of their models, are disadvantaged, especially when such models are predicated on complex analyses of long-term change processes. In anthropology, the problems posed by this dilemma have been exacerbated by a virtual lack of agreement on appropriate explanatory frameworks and research methods. Moreover, anthropologists who study political evolution and emergent political systems must necessarily rely on archaeological data to provide time depth. They often fuse archaeological and ethnographic data into a kind of "hybrid ethnology" without due consideration of the strengths and limitations of the data, clear definition of terms, coherent analytical strategies, or unified interpretive models. In addition, there is confusion over issues as basic as the nature of behavioral and cultural variability (continuously or discontinuously variable?).

I do not pretend to be able to resolve all of these problems, but I can examine several theoretical issues arising from the divergent approaches used to study the evolution of political systems. These issues include (a) taxonomic and processual approaches to social and political evolution, (b) the use of categorical and continuous variables, and (c) the nature of change and explanation in studies of political evolution. A tendentious paper of this sort would not be complete without presenting a format for studying the evolution of political systems that seeks to unify theoretical and methodological differences, and the last portion of this chapter is devoted to an outline of just such an approach.

VARIATION, PROCESS, TYPES, AND CHANGE

Thinking categorically as an anthropologist can prove perilous. The anthropologist who routinely confuses measurement scales, for example, might equate the nominal assignment of political complexity to a group (e.g., tribe, chiefdom) with an absolute measure of complexity monitored along any of several axes of organizational variability (e.g., number of decision-making or administrative levels, number of sumptuary rules). One result of such conflation might be to conclude that all tribes or chiefdoms containing n administrative levels can be characterized by a certain number of sumptuary rules. Even more insidiously, one might argue that the presence of certain sumptuary rules indicated the presence of a tribal or chiefdom level of organization. Both kinds of conclusions have been proffered in anthropological studies of emergent political systems, despite the absence of logical connections between the two kinds of measures (see Feinman and Neitzel [1984] for a detailed treatment of this issue).

One of the driving forces behind the kind of pseudo-correlations described above is the misunderstanding and misuse of Elman Service's (1962) and Morton Fried's (1967) classic cross-cultural studies of generalized societal types. The motivation for designating societal types is deeply rooted in anthropology's historical ties to evolutionary theory. Yet, there is no necessary isomorphism between the traits and institutions identified as characteristic of these ideal types and the *developmental sequences* leading to the different social and political forms described by Service and Fried. This lack of congruence results directly from the fact that the societal types of Service and Fried are composites and do not exist in their entirety in the real world; they are categorical representations of reality that condense meaningful variability.

The concern with evolutionary "stages" and cultural taxonomies, however, cannot be laid solely at the feet of Service and Fried. Beginning with Lewis Henry Morgan, the list of anthropologists concerned with societal types is virtually identical with the list of anthropologists concerned with positing more general evolutionary frameworks (Morgan 1963 [1877]; Steward 1949; White 1949, 1959; Oberg 1955; Steward and Faron 1959; Service 1962; Fried 1967; Sanders and Webster 1978). At the same time, a number of anthropologists have offered more restricted societal typologies independent of broader evolutionary formulations (Sahlins 1958; Goldman 1970; Renfrew 1974; Taylor 1975; Steponaitis 1978). One theme that unites all of these works, particularly with respect to the issue of cultural taxonomies and evolving political systems, is an overriding concern with explaining why the presence of certain traits, institutions, and environmental circumstances, or the unfolding of particular cultural processes, represents a given "stage" in cultural evolution.

As more anthropologists confront the range of variation evident in the organizational structures of ethnographically known groups, it has become plain that the notion of "ideal types" in the study of social and political organization is analogous to the use of "jural norms" in studies of marriage patterns and post-marital residence. In short, if the goal is explanation, the use of ideal types truncates any arguments based on the definition of those types. F. Plog and I commented on this problem previously:

> If some key attribute in the typology is used in classifying the political organization of a particular site or region, the range of explanatory statements that can then be explored is either sharply curtailed or the arguments become hopelessly circular. When, for example the size of the largest settlement is used to identify state organization, it is impossible to explore the relationship between state organization and population aggregation since the latter was used to define the former (Plog and Upham 1983:199–200).

The move away from the use of ideal types is consistent with the trend in anthropology to examine organizational variability in a continuous as opposed to a categorical fashion. It should be noted, however, that this developing trend has left an interpretive vacuum in studies dealing with the evolution of organizational complexity. Are the general evolutionary formulations of Service, Fried, and others still a primary anthropological goal or are more particularistic explanations now desirable? Are stage-based approaches and cultural taxonomies necessary and sufficient methodologies in such studies, or are processual studies required? Is the emphasis on continuous variability productive or counter-productive in the search for structural regularities, or must we also incorporate measures of discontinuous variation?

In seeking answers to these questions, a few investigators have recognized that the ideal types of Service and Fried are an attempt to represent complex continua as simpler categories. Fried has observed (1967:14) that the ideal types are useful because they isolate key aspects of variation, something that is critical in the search for structural regularities. It is the complex patterns of variation, however, that 'are crucial for understanding why the most typical outcomes of evolutionary processes are the relatively few ideal types" (Plog and Upham 1983:200). Research during the last decade has made less use of the ideal types and has focused more on the processes involved in the organizational change (e.g. Johnson 1978; Sanders and Webster 1978; Cordell and Plog 1979; Smith 1978; Helms 1979; Blanton et al. 1981; Upham 1982, 1987; Feinman and Neitzel 1984). This new focus is significant because it has forced study of variation in the processes themselves Thus, some anthropologists have moved away from using societal types, granting that the typical outcomes of evolutionary processes are few, and have embraced processual approaches.

Analog or digital?

A number of processes have been identified as a set of interrelated phenomena that lead to the development of organizational complexity. These include, minimally, population growth and aggregation, the organization and management of labor, the development of productive specialization, the elaboration of exchange systems, the centralization of storage, warfare, agricultural intensification, and surplus production. In most considerations of these processes, the role of the natural environment is also recognized as important. In some cases, the interaction of these processes is argued to result in more centralized, hierarchical organization, and social stratification, culminating in the formation of state-level political systems. The number of possible connections in this welter of processes is so enormous that one might legitimately conclude that any kind of meaningful generalization regarding structural or developmental regularities would be impossible to formulate. More parsimony and elegance are clearly required.

Directions: analog or digital?

The shift in emphasis in anthropology away from ideal types to multivariate processual models, away from simple categorical representations to a focus on complex continua, mirrors an interesting technological confrontation taking place in the modern world between analog and digital instrumentation. That confrontation, although seemingly relegated to the arena of "consumerism," illustrates a basic psychological dichotomy that is relevant to theoretical and methodological approaches used to study evolving political systems.

Digital does not just look more modern. It is more modern. Analog devices represent reality as a continuum on which things . . . are assigned a location. Romantic, but not quite as practical as digital devices. They [digital devices] represent reality as discrete intervals, each assigned some numerical value. And once chopped into numbered bits, reality can be manipulated with unnatural ease and in an infinity of ways by microprocessors. Digital is ideally suited to crunching, shaping, and twisting by modern computers . . . But now the counter-revolution (Krauthammer 1986:84).

Few would doubt the immediate and widespread acceptance of digital technology by industrialized nations. But the counter-revolution noted above is witness to a resurgence of analog technology, including a 50 percent decline in imports of digital technology to the United States and Canada during 1985–86, the labeling of digital audio technology as "the

91

greatest step backward" by the president of a major sound and recording laboratory, and the installation of all analog gauges in one of the greatest symbols of Western capitalism, the new Lincoln Mark VII LSC (Krauthammer 1986:84). The resurgence of analog instrumentation and the competition for market shares by the manufacturers of digital and analog technology appears as a post-modern rejection for more traditional technology, providing a parallel to the tug-of-war that has taken place in anthropology during the last few decades between processual and taxonomic approaches to social and political evolution. Unlike the marketplace, however, anthropologists must be concerned with the demands of explanation and must identify approaches that are compatible with cultural evolutionary theory. A number of issues must be considered before such approaches are constructed:

1   *Categories and continua: how did we get here?* Like the changing trends favoring digital or analog instruments, the debate over categorical versus continuous approaches in anthropology has a history. There can be little doubt that the emphasis in anthropology during the last few decades has been on process and continuous variation, in a move away from the use of historical approaches and cultural taxonomies. This trend can be traced to three separate developments in American anthropology: (a) the reassertion of cultural evolutionism, especially through cultural materialism (Harris 1968) and cultural ecology (Steward 1955, 1968; Netting 1965a; Damas 1969), the two dominant, if competing, evolutionary schools; (b) a disaffection with both cultural historical interpretations (Binford 1962; Flannery 1967; Trigger 1970, 1973) and functionalist arguments (Harris 1968); and (c) an acceptance of a few of the stated aims of the "new archaeology" that identified regional approaches, model building, and the explanation of change as scientific goals of the discipline (see especially Binford 1968; Plog 1973).

These developments implied that the anthropological studies offering the greatest potential to contribute to the newly restated evolutionary goals were those that were diachronic, focused on broad geographical areas, and sought to explain the processes of long-term change (especially those that emphasized technology, the organization and management of labor and production, and human adaptive strategies tempered by environmental variability). Since the mid 1970s, however, confusion about just how to operationalize this approach has existed.

2   *The conflation of continuous variation, time, and change.* The

92

redefinition of goals that occurred in anthropology during the 1960s and 1970s was stimulated largely by archaeologists who identified the explanation of change as a principal objective of the field. Along with this stated objective, it was suggested that anthropologists should be concerned with regularities of process, not events, and should measure behavioral variability in a continuous as opposed to categorical fashion (cf. Plog 1973, 1977). There was a tacit acceptance of the idea that continuous measures were the only appropriate ones for complex cultural and behavioral phenomena. Discontinuous measures and categorical representations were criticized for their simplicity and normative character. Moreover, it was argued that an explicit concern with time, at least as archaeologists measured time by constructing chronologies, was of less importance than identifying patterns of behavioral variability. In fact, chronological studies, because of the way they arbitrarily partitioned time into discrete units, were seen as antithetical to the goals of explaining change.

In the exuberance that accompanied the explicit change in interpretive philosophies, the theoretical position of several archaeologists (e.g. Plog 1973, 1977; Watson, LeBlanc, and Redman 1971) was distorted so that the ideas of process, continuous variation, and change were conflated and were often used as proxy measures of each other and of time. Some of the confusion resulted from the polemic of arguments about the new approach; some from attempts to simplify more complex issues. Statements from one of F. Plog's important papers on explaining change (1977) illustrate this problem:

Change is ubiquitous, it is everywhere (1977:42).

Processes have a temporal dimension (in fact, most definitions of the term *processes* refer to changes-in-time [1977:31]).

The measures of behavior appropriate to the study of change are usually continuous rather than categorical (1977:43).

Some archaeologists (although not necessarily F. Plog) who sought to operationalize this new approach used the notions of change, continuous variation, and regularities of process as isomorphic concepts. Moreover, concern with time and temporal variability, because they were properties of all three concepts, was viewed as "historical" and unscientific. Ironically, some efforts to construct a record of continuous variation through time superseded all chronological studies, despite the inability of investigators to control for time in their work!

The extreme positions that existed just ten years ago in our field have moderated, yet many of the exuberant overstatements persist. We now know that reasonable positions are found on both sides of this argument. As Wallerstein (1974) reminds us in his opening statement to *The Modern World System*, "all things change; all things stay the same." Both statements can be either true or false depending on the context, level of specificity, or scale of one's observations. The statement that processes have a temporal dimension is redundant, yet our ability to perceive time and process is dependent on whether our time frame is a nanosecond or a millennium. A record of continuous variation may be invaluable for explaining some change processes; discontinuous variation, like phenotypically discontinuous traits and polymorphisms, may also be important to explain change.

3 *Quantum effects and rates of change.* The history of the natural sciences offers an interesting parallel to the shifting tides of interpretation in anthropology that alternately ebb and flow in favor of continuous or categorical models. The successive dominance of Aristotelian, Galilean, Newtonian, and Einsteinian conceptions of the universe, for example, actually represents changing conceptions of physical phenomena based on categorical or continuous measures (Lewin 1935). Today in physics, the smooth, continuous universe depicted by Newtonian mechanics has given way to more discontinuous ideas, to quantum mechanics and a universe that is seen as jerky and grainy.[1] Yet it would be a mistake to assume that conceptions of physical phenomena based on continuous measures have somehow fallen by the wayside. Einstein's relativity proved that the laws of nature are absolute and are not dependent on the motion of the system. Time and space prove to be relative, but the system based on the laws is in continuous, invariant operation. If we were riding Einstein's light beam, we could not tell if we were moving or at rest because of the continuous nature of the system. The continuous operation of such a system, particularly in the face of quantum effects, would thus seem to pose one of the ultimate philosophical paradoxes of our time.

Quantum mechanics tells us that in our universe energy, momentum, light, force, matter, and everything else exists in quantum amounts that are fixed and can only occur as multiples of certain amounts. At this most basic of physical levels, categories prevail; quantum amounts exist without intermediaries. The idea of process as it relates to transitions between quantum states at this level of observation is meaningless since there are no transitions between quantum states. The idea of process applies only to the cycling of things between quantum states, to the energy inputs that are required to excite quantum leaps, and to the *rates of change* that are the unique properties of things in a quantized universe.

What does all this have to do with anthropological studies of emergent political systems? Philosophically, it means that the idea of categories and continua are not mutually exclusive, but are the dependent properties of all kinds of things and phenomena. In the study of sociopolitical evolution, a recognition of this fact necessarily forces consideration of behavioral and cultural phenomena using both kinds of measures. It also means that the explanation of change is defined by (a) the identification and description of the different "quantum states," individually or in series, of cultural and behavioral phenomena, (b) the specification of the energy levels required to produce quantum leaps in these phenomena, and (c) the measurement of the rates of change that are the unique properties of all such phenomena. Thus, the issue is not a polemic about change being ubiquitous, processes having a temporal dimension, or categorical versus continuous measures, but is an epistemological question about explaining change using the expectations of a quantized universe. In such a universe, rates of change for different kinds of behavioral and cultural phenomena are expected to vary, and the operation of cultural systems through time is expected to be jerky, grainy, and characterized by quantum leaps in all kinds of state variables.

I equate the identification and description of different "quantum states" of behavioral and cultural phenomena with the taxonomic approach to cultural evolution. At this most basic descriptive level, all kinds of culture phenomena are considered statically and synchronically, even though they may be linked in serial order. For example, when cultural traits, institutions, or other cultural features are described synchronically (that is, as existing in a single quantum state) by cultural anthropologists, especially when the features pertain to a single cultural or ethnic group, ethnographic description is produced. Similarly, when quantum states are described serially by cultural anthropologists, when the effort is cross-cultural and comparative and the aim is to generalize about broad patterns of cultural development, the emphasis is on normative characteristics and ideal types, and classic ethnological description is produced. Archaeologists also describe quantum states when they identify single cultural "phases" or "phase sequences." But broader periodization schemes and developmental typologies are the equivalent of the more general serial descriptions developed by cultural anthropologists, although these taxonomic devices rarely achieve the generality of the ethnologists' formulations. Because all such descriptions condense meaningful cultural variation and emphasize cultural and behavioral norms, they are of secondary importance in developing explanations of change. They are, nevertheless, a fundamental part of holistic approaches to explaining change.

The specification of energy levels required to produce quantum leaps in state variables is analytically distinct from the ideas of energy and progressive energy capture elucidated by White (1959). It also deviates substantially from the idea of "trophic levels" found in theoretical ecology, because quantum changes in state variables have no necessary connection with nutrition, metabolic exchanges, food chains, feeding cohorts, or feeding strategies. What is meant by the specification of energy levels in this case is measurement of changes in the value of any state variable. Changes in the value of state variables may refer to either increases or decreases in the quantity, magnitude, intensity, amplitude, or frequency of those variables. The idea of quantum leaps presupposes that threshold values exist for all such state variables and that when threshold values are met or exceeded, quantum changes in the states of those variables occur. Thus, analysis of cultural phenomena at this level is directed to measurement of changes in the value of state variables and to the identification of threshold values.

I define rates of change as changes in the value of state variables measured per unit of time. Measurement of the rates at which state variables change requires relatively precise chronometric techniques to calibrate the duration of specific behavioral and cultural phenomena. In cultural anthropology and archaeology, time is most frequently measured using units of seasons, years, decades, centuries, or millennia. Measuring rates of change requires that specific scales of observation and analysis be identified and maintained and that sufficient observational standards be employed. It is here that more recent contributions from archaeology to general anthropology (that actually derive from some of the original precepts of the "new archaeology") are important. F. Plog's (1979:224–27) idea of observational adequacy, for example, identifies the types of analyses and observational standards required to measure rates of change.

CONSTRUCTING THE APPROACH

Given the above background and the perspective it provides, I state explicitly my own biases regarding anthropological efforts to explain the evolution of social and political systems.

1.   All studies of social and political evolution ultimately have as their underlying goal the description and explanation of changes in the complexity of cultural systems. Such studies, if they are to contribute to general evolutionary theory, must also be explicitly concerned with measuring the rates at which changes in complexity take place. I believe the former statement defines the primary anthropological goal of "explaining change" while the latter statement defines the term "process." Both concepts are essential if anthropology is to be considered a social science.

2.   The term "process" as defined above is simply another term for history. The goal of studies concerned with social and political evolution is to identify and explain changes in the complexity of cultural systems that are the product of shared developmental histories. Like cladism, the purpose of studying social and political evolution is to identify homologous similarities of development. History defined in this manner is thus scientific and of great relevance to anthropology. By pursuing issues related to social and political evolution, anthropologists are actually contributing to a general theory of history.

3.   Entire cultural systems are not units of analysis in studies of social and political evolution. Although the goal is to generalize about the evolutionary history of such systems, they are too inclusive to be used as analytical units. In much the same way that biologists focus on change in a few key characters to define different species, anthropologists should focus on change in a few key societal dimensions in their efforts to develop a theory of history and explain the evolution of culture and human behavior.

4.   Because cultural systems are too inclusive to be used as analytical units, taxonomic approaches that seek to identify "stages" of cultural

evolution are scientifically inadequate to explain changes in the complexity of cultural systems. Consequently, the use of terms like band, tribe, chiefdom, and state in studies of social and political evolution are counterproductive since they define constellations of variables that may or may not covary and certainly cannot be measured.

5.   Social and political evolution is a mosaic process; changes in the complexity of one variable may or may not be independent of changes along other axes of cultural variability. Because of this fact, different processes of development (e.g. demographic, economic, social, political, etc.) change differentially and exhibit different rates of change. The use of multivariate analytical techniques to model change processes presupposes that the rates of change in all variables are equivalent. Consequently, the use of such models is inappropriate *unless* it can be independently demonstrated that rates of change among variables are autocorrelated.

These five statements suggest a clear direction for studying questions related to social and political evolution. In the following section of this chapter, I outline what I call a generic framework for explaining the development of social and political systems. I use the term "generic" because of the fact that all of the issues I am concerned with are common to or characteristic of all cultural systems, regardless of the system's size and complexity.

A GENERIC FRAMEWORK FOR EXPLAINING THE DEVELOPMENT OF EMERGENT POLITICAL SYSTEMS

Most anthropological studies of social and political evolution have used the emergence of state-level polities as the *regula norma* by which all other such developments are measured. I have argued, however, that the goal of evolutionary studies is to identify and explain changes in the complexity of cultural systems that are the product of shared developmental histories. Accordingly, the state *per se* cannot be an analytical unit since state-level polities, as a class of phenomena, do not have shared developmental histories. Although such an idea is theoretically plausible, it is statistically unlikely that the constellation of traits and institutions comprising the state at different times and places would evolve in an homologous fashion. Rather, the developmental regulari-

98

ties sought by anthropologists must be identified at a more particularistic level. The specific axes of variability that relate to people and production within such systems thus become the focus of analysis. I define four such axes that are relevant to the complexity of any cultural system: demographic, economic, social, and political.

Demographic variability

Demographers use a variety of measures to describe the structure of human populations and the way that structure has changed through time. Age/sex ratios, fertility and mortality rates, migration, and the like are all viewed as essential measures in comparative demographic studies of modern populations. Because of demographic research, however, anthropologists are keenly aware that modern states have very different population structures, and fertility and mortality rates, depending on the position of the state in the developed or developing world. Such populations also have very different developmental histories because of the divergent historical forces of colonialism and modernization. Consequently, the identification and explanation of changes in the complexity of cultural systems resulting from demographic processes that are the product of shared developmental histories would appear too complex to be of value in the search for structural regularities.

Two axes of demographic variability, however, are properties of all human populations: population size and population density. Although these measures are rarely used analytically by demographers in the study of modern populations, they are of key interest in the study of social and political evolution. This interest results from the fact that measures of changing population size and density, when viewed diachronically, reflect rates of population growth or decline, aggregation or dispersal. Because particular political and social systems are really nothing more than solutions to specific problems of management and production, the size and density of human populations on the landscape are directly linked to the complexity of the decision-making system. In other words, the complexity of social and political systems, and especially decision-making, are regulated in a fundamental manner by the size and density of populations. Thus, I suggest that a beginning point for all studies of social and political evolution is to compile longitudinal data on changes in population size and density.

Elsewhere (Upham 1987), I have sought to clarify the relationship between increases in social and political complexity and the two demographic variables of size and density by reevaluating a detailed comparative study of social and political organization undertaken by Feinman and Neitzel (1984). Based on the data they compiled for 106 ethnographically known New World groups, I constructed a series of statistical analyses to evaluate how various indicators of political control (number of administrative levels, craft production, form of political control, etc.) were correlated with the demographic variables. Although my results remain tentative, overall population size was strongly correlated (correlation coefficient = 0.929779, explaining more than 86 percent of the variance) with seven variables related to centralized (and sometimes coercive) political control.[2] More significant, however, was that fact that population threshold values were identified for each of the variables. The mean threshold value for all of the variables was approximately 10,500 people, meaning that many of the attributes of political complexity identified by Feinman and Neitzel have a statistically higher probability of occurrence in total regional populations larger than this figure. From this analysis, it became clear that *population density* and not merely total population size was also an extremely important variable. Unfortunately, my analysis was exploratory and the ethnographic data were not sufficiently fine-grained to examine this axis of variability.

There is little question that population density is an important variable in explanation of change in social and political systems. To measure population density, especially during periods in prehistory when the first emergent social and political hierarchies formed, archaeological data must be of superior quality. At the present time, archaeologists use a variety of different proxy measures to calculate total population size (number of rooms, floor area within rooms, site size, number of vessels, vessel capacity, etc.), each of which has both strengths and weaknesses. Extrapolating total population counts based on these proxies to measures of population density, however, presupposes a knowledge of the past that would be difficult to validate even under the best of conditions. Consequently, another kind of indicator is required to examine population density prior to the advent of detailed census data. I suggest that along with total population, the total population size of individual communities can also prove useful.

Naroll (1956) has shown, for example, that communities larger than about 500 people generally have more centralized political leadership.

100

This finding is not remarkable in that as community size increases, face-to-face interaction also increases and the potential for disputes and conflict is greater (cf. Flannery 1972; Johnson 1983). Community populations larger than 500 must also work out strategies for resource allocation and mate selection. I find Naroll's result particularly intriguing since a community of 500 is also the approximate size of the minimum local population in which endogamy is possible on a regular basis (see Wobst 1974). Community endogamy can facilitate marriage strategies used by small local groups to gain access to or maintain control of strategic resources. Consequently, when communities larger than approximately 500 people exist in conjunction with total regional populations of 10,500, the potential for emergent social and political hierarchies to form is greatly increased.

Such a conclusion is neither new (see, for example, Michels 1915:26–27) nor surprising. Several previous researchers have explored the relationship between demographic variables and the formation of political hierarchies (Niemi and Weisberg 1972; Dahl and Tufte 1973; Noell 1974; Mayhew 1973; Mayhew and Levinger 1976). Their work indicates that centralized political bodies are more likely to evolve as the size of a system increases. "In fact, Michel's 'iron law of oligarchy' was originally hypothesized to hold only after a critical point in size had been reached: a point somewhere in the range of 1000 to 10,000" (Mayhew and Levinger 1976:1017).

By advocating a primacy for demographic data in the search for structural regularities, I am not suggesting that demographic prime-mover arguments or Boserupian solutions are required to explain the emergence and subsequent evolution of specific political or social systems. One must also explain why the size and density of populations change. Recourse to pat prime-mover arguments or Boserupian models is antithetical to the general anthropological goal of explaining change.

There may be an illusion of "magic numbers" in the above discussion. It should be recognized, however, that these population figures are simply estimates. Such numbers are not a panacea for explanation, nor are they substitutes for empirical data. Threshold values in state variables do exist, however, and when such values are met (within certain prescribed ranges), quantum leaps in the form and structure of social and political systems occur.

Economic variability

Since the time of Karl Marx, social scientists have actively sought to demonstrate how economy and the mode and relations of production either determine or are determined by various political and social configurations. Particular economies and production strategies, as aspects of social and political systems, are merely solutions to problems of management; management needs pertaining to production are intimately related to demographic variability. Strong connections exist between the relations of production in any economy and the size and quality of the productive base (see Gall and Saxe 1977). These relationships, when filtered through populations of varying size and density, give rise to distinctive economic forms and institutions. When such connections are considered on a worldwide basis, the incredible variety of relationships found among just these few variables would seem to preclude anthropologists' ability to offer more general, evolutionary formulations. Yet there is one change in the relations of production that divides all economies into two distinctive, wholly separate groups: the change from subsistence production to production for exchange. This change thus identifies a boundary, and that *boundary* can be viewed as a general property of all economic systems.

The boundary between economic systems based on subsistence production and those based upon exchange is not arbitrarily placed. Because the relations of production are reflections of management considerations more broadly construed, fundamental changes in such relations mirror like changes in the form and structure of management and decision-making. Frederick Engels (1972 [1884]) may have been the first to recognize how strategies of production for exchange stimulated specialization in labor, the emergence of social classes, and the development of private property. But his ideas have become unfortunately politicized and because of this fact, foster polemic in scientific arguments. Leacock (1975, 1978, 1982), in her work on gender hierarchy and hierarchy in general, has taken a less doctrinaire (but no less political!), more social scientific approach to this issue and has also recognized the importance of this boundary. On the basis of her work, one can define two mutually exclusive organizational modes that coincide with subsistence production and production for exchange, respectively. They are found in systems of group dependence (usually hunting and gathering familial groups or patribands) on the one hand,

and systems of hierarchy on the other (supra-household systems). In the vast middle ground between these two organizational modes are found dyadic (male–female) structures of dependence and decision-making that exist as horticulturally or pastorally based households (although not necessarily sedentary ones). As Netting (1965b, 1979) and Wilk and Netting (1984) have shown, the household as a primary unit of production, distribution, transmission (inheritance), reproduction, and consumption is enormously variable across cultures. Yet it is within the context of these dyadic structures of dependence that the change from subsistence production to production for exchange occurs. So that we can understand the emergence of more complex vertically and horizontally specialized decision-making structures (bureaucracies) that characterize all supra-household systems, investigation must then center on the relations of production found in the household.

It is clear that if we focus on the important boundary between subsistence production and production for exchange, a host of other economic processes become relevant. The intensity of agricultural production, storage, productive specialization, as well as the local and regional procurement, supply, and distribution of commodities are all variables that must be measured. Moreover, all of these variables must be considered in conjunction with demographic processes.

Social variability

A third major axis of variability relevant to the complexity of any cultural system pertains to social organization and to the social arrangements found in human societies. It is clear from the past work of ethnographers that the variety of social institutions found cross-culturally is immense. Systems of kinship, cross-cutting associations and sodalities, patterns of post-marital residence and so on are so diverse in the literature as to appear nearly unique for each human group. Although the previous sentiment is no doubt an overstatement, such uniqueness has been compounded by the facile manner that anthropologists describe such systems as "localistic" developments. Moreover, anthropologists are willing to identify unique traits and institutions over more general features of social organization. The resulting welter of organizational forms found in the ethnographic literature would thus seem to preclude more general formulations.

Again, however, there is a dimension of social variability that stands apart from the details of any specific organizational form, and mirrors specific changes in the complexity of social organization. That dimension is social symboling, embodied in the concept of "style," and it can be used to distinguish significant evolutionary changes in the complexity of human social systems. These changes in complexity can be identified and measured based on the way various cultural and ethnic groups employ stylistic criteria to signal individual or group identity. The recent exchange between Sackett (1985) and Wiessner (1985) on the interpretation of stylistic data has called needed attention to this important area of anthropological inquiry. More recently, S. Plog (1987) has sought to clarify and elaborate on the ideas of Sackett and Wiessner and show how stylistic data are relevant to the evolution of social and political systems. On the basis of his work and of the work of Sackett and Wiessner, I distinguish between three different kinds of "stylistic" behavior: isochrestic, symbolic or iconographic, and heterochrestic.

At the most basic behavioral level, isochrestic variation refers to stylistic criteria that are both idiomatic and diagnostic of ethnicity (Sackett 1985:157). Yet isochrestic variation (meaning literally "equivalent in use") specifically refers

to the fact that there normally exists an appreciable range of equivalent alternatives, of equally viable options, for attaining any given end in manufacturing craft products. Style enters the equation when it is recognized that the choices artisans make along the range of options potentially available to them tend to be quite specific and consistent, and that these are directed largely by the craft traditions within which the artisans have been enculturated as members of social groups (ibid.).

In other words, stylistic variability that is isochrestic derives from the unique properties of each cultural group's historical development and reflects patterns learned by rote by all participating members of that social system. Conkey (1978, 1980) has argued that the kind of standardization in material culture resulting from isochrestic behavior is not found prior to the Mousterian (*ca.* 100,000 B.P.). Today, isochrestic variability is a measurable property of all classes of material objects, but is not a *primary* means of signaling cultural or ethnic identity. Because of that fact, isochrestic style similarities and differences are of little interest in the search for structural regularities.

The second stylistic category, stylistic variability that is symbolic or

104

iconographic in content, corresponds to Wiessner's "emblemic" designation and refers to

> styles [that have] a behavioral basis in the fundamental human cognitive process of personal and social identification through stylistic and social comparison. In this process, people compare their ways of making artifacts with those of others and then imitate, differentiate, ignore, or in some way comment on how aspects of the maker or bearer relate to their own social and personal identities. Style is thus not acquired and developed through routine duplication of certain standard types, but through dynamic comparison of artifacts and corresponding social attributes of their makers. Stylistic outcomes project positive images of identity to others in order to obtain social recognition (Wiessner 1985:161).

No doubt Leslie White (1959) would have viewed the kind of stylistic behavior identified by Wiessner and S. Plog as beginning with cave art during the Upper Paleolithic about 40,000 years ago. Symbolic content as a primary form of stylistic behavior is enduring. Wiessner, for example, has shown how modern !Kung San projectile points symbolically communicate individual and language group identity (Wiessner 1983).

Many other examples of symbolic or emblemic styles can be found today as a primary means of expressing individual or cultural identity. Often symbolic variability takes the form of iconographic representation. I define iconography as the use of styles that are fixed by convention to convey the identity of a specific subject (an individual or group) *and* the set of conventions or principles that govern the use of such imagery. Wiessner (1985:161) and S. Plog (1987:3) have both suggested that iconographic variability is a "special case of stylistic behavior" that is symbolic in content, information-rich, and aimed at a specific target population. The most important characteristic of both symbolic and iconographic behavior is that they communicate identity and membership at the level of the entire cultural or ethnic group; they are boundary-setting, but their use is inclusive at the level of the entire group.

The final category of stylistic behavior refers to variability that is *heterochrestic*, a neologism literally meaning "unequal in use." As the opposite of isochrestic, I have reluctantly chosen this term to represent stylistic identities that are differentially shared within and between cultural and ethnic groups. Such differential sharing of heterochrestic styles is conscious and directed and, like iconographic variability, is governed by rules and conventions. Heterochrestic behavior, however, demarcates subgroups that possess and maintain distinct stylistic identities. Most commonly these identities are status related, and access to heterochrestic styles is determined by membership criteria that are ascribed.

As a primary form of stylistic behavior, heterochrestic variability is found in societies that publicly identify the rank or status of individuals or groups. The corollaries to this kind of public identification may vary, but the possession and use of heterochrestic styles always defines a distinct status for an individual or subgroup within a larger interacting population (the most studied are styles that define "elites," but heterochrestic styles also demarcate slaves, serfs, peasants, or the "poor" from other segments of a population). Like symbolic or iconographic styles, the identification of heterochrestic behavior is as much a study in the distribution of specific styles as it is an exercise in defining their information content, and the rules or conventions that govern their use. Many different examples of heterochrestic variability have been identified in both the archaeological and ethnographic literature. Unlike broadly available symbolic or iconographic stylistic elements, differential access and use of heterochrestic styles always results in inhomogeneous distributions of key style elements.

The distinction between symbolic and heterochrestic styles defines a boundary between two distinct social and political forms. In any society, style in material culture (or speech) is a social resource. Because public style displays are always for public consumption, they reflect directly on the nature of access to resources in a society. The boundary that separates symbolic from heterochrestic styles also distinguishes the boundary between unrestricted and restricted access to social resources. In all societies, when access to social resources is restricted there are corresponding restrictions, albeit of varying intensities, to natural resources that divide a given population into subgroups of varying rank or status. The emergence of these subdivisions, from the standpoint of social and political evolution, is of paramount interest.

Many anthropologists have identified these fundamental changes in styles and access as a meaningful sociopolitical boundary. A few anthropologists have also sought to describe the corresponding organizational features of the two broad groups of societies that result

106

from this type of classifying. Leacock and Lee (1982:7–8), for example, discuss the essential forms of "group dependence," and I believe their definition conforms to the kind of social and political systems that rely solely on the use of symbolic styles. The attributes, found most typically in hunting and gathering societies, include "egalitarian patterns of sharing, strong anti-authoritarianism, an emphasis on the importance of cooperation in decision-making, conflict resolution, sharing, exchange, the allocation of rights to lands and resources, the socialization of children, and the ritualization of potential conflict between the sexes" (ibid.). It is significant to note that the virtual opposite of many of these attributes defines what have been described as state-level polities (see, for example, Haas 1982). These latter systems are dominated by heterochrestic style behaviors. Occupying the vast middle range between these two forms of human organization are most societies. It is among these groups that the use of symbolic and heterochrestic styles is of greatest interest, since the public identification of rank or status that is correlated with a restriction of access to social and natural resources represents a quantum leap in the complexity of social and political systems. Styles and their context, then, become a focus for inquiry into the evolution of social and political organization.

Political variability

The final axis of variability in the generic framework I have constructed pertains to political decision-making and to the way decision-making systems articulate with the three axes of variability described above. In a previous study (Upham 1982:4), I defined the political processes in the following manner:

I equate the decision-making process with the political process, defining the latter as the ability of an individual or group to instigate and link together the behavior and acts of others by the power of persuasion or coercion so as to create a necessity for action within the perceived common good. The concern . . . then, is with the managerial structure, the decisions of which affect the behavior and economy of the general population.

In a more recent study, F. Plog and I have sought to elaborate on this definition to clarify how political decision-making might demarcate societies into broad classes that are managerially distinct. We also sought to develop a model of political decision-making that would have material correlates and, consequently, would be useful to archaeologists:

Although status and role are pertinent concepts for the study of political systems, the archaeological record, to the extent that it reflects political organization, is the product of managerial decisions broadly construed. In any society, the most basic of these decisions involve access to space, access to human and natural resources, and access to social resources including statuses, organization, and symbols. Across societies access to space, natural resources, and social resources varies *in the extent of its restriction to particular individuals or groups and whether the restrictions are consensual or cooptative* (Plog and Upham 1983:201; my italics).

In much the same way that symbolic and heterochrestic variability are manifest in content, use, and ultimately, in homogeneous or inhomogeneous distributions of particular style elements, decision-making by consensus or cooptation produces different kinds of distributions of material culture that can be used to distinguish major differences in the complexity of decision-making systems. Because political decision-making often pertains to problems of access to various kinds of resources, distinguishing between consensual and cooptative systems also distinguishes between systems of free and restricted access. As I argued for styles and social resources, I would again argue that this fundamental difference in access identifies two separate trajectories of social and political evolution.

There is general consensus among anthropologists, a few dissenters notwithstanding (e.g. Cashdan 1980), that most hunting and gathering societies now and in the past can be characterized by a socio-political ethos that emphasizes egalitarian patterns of sharing and free access within the group to basic natural, human, and social resources. Similarly, most anthropologists would also agree that the large, vertically and horizontally specialized bureaucracies found in pre-industrial and industrial societies are characterized by a socio-political ethos that emphasizes disparities in access to natural, human, and social resources. Between these two extremes the vast majority of societies are found. At just what point political decision-making changes from a system of consensus to one of cooptation is an empirical question that can be determined by studying patterns of access to key resources.

Other considerations

The four axes of variability discussed above are graphically presented in figure 4.1. I have dichotomized the pathways of evolutionary development into mutually exclusive alternatives that exist as quantum states. Only two outcomes are possible in the model. The first, undifferentiated political systems, refers to the basic, and possibly the only abiding, form of human organization: systems of group dependence. Systems of group dependence are historically linked to small hunting and gathering

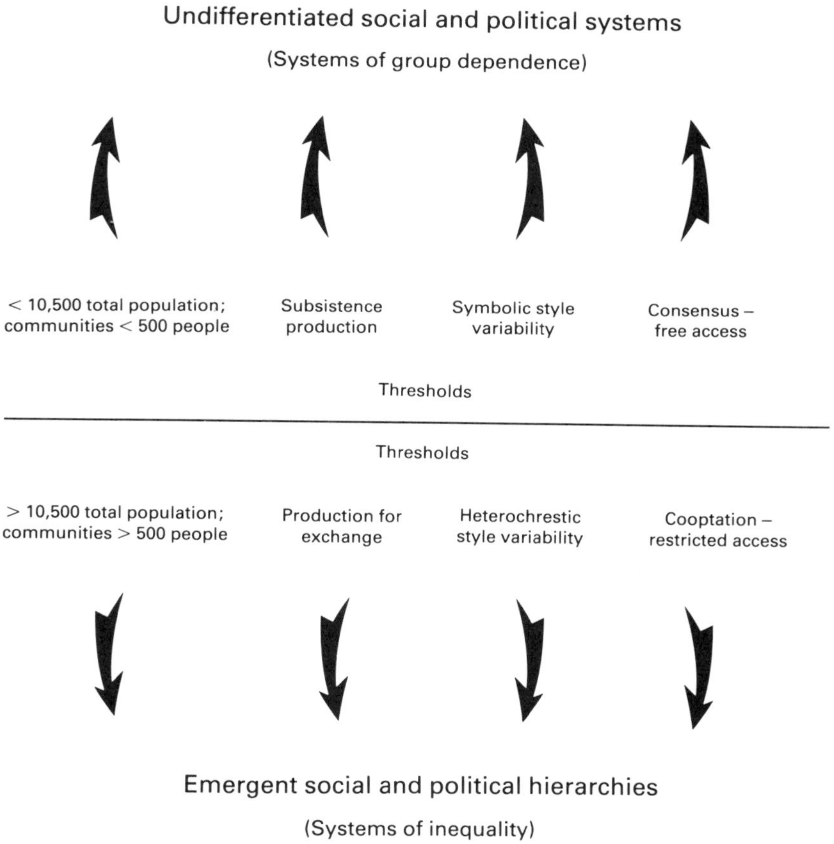

Undifferentiated social and political systems

(Systems of group dependence)

| < 10,500 total population; communities < 500 people | Subsistence production | Symbolic style variability | Consensus – free access |

Thresholds

Thresholds

| > 10,500 total population; communities > 500 people | Production for exchange | Heterochrestic style variability | Cooptation – restricted access |

Emergent social and political hierarchies

(Systems of inequality)

Figure 4.1   A graphic representation of the generic framework. Only two outcomes, undifferentiated social and political systems and emergent social and political hierarchies, are recognized from the four state variables.

populations (although they occur under other subsistence modes as well) and, as a class of phenomena, have existed since the Lower Paleolithic. A few anthropologists have argued that other kinds of social configurations, especially those formed during what Braun and Plog (1982) identify as the process of *tribalization*, would conform to the definition of an undifferentiated political system. The second outcome, emergent social and political hierarchies, represents the only alternative to systems of group dependence. These emergent hierarchies are a class of phenomena and are best described as systems of inequality. Obviously the intensity of both group dependence and inequality varies between systems and through time so that there are more and less intense egalitarian patterns of sharing or inequality in different social and political systems of the same class.

The general patterns of world history suggest that a prerequisite for the development of emergent social and political hierarchies is a sedentary or semi-sedentary lifestyle, in which substantial portions of each year are spent in permanent settlements. Social and political systems characterized by emergent political hierarchies thus probably existed in very small numbers before the origins of agriculture and other strategies of food production. Based on archaeological and ethnographic data, their occurrence would be predicted in resource-rich environments, like those seen in temperate zones along the Pacific coast of North America at the close of the Pleistocene. Following the origins and spread of agriculture, the number of emergent social and political hierarchies increased rapidly.

Traditionally, sedentarization is linked to groups involved in food production, groups residing in those regions where sufficient natural resources permit the establishment of permanent settlements, or, more recently, groups in the throes of modernization or development. As such, sedentarization is normally associated with (a) certain kinds of environments (those either conducive to agriculture or naturally resource-rich), (b) surplus production (at least production sufficient to carry a group through the four seasons of the year), or (c) the availability of resources or capital from more developed groups, a slightly different kind of "natural resource" (Kenyon 1959:35; MacNeish 1964:531; Braidwood and Braidwood 1953:278). I term this process "sedentarization through abundance." Many discussions of sedentarization through abundance, especially in the archaeological literature, are thus directed to the study of purely environmental considerations (availability of water, amount and quality of arable land, abundance of natural resources, climate, etc.). If one were to survey the anthropological literature on sedentarization, this pathway to sedentary life would appear virtually exclusive.

A focus on purely environmental issues and on sedentarization through abundance, however, obscures a very important issue. Another alternative, "sedentarization through impoverishment," is just as common, if not more common, than the traditionally accepted explanation. Sedentarization through impoverishment has been occasionally described in the anthropological literature (see Barth 1961). Sedentarization through impoverishment can occur in a variety of ways, but most often begins when population increases and a given landscape becomes "packed." Among pastoralists, a packed landscape decreases the amount of available pasturage, stimulates herd reduction strategies, and can result in the eventual loss of animals. If unchecked, entire herds can be lost and households can be forced to join existing settlements, almost always in dependency relationships with other households or supra-households and in circumstances of greatly reduced status.

Among hunter-gatherers, a packed landscape decreases foraging range, increases competition for increasingly scarce resources, and may stimulate intensified procurement strategies. In prehistory, many such hunting and gathering populations may have responded to increased population densities by joining agricultural or pastoral communities. Such communities existed as "magnets" on the landscape in much the same way that trading posts or mission stations do today in remote regions (Lee 1972a, 1972b). Exactly which communities were selected by hunter-gatherers may relate to long-term social relationships between foragers and farmers and to the kinds of "alliances" described by Bender (1978:210–13). Hunter-gatherers, like pastoralists joining sedentary communities, also existed in positions of greatly reduced status.

Arguments seeking too strong a link between environmental variables and the process of sedentarization often mistake the environmental setting as causal. As I intended to show above, sedentarization through impoverishment is fundamentally a demographic process (Cohen 1977:83). As Hitchcock (1982:231) points out,

Simple availability of resources (is) insufficient to bring about residential stability for an extended period of time . . . Long term residential stability comes about when a group's mobility options are restricted due to the fact that there are too many other groups occupying the habitat.

CONCLUSION

Significant changes in the complexity of social and political systems, resulting in the fundamental transformations discussed in this chapter, occur in only a few of the many societal dimensions studied by anthropologists. I have sought to identify the four basic axes of variability that are both preconditions and indicators of cultural evolutionary change. I would argue that change in these four axes in effect "drives the system"; that other more particularistic societal dimensions respond to these axes of variability and change in kind. In this sense, elements of any cultural system that fall outside the four basic axes of variability I have described can be considered as epiphenomena.

I have argued that demographic variability as it relates to total population size and to population density, viewed by its proxy indicator of community size, is the most significant axis of variation because it provides a set of preconditions that must be met *before* significant evolutionary change can occur. When these preconditions are met, a threshold is crossed and economic, social, and political systems also begin to change. Clearly, the rates at which change occurs in these latter three societal dimensions is an empirical question of great interest. In the natural sciences, systematists have devoted substantial energy to classifying phenomena based on homologous rates of change (e.g. Simpson 1944, 1952, 1953). Given the perspective of the present chapter, I argue that a major goal for anthropology is the development of what might be considered "cultural taxa" based on homologous rates of change in economic, social, and political systems that derive from different demographic inputs. It is at this level that the idea of shared developmental histories becomes truly meaningful.

I have also suggested that the major social indicator of change from systems of group dependence to emergent political hierarchies is stylistic; that the change from symbolic to heterochrestic style behaviors clearly identifies this important boundary. Identifying the heterochrestic or symbolic "signature," especially for archaeologists who do not work with living systems, is explicitly a distributional exercise whereby the context of use and discard for items of material culture are critical dimensions of any reconstructions of past social and political systems. Cultural anthropologists, on the other hand, can investigate

112

the material patterns along with the jural systems governing access and use of styles marking social identity.

In the generic framework, the remaining two axes of variability, economic and political, are located structurally between the demographic preconditions and the stylistic manifestations of social and political complexity. I have suggested that the change from subsistence production to production for exchange, for example, occurs in the context of the household. Wilk and Netting (1984:7–8) have shown that the most important kind of variation in production occurs in scheduling at the household level. They define scheduling as "the timing (in the yearly cycle) of productive tasks and the sequencing (the order) of the tasks themselves" (ibid.) They go on to identify simple and diverse production systems. In simple productive systems, the sequencing of tasks is relatively uncomplicated and productive activities can be ordered without conflict. When household production systems are diverse, however, the performance of major productive activities must be simultaneous. Consequently, scheduling conflicts can arise. Theoretically, a variety of solutions to scheduling conflicts are possible, but Wilk and Netting show convincingly that one solution, to increase the size of the household, is far more common than any other.

Because scheduling conflicts most often arise when populations increase, there is a general relationship between labor demands within the household and local and regional demographic conditions. Moreover, there are indications that specialization and differentiation in task performance are used by large households with diverse productive strategies to linearize scheduling conflicts (see Befu 1968a, 1968b; Hughes 1975; Sahlins 1957). Specialization in task performance, a basic condition of production for exchange, may thus result from scheduling conflicts in diverse production systems and be related to local and regional demographic conditions.

I have argued in this chapter that change from subsistence production to production for exchange would be far more likely to occur when village and total regional population threshold values were met or exceeded. These demographic preconditions are linked to the household through labor demands and scheduling. Once specialization in task performance begins to occur, individuals are separated from the full range of subsistence activities and a related process, the separation of food producers from consumers, can also be seen to have its roots in the

113

household. This kind of separation presents a unique challenge to any decision-making system, and especially to those predicated on egalitarian patterns of sharing. How does one evaluate (and valuate) human labor performed at different tasks? Are all tasks of equal value, or are some more valuable than others? While this is a complex issue, the basis for the change in decision-making from consensus to cooptation, and the concomitant dimension of access to all human, natural, and social resources resides in the process of valuating human labor performed at different tasks. The way such decisions are ultimately made is manifest in the social styles of any society.

I have attempted to bring together a series of tangible and measurable attributes of human societies that are sensitive to one of the most important changes in the human cultural past: the change from systems of group dependence to systems of inequality. I have also tried to suggest, using the example of technological change in analog and digital instrumentation, that attention to both categorical and continuous measures is necessary to identify important axes of cultural variation and to explain change. I have further suggested that threshold values in key state variables exist and that quantum change in the organization of social and political systems occurs when such values are met or exceeded. More importantly, however, I have identified the measurement of rates of change in major axes of variability as the most important long-term goal for anthropologists. Our success in these efforts will determine the scale and importance of our contributions as social scientists to general evolutionary theory and to the development of a general theory of history.

NOTES

Linda S. Cordell, Gary Feinman, Scott Rushforth, Edward Staski, Wenda R. Trevathan, and Richard Wilk provided critical commentary on a pre-seminar version of this chapter. Their views are greatly appreciated. The seminar participants added further insight to the thesis presented here. I am indebted to the participants for their perspicacity and advice.
1. It is ironic to note that as this chapter is being written, high-energy physicists are again seeking to model a more continuous universe by developing "string theory" and ideas of "supersymmetry."
2. The seven variables correlated with total population size in Feinman and

114

Analog or digital?

Neitzel's data are a leader's control of storage, special burials for leaders, treatment of the leader with obeisance, provisioning the leader with special food, special residences for leaders, increased size of the administrative organization, and increased size of the largest community.

115

The role of decision-making, productive, and environmental processes in political change

5

Maintaining economic equality in opposition to complexity: an Iroquoian case study

BRUCE G. TRIGGER

McGill University

In this chapter I present an account of Iroquoian prehistory and ethnohistory in order to call into question certain general concepts about the nature of power and social change in small-scale societies. These concepts, which have become increasingly popular among self-styled critical archaeologists in the last decade, have repudiated many traditional archaeological and ethnographic interpretations, including those based on the tenets of classical Marxism (Miller and Tilley 1984).

Karl Marx and Friedrich Engels interpreted "primitive" societies as being in many respects the opposite of class ones, which were their main object of study. They believed that these small-scale societies were egalitarian collectivities that had not yet developed social classes, exploitation, or class conflict. They believed further that these phenomena were the principal dynamic forces in more developed societies. To a large degree primitive societies were viewed as static, at least with respect to their principal structural features, and such changes as did occur were largely attributed to ecological or technological factors (Bloch 1983:1–94). One of the great attractions of these societies for revolutionary Marxists was their demonstration that hierarchical organization and exploitation are not inherent in human nature and therefore inevitable features of all human societies (for recent discus-

119

sions of Marxist views of human nature, see Fuller 1980:230–64; Geras 1983).

A similar view was independently adopted in the 1950s by American neo-evolutionary anthropologists, who interpreted band and tribal societies as economically egalitarian. The power of chiefs or "big-men" was based on their ability to win renown by producing and giving away more goods to their supporters than they received from them (Sahlins 1968; Service 1962). Yet in recent years, there has been a tendency to restrict these features to nomadic hunter-gatherer societies and to stress the hierarchical characteristics of more sedentary collecting and agricultural groups (Testart 1982). Anthropologists have also emphasized the rapidity with which egalitarian structures are transformed into hierarchical ones, as surviving hunter-gatherer peoples enter into relations with more complex societies (Cashdan 1980; Leacock and Lee 1982; Lee 1984). The implication of both observations is often taken to be that equality is far more fragile and short-lived than anthropologists had previously believed.

At the same time, Marxist and self-styled Marxist anthropologists in France, such as Terray, Rey, and Meillassoux, have sought to extend the Marxist explanation of class conflict as the major cause of social change to account for change in all societies. They argue that the differences of age, gender, and personal prestige found in small-scale societies give rise to conflicts that are similar to those that occur between classes in more complex ones. All social change is thus viewed as being the result of conflict among interest groups. Rey and Terray assert that all societies are in some sense class societies, with Terray differentiating between simpler societies in which age and sex groupings constitute "classes in themselves" and the hierarchical divisions of more complex societies, which constitute self-conscious "classes for themselves" (Bloch 1983:163). We thus witness what, in traditional Marxist terms, must be accounted a Pyrrhic victory. These anthropologists have extended a Marxist-style analysis of internal factors that promote development to include small-scale societies only at the cost of abandoning the equally important Marxist argument that human behavior is radically different in small-scale as opposed to class societies. In accepting the universality of social conflict, these self-styled Marxists have embraced a favorite doctrine of right-wing social analysts (Ardrey 1961, 1966).

This was precisely the point denied by Pierre Clastres (1977:6) when he maintained that coercion and subordination of one individual or group by another do not constitute the essence of power in all societies. He asserted, as do orthodox Marxists, that society as a whole was the locus of power prior to the development of the state. He argued more creatively that both conflicts between groups within a society and the exercise of power by one individual over others are seen in small-scale societies as tendencies that have to be subdued and negated (1977:35). He also believed that primitive peoples intuitively understand the danger of the state and are prepared to use force to prevent the development of private power (1977:158, 180). Thus, "the history of peoples without history is the history of their struggle against the State" (1977:185–86). Clastres saw demographic growth as unsettling to egalitarian societies and ultimately subverting their political institutions. The Tupi-Guarani peoples of South America, with their high population densities and communities of over a thousand inhabitants, were cited as an example of the extreme upper limit at which an egalitarian political structure could be maintained. He argued that their chiefs sought power but that their ambitions were thwarted by the "Land Without Evil," a powerful religious movement which identified political power with evil and hindered its development by encouraging the relocation and dispersal of social groups (1977:182).

Clastres's position is very interesting, but his analysis of how small-scale societies maintain egalitarian structures remains sketchy and particularistic to the Indians of South America. I will take up his arguments with reference to the Iroquoian-speaking peoples who lived in northeastern North America in the seventeenth century, especially the Huron and the Five Nations Iroquois, who are the best documented of these groups. Both were confederacies composed of four or five tribes and embracing 20,000 to 30,000 people, whose settlements in the case of Huron were concentrated in an area of less than 2,000 km.[2] Like the Tupinamba, the Iroquoians lived in multi-family longhouses and often in large, heavily fortified villages, practiced slash-and-burn agriculture, had hereditary chiefships, and routinely engaged in warfare and the ritual sacrifice of prisoners. While the Tupinamba were patrilineal and polygynous, the Iroquoians were matrilineal and monogamous. There is also no evidence that the zone of Iroquoian settlement was expanding in early historical times, while that of the Tupinamba was. There is excellent historical-ethnographic documentation for the Huron prior to their dispersal by the Iroquois in 1649 (Trigger 1976), and for the

121

Iroquois beginning in the 1630s, as well as a continuous tradition of
ethnographic studies of the descendants of these groups starting early in
the nineteenth century (Morgan 1851; Tooker 1985a, 1985b, 1985c).
There is also a detailed archaeological record which documents the
rapidly changing nature of Iroquoian societies in prehistoric and early
historical times. These data provide a broad basis for understanding the
nature of power in Iroquoian societies at the beginning of recorded
European contact in the seventeenth century.

PREHISTORIC DEVELOPMENT

Historical linguists have concluded that the Iroquoian-speaking peoples
originated in the northern part of the deciduous woodlands of eastern
North America (perhaps to the south of the Great Lakes in what is now
Ohio, Pennsylvania, and New York State, rather than in Ontario), and
began to disperse 3,500 to 4,000 years ago (Lounsbury 1978:334–36;
Buell 1979; Mithun 1984). Archaeological and physical anthropological evidence indicates a continuity of population between the
Middle Woodland (500 B.C.–A.D. 1000) hunter-gatherer populations
of southern Ontario and the historical Iroquoians (Wright 1972, 1984;
Molto 1983:234). This continuity suggests that the growing of maize,
and later of beans and squash, was adopted by an indigenous Iroquoian
population beginning sometime after A.D. 500. The earliest evidence
of agriculture in this region appears in the Princess Point culture of
southwestern Ontario, and somewhat later in south-central Ontario,
upper New York State, and the St. Lawrence Valley (Fecteau 1985;
Timmins 1985:159–61). The Princess Point people as well as contemporary and later Owasco groups in New York State dispersed in
small hunting groups each winter, as hunter-gatherers had done
previously, but they grew small amounts of corn on the flood plains
when they gathered in groups of several hundred people to fish in the
warmer weather (Stothers 1977; Ritchie and Funk 1973:179–94; Niemczycki 1986). It is not known whether they cached their seed corn or
carried it with them over the winter. Either practice would have differed
radically from nut or wild rice collecting, which did not require the
conservation of part of the harvest until the following year.

In the following Early Iroquoian period (A.D. 1000–1300), the
Ontario Iroquoians were living in small, year-round villages and
growing corn on adjacent, easily worked, sandy soils. These villages

were relocated periodically as adjacent soil, firewood, and other resources were depleted. They were often palisaded, which has been interpreted as evidence of warfare, although the single rows of small poles that were erected at this time may have served mainly as fences to keep out snow or dangerous wild animals (Pearce 1984:318). People lived in small multi-family houses of a sort already attested in Middle Woodland times (Brose 1970). Provisional studies of pottery suggest that matrilocal residence may already have been established (Whallon 1968; cf. Richards 1967, Hayden 1979:182, but see Trigger 1978). It is unclear whether band exogamy continued to be practiced, as it had been in Middle Woodland times, when physical anthropological evidence also indicates that continuity in band membership was patrilineal (Spence 1986; Spence et al. 1979). Williamson's (1985) study of Early Iroquoian settlement patterns on the Caradoc sand plain in south-western Ontario shows a continuing heavy reliance on wild plants and animals, with parties of men, women, and children spending long periods at collecting camps far from their main villages. Cultural change appears to have been occurring relatively slowly at this time, although in the Caradoc area there was a growing emphasis on locating villages adjacent to soils that were suitable for agriculture (Williamson 1985:326). There is little evidence of intertribal trade (Ritchie 1965:293; Pearce 1984:334–36) or of elaborate burial rituals. Both had been more developed in parts of southern Ontario and New York State in the late Archaic and Middle Woodland periods when those areas were involved, if only peripherally, in the widespread Adena and Hopewellian interaction spheres (Johnston 1968; Ritchie 1965:213–14). Recent studies of Eastern Woodland religious beliefs that survived into historical times suggest a close relationship between exotic substances, such as native copper, marine shells, and quartz crystals, and burial cults (Hamell 1983).

The Middle Iroquoian period (A.D. 1300–1400) was an episode of revolutionary change (Lenig 1965; Wright 1966). It was marked by the first appearance of large Iroquoian communities of a thousand people or more. Where this process has been studied in detail, it appears that such towns developed as a result of two or more Early Iroquoian villages joining together (Tuck 1971; Pearce 1984). The Iroquoians now relied almost as heavily on agriculture as a source of food as they did in historical times, and they cultivated heavier, more drought-resistant soils than before (Pearce 1984:287). The average length of longhouses

123

increased at this time; ones over 100 meters long were recorded for the beginning of the Late Iroquoian period (MacDonald 1986; Tuck 1971). There was also growing variation in the length of these houses, and in the number of families that lived in them (Dodd 1984:267; Tuck 1971:79–85). Among the ancestors of the Huron and Petun, ossuaries began to appear in which the bones of the dead, initially deposited above ground in village cemeteries, were communally interred when a community relocated at intervals of a decade or longer (Anderson 1964). There is still, however, not much evidence of long-distance trade, although some marine shell from the south and native copper from the upper Great Lakes was entering the area at this time (McPherron 1967:106).

Massive stylistic changes can be observed in pottery and pipe styles, which once suggested to archaeologists that spectacular population movements and conquests had occurred at the beginning of the Middle Iroquoian period (Wright 1966:53–65). Now, however, there is a growing tendency to correlate these alterations with the massive social and political changes that accompanied village fusion (Pearce 1984:233–34). There is also evidence of cannibalism, which suggests that the ritual sacrifice of prisoners of war, a prominent feature of Iroquoian societies in the historical period, had begun by at least A.D. 1400 (Wright 1966:56–57, 60, 64). The earliest evidence of cannibalism dates from late Owasco (Early Iroquoian) times in New York State (Ritchie and Funk 1973:361).

At least for south-central Ontario, the Middle Iroquoian period has been shown to be one of rapid population increase. Over a period of 100 years, the population multiplied several times, reaching a level resembling that found in historical times by the fifteenth century. This was followed by 150 years of population stability (Warrick 1989; for earlier studies of long-term population trends, see Clermont 1980 and Snow 1985). The increase appears to have been a consequence (Ritchie 1965:296; Wright 1966:59) rather than a cause (Smith 1972:418) of growing reliance on horticulture. In the historical period the Jesuits commented on the small number of children in Iroquoian families by comparison with European ones. They also noted that Iroquoian women nursed their children for two to three years and during that time avoided sexual intercourse, apparently because they believed that lactation was not a sufficient contraceptive (JR 8:127; Engelbrecht 1987). Thus, almost a millennium after the adoption of agriculture and

600 years after beginning a sedentary way of life, the Iroquoian nuclear family once again resembled demographically that of Algonquian hunter-gatherers to the north.

It is also noteworthy that, while historical Iroquoian populations were heavily concentrated in villages and tribal clusters, their overall population densities remained below one person per square km. It seems that a maximum limit was set by the inflexible fish and game reserves on which they relied for protein and clothing (Gramly 1977). Into historical times, the Iroquoian population continued to be much lower than could have been supported by the cultivation of available land, even without improvements of their simple techniques of long fallowing (Heidenreich 1971:189–200; Trigger 1976:132–33).

It is possible that larger Iroquoian communities were a response to increasing warfare, which is also attested by stronger fortifications and prisoner sacrifice. Dincauze and Hasenstab (1986) have suggested that the introduction of agriculture into the lower Great Lakes region and these later developments were Iroquoian responses to the growth of large-scale Mississippian political and economic networks. They argue that the Iroquoians were first drawn into Mississippian trading patterns, perhaps as suppliers of deer skins to Cahokia, and later were forced to defend themselves against secondary centers that developed in the Ohio Valley. Generalized southeastern influences are found in the Iroquoian agricultural complex, the incised vessels used to cook corn, and prisoner sacrifice. The latter was a ritual closely related to agricultural fertility and was also practiced farther south in the United States and in Mesoamerica (Knowles 1940; Rands and Riley 1958). Yet there is little clear evidence in Early or Middle Iroquoian times of specific Mississippian influences in the form of either religious iconography or long-distance trade.

It is possible, however, that Iroquoian social organization was significantly influenced by efforts to avoid domination by neighboring Mississippian or Mississippian-influenced cultures. An external challenge seems to provide as convincing an explanation for the escalation of warfare in the Middle Iroquoian period as do recent efforts to attribute it to environmental pressures resulting from population increases or climatic change (Gramly 1977; Warrick 1984:65–66). Large Middle Iroquoian sites appear first on the western extremity of Iroquoian settlement in southwestern Ontario, where there is evidence of warfare against Central Algonquian peoples in Michigan and Ohio that con-

125

tinued into the historical period (Pearce 1984:320–34). Communities of this type might have spread throughout the whole Northern Iroquoian culture area as small villages amalgamated to defend themselves against their larger Iroquoian neighbors (Braun and Plog 1982). This interpretation is in accord with the current understanding of radiocarbon dates, which suggests that the Middle Iroquoian revolution began in southwestern Ontario and diffused eastward to the St. Lawrence Valley over a period of about fifty years (Timmins 1985:162–64).

The larger and more varied sizes of Iroquoian houses have elicited various explanations. They are unlikely to have resulted merely from the unequal reproduction of extended families. While some of the increase in size of extended families may reflect the growing importance of female work teams (Ember 1973), not all of it can be explained in terms of the greater economic security that larger households would have enjoyed as productive units. Food stored under a single roof would have been more at risk as a result of fires, which not infrequently destroyed Iroquoian bark houses (JR 8:95, 105; 10:35, 65, 145, 169). Moreover, while the nuclear family and the household were the units that routinely produced and consumed food, the village as a whole probably pooled its resources in the Middle Iroquoian period as it did in historical times when one or more households suffered major losses (JR 14:43–45). Rivalry to control long-distance trade or exotic resources cannot have been a significant factor encouraging the growth of large extended families, since these were not major activities at this time. Defense, as expressed in the building of strong fortifications, was a community activity. This aspect of Iroquoian settlement suggests that the development of very large households may reflect lineage rivalry within communities formed by the amalgamation of smaller ones, as the Iroquoians experimented with new forms of social control. The largest households may have been the ones whose spokesmen played the most important roles in guiding the affairs of the community. Yet there is no archaeological evidence that the per capita storage capacity of large houses was greater than that of smaller ones, or that the people who lived in them were richer than their neighbors (Warrick 1984:41).

By Late Iroquoian times (A.D. 1400–1600) tribal clusters can be delineated, some of which are ancestral to specific tribes known in the historical period. Each cluster contained one to several settlements at any one time (Tuck 1971; Ramsden 1977). Maximum town size increased, with some heavily fortified communities having as many as

3,000 inhabitants. Village planning also became increasingly elaborate and regular (Warrick 1984:67–68). As in earlier times, large communities were formed through the union of two or more smaller ones. The largest communities tended to be unstable and frequently split apart to form two or more villages (Heidenreich 1971:129–34), a process that was made easier since the rapidly declining fertility of cultivated soil and diminished supplies of firewood required frequent relocations of all communities. There were also, however, many settlements that had only a few hundred inhabitants.

In recent years archaeologists have speculated that very large communities developed as "gateways" to control trade routes used in connection with the fur trade (Hayden 1978, 1979:7–9). It is now evident that many of the largest communities date from the late prehistoric period and hence from before the development of this trade (Finlayson 1985). While there was some increase in the amount of marine shell and native copper being exchanged at that time, such an increase does not appear to have been important enough to account for major changes in the settlement pattern. Nor is there archaeological evidence within these sites of chiefs who monopolized this trade. The largest historical Huron communities, which were located along the southern and eastern margins of Huron settlement, superficially look like gateways, but we know from historical records that they were formed to defend their inhabitants against Iroquois attacks from the south. This ring of heavily fortified towns also sheltered Huron settlements to the north, which remained smaller. This meant that their inhabitants lived closer to their fields and did not exhaust nearby resources so quickly. Yet the smaller northern Huron villages played an important and perhaps a leading role in the fur trade (Trigger 1976:290–92). The evidence suggests that defensive considerations rather than trade were the major determinants of Iroquoian community size in prehistoric as well as historic times.

Although longhouses reached their maximum length in early Late Iroquoian times (MacDonald 1986), they later declined in size until, by the historical period, most of them were no larger than Early Iroquoian ones had been (Dodd 1984:270). Yet within communities a few houses remained much larger than the rest. Historical and archaeological evidence suggests that these houses were associated with the chiefs of the various clan segments that made up a community; peace chiefs and war chiefs sometimes each had their own council house (Pearce 1984:305–

127

308; Finlayson 1985:416). Public feasts, rituals, and political meetings were held inside these houses (Sagard 1939:115; JR 10:181, 233; 13:59). There is still no evidence that chiefs monopolized the redistributive networks of their communities, or that they and their families possessed more food or were richer than other members of their communities (JR 10:231).

The new community plans suggest a changing emphasis in Iroquoian social organization in which clans replaced extended households as basic elements of local organization. Membership in clans was determined through matrilineal descent, and clans were named after mammals, reptiles, and birds (Tooker 1970). People who belonged to clans named after the same animal regarded themselves as kinsmen, to the extent that intermarriage was considered incestuous even between members of different tribes. Clans were further grouped to form phratries and moieties that played an important role in major rituals, including funerals. Clan segments, made up of the households in a single community whose matrilineal core belonged to the same clan, became an important element in Iroquoian community organization. They were internally self-governing in all matters and were represented at the village, tribal, and confederacy levels by their chiefs. A wider range of individuals, however, participated in community councils. Clan segments may have been descended from Middle Woodland hunter-gatherer bands. Such bands had persisted in the form of the Early Iroquoian villages that had joined together to form larger communities beginning in Middle Iroquoian times (Trigger 1976:134–35). Community endogamy may have first become possible in Middle Iroquoian times, and sometime during the late Middle Woodland or Early Iroquoian periods the basis of membership in these groups must have become matrilineal instead of patrilineal (Spence 1986).

It is possible that Middle Woodland Iroquoian bands already had quasi-hereditary chiefs, as Ojibwa, Algonquin, and Montagnais bands did in historical times. This mechanism would have allowed an age-old unit of social organization to be represented at progressively higher political levels by men who sought to coordinate activities but had no power to override the autonomous rights of clan segments or their members. The emergence of ritually constituted village councils may have lessened the need for clans or lineages to express their solidarity by forming single households, and this gradually may have resulted in a decline in the average size of longhouses (Engelbrecht 1986). The decline of household size beginning in late prehistoric times counters the suggestion that it resulted from the male-dominated fur trade undermining the traditional matrilineal structures of Iroquoian society (Smith 1970; Hayden 1979).

In the protohistoric period (A.D. 1525–1600), evidence of long-distance trade increases dramatically in the archaeological record. European goods as well as native items, such as marine shell, occur in growing numbers. At first these goods are found primarily associated with burials rather than living sites, indicating a continuation, after an apparent lapse of many centuries in this region, of a millennia-old association in eastern North America between exotic goods and burial ceremonialism (Hall 1979; Hamell 1983; Miller and Hamell 1986). Among the Huron, communal reburials of the dead make it impossible to study individual associations of grave goods, but for the Iroquois there is some indication that more exotic goods were buried with men and children than with women (Wray and Schoff 1953:55–58).

In recent years, there has been much discussion about whether there was a major decline in Iroquoian population as a result of the introduction of European diseases during the sixteenth century. Depopulation could have resulted in major changes in Iroquoian social and political organization, as well as in their patterns of ecological adaptation prior to earliest European descriptions of their cultures. Evidence of what appears to be population decline has been noted in cemeteries and settlements, especially among the Seneca (Dobyns 1983:313–27; Wray 1973:27–28). In other instances, findings have proved inconclusive (Jackes 1986; Ramenofsky 1987). Recent settlement pattern studies suggest that there was no significant decline in population prior to the first historically recorded epidemics in the 1630s (Snow 1985; Sullivan 1983; Warrick 1989).

It is also debated to what extent Iroquoian confederacies originated in the course of the sixteenth century as a response to the developing fur trade. Unfortunately, no archaeological data have shed light on this process (Engelbrecht 1974). The Huron claimed that the nucleus of their confederacy dated from the fifteenth century (JR 16:227–29), while Iroquois traditions suggest various dates for theirs in the fifteenth and sixteenth centuries (Tooker 1978:418–22).

In general, confederacies appear to be products of the same forces that led to the creation and enlargement of tribes. Hence, there is no reason why they may not have begun to develop prior to European influence.

The process of confederacy formation was complete by the beginning of the seventeenth century. Hereafter, apart from the qualified acceptance of the Tuscarora into the Iroquois confederacy in the eighteenth century, refugees joined existing tribes, but no tribes as such are recorded as joining confederacies.

The archaeological record documents major changes in the Iroquoian way of life. They became more numerous and sedentary and beginning in Middle Iroquoian times, warfare produced much larger communities. Long-distance trade does not appear to have been of major importance prior to the sixteenth century. There are no indications that significant individual variations in wealth developed in prehistoric times. Chiefly councils appear to have come into existence in response to a need to coordinate activities on an ever larger scale. Yet there is no evidence that these political developments had provided a basis for economic inequality or exploitation.

ETHNOGRAPHIC EVIDENCE

The archaeological record reveals that Iroquoian societies were changing rapidly in prehistoric times. To what extent can the historical-ethnographic and the archaeological record be combined to provide clearer insights into the nature of Iroquoian societies in the early historical period?

The Iroquoians are no exception to the rule that in no society are all roles homogeneous, in the sense of being freely interchangeable among all members. Seventeenth-century Iroquoian behavior, like that found in all human societies, was differentiated according to age, sex, and personal prestige.

The division of labor was overwhelmingly along gender lines (Quain 1937). According to the French, from an early age, boys refused to perform "women's work" (Sagard 1939:132). Men cleared new fields (a more or less continuous activity among swidden agriculturalists), built houses, hunted, fished, traded, waged war, and conducted the public affairs of their communities, tribes, and confederacies. Women grew and harvested crops, gathered firewood, cooked, looked after children, and engaged in craft production. They also aided men in hunting and fishing, but their role was limited to helping process and transport the catch. In all of these activities there was strong emphasis on work teams made up of individuals of the same sex, who were often also members of the same household or clan. Individual men and women were often separated from one another for long stretches as they went about their respective tasks. Except for a period of teenage promiscuity, public relations between men and women were characterized by considerable reserve and a measure of avoidance, which was accentuated by menstrual and various other religiously based taboos (Sagard 1939:67; JR 15:181). Iroquoians preferred female babies to male ones, since they increased the membership of the extended family into which they were born (JR 15:181–83).

While men frequently engaged in activities that took them far from their communities, women rarely ventured beyond their clearings unaccompanied by men. Iroquois women, however, may have moved more freely between villages during periods of relative peace (Engelbrecht 1974:62). The distinction between clearing and forest was of great symbolic importance to Iroquoians, and male participation in faraway councils was part of their general confrontation of the physical and supernatural dangers that lay beyond the village (Fenton 1978:298). Men held all public offices but were elected to and could be dismissed from them by the women of their matrilineages. They were also advised by women on matters of policy (Fenton 1978:314). In general, both men and women appear to have had a stronger voice in those issues that affected their lives more closely. Thus, women had a preponderant role in deciding matters relating primarily to village life, while men had a stronger say in relations between communities (Trigger 1978; cf. Brown 1970; Tooker 1984). Iroquoian women were the guardians of family and community traditions, while men were more aware of cultural differences and more accustomed to tolerating such differences. Yet no clear line could be drawn between interests relating to these two spheres. For example, war chiefs had to obtain permission from women before they could take teenage boys on a raiding expedition (Fenton 1978:315). Hence, men and women appear to have had a significant input into most discussions of public policy.

While men conducted intergroup diplomacy and enjoyed the public show of political office, even the symbolic role of women in political life may not have been compromised in a culture that at the same time esteemed oratorical abilities and equated silence with strength. Most women also enjoyed the security of lifelong membership in a matrilineal extended family, while adult men had to contend with divided responsibilities to their mothers' and wives' longhouses, which included provisioning them and avenging murders (Tooker 1984). They also had to avoid a barrage of criticism for slackness that, at an extreme, could lead to a man's expulsion from his wife's longhouse and his forced return to the one in which he had been born. To win esteem, men had to work hard, face dangers, and hide fear. Ultimately, as warriors, they had to risk their lives so that on a supernatural plane their shed blood would ensure the continuation of the natural cycles on which human beings depended. While men and women led separate lives there is no evidence that women were inferior to men in Iroquoian societies.

Older men and women were generally more esteemed than younger ones. Women and men of the senior generation served as heads and spokesmen for their extended families. The senior women appear to have played an essential role in organizing their household's female work teams. They could also bring considerable pressure to bear on younger women, especially those who did not yet have children, to divorce a husband who was lazy, unproductive, or otherwise objectionable (Fenton 1978:299–300; JR 23:127). Young men were not regarded as reliable witnesses or trustworthy bearers of messages between one community and another (JR 16:169–71). They were suspected of trying to stir up warfare in the hope of being able to acquire personal prestige by performing deeds of valor. This tendency was opposed by older men who were more interested in trade and friendly relations with other tribes, and perhaps not inclined to hurry the process by which younger men could win prestige and challenge their authority. Hence, political offices tended to be held by older men, while younger ones were excluded from decision-making to a considerable degree (JR 10:251). Yet at all levels of Iroquoian society, care was taken to avoid the appearance of coercion or of one person being given orders by another.

Europeans were scandalized when they discovered that young children were never slapped, violently restrained, or reprimanded (Sagard 1939:130–31; JR 33:177–79). In addition to believing that the dignity of a child as a human being precluded such treatment, the Iroquoians feared that children who were publicly humiliated might become ill or commit suicide (JR 14:37; Fenton 1941). The social control of children was achieved through praise, gentle ridicule, and inculcating feelings of guilt. Europeans were impressed by the harmonious nature of all aspects of human relations within Iroquoian communities.

There was also considerable variation in personal prestige. Women enhanced their reputations through exceptional industry and skill in growing corn and as homemakers. In keeping with general Iroquoian attitudes toward family size, having many children is not mentioned as increasing a woman's prestige, although it would seem likely that numerous adult daughters would have enhanced a woman's position within a matrilineal extended family. Men sought personal prestige by demonstrating their ability to hunt, fish, trade, clear trees, and provide feasts, and as orators (JR 10:229–35). This ethos encouraged hard work and individual initiative, even in tasks that depended on cooperation. The most important opportunity to win personal prestige for men was success as a warrior (Witthoft 1959). The Iroquoians conceived of all warfare as blood-feuds, and enemies were killed or captured to avenge murdered kin or tribespeople (JR 10:225–27; 17:111). Just as warfare was a supreme test of courage, the taking of prisoners or scalps was an unparalleled source of individual prestige.

The Iroquoians also had institutionalized titles and offices. Among the Iroquois, the title of Pine Tree Chief was bestowed on any man who had sufficiently distinguished himself (Fenton 1978:314). Other positions, including the peace and war chiefs of each clan segment, were hereditary in particular lineages, although they too were achieved in the sense that there was no rule prescribing the individual order of inheritance of these offices within the lineage. Chiefs were selected and could be removed by the members, especially the female members, of the lineages and clan segments (Fenton 1957:310; Tooker 1978:424–26). Yet, since the installation of a chief involved feasting and the reciprocal exchange of presents with all clan segments of a particular tribe or confederacy, it required the approval of a large network of cooperating clan segments. Among at least the Iroquois, members of lineages that supplied the chiefs who sat on the confederacy council were called *agoiander*, or eminent persons, a term that to the French had connotations of royalty or nobility (Fenton 1978:312).

The material benefits of chiefly office were more than counterbalanced by its expenses. Chiefs and their families lived in larger houses than did other Iroquoians, although these houses were not more lavishly constructed or furnished than other ones and served as community meeting places (JR 10:181; 13:59). Apart from these, the Iroquoians did not construct any buildings specifically for political or religious purposes. To ensure that clan chiefs continued to live among their clanspeople, they may have observed an avunculocal, rather than an uxorilocal, post-marital residence pattern; the evidence for this pattern is indirect and highly inconclusive (Trigger 1978). Peace chiefs played a major role in entertaining foreign visitors to the community, which was an expensive duty as well as a source of prestige. They controlled trade routes and had the right to collect presents from clansmen or strangers who made use of them, as well as tolls from individuals passing through or making use of clan territories (Sagard 1939:99; JR 10:223–25). The peace chiefs also controlled their clan segment's treasury, which contained the shell beads and other valuables used to conduct diplomacy with other groups and to provide compensation for murders and serious injuries committed by members of the clan segment against other families belonging to the same confederacy (Sagard 1939:163–64; JR 28:87). Peace chiefs played a leading role in conducting councils and community projects, and were treated with special respect. They were also expected to play a leading role in providing the hospitality associated with council meetings, collective activities such as erecting palisades, and an elaborate annual cycle of public celebrations and rituals (JR 10:229–31; 16:229). In providing the food for such events, the chief was actively supported by his entire clan or even the whole village, although he and other members of his lineage were expected to exert themselves more than anyone else. Although peace chiefs were in a privileged position to obtain exotic goods through diplomatic exchanges and foreign trade, they were required to dispense these goods generously to other members of their community or tribe in the course of rituals in which gift-giving played a major role. In return, their advice appears to have been listened to more than that of other people (JR 10:233–35). More community support could also be mustered for curing rituals for chiefs and their families than for other people (JR 10:175).

While peace chiefs played a major role in organizing community religious rituals, they did not possess any special supernatural powers. At puberty most boys sought the personal support of a supernatural being through vision quests. Shamans likewise acquired their powers individually in this fashion. Much supernatural power was controlled by curing societies, which cut across clan, community, and even tribal divisions. Membership in these societies was gained as a result of being healed by them. While chiefs inherited the office name of their predecessor, the Iroquoians feared the spirits of the dead and sought in the long run to sever relations with them. Hence peace chiefs were not in a position to acquire supernatural powers through special relations with the spirits of dead ancestors.

War chiefs played a more restricted role than peace chiefs, to whom they were normally closely related. Indeed some war chiefs may have become peace chiefs as they grew older. War chiefs led raiding parties and had the right to dispose of prisoners and scalps, which they generally gave to families whose members had been slain by the enemy (Champlain 1922–36, 3:159). War chiefs were also responsible for the interrogation and slaying of witches. In times of major epidemics or other disasters that were attributed to witchcraft, as well as during prolonged conflicts with other groups, war chiefs might temporarily take over many of the functions of peace chiefs (JR 15:53; 14:37–39; Fenton 1978:315).

Iroquoians, like all human beings, recognized the unequal power of individuals and groups, including the ability of some individuals and groups to dominate others by brute force. Similarly, in the supernatural sphere some spirits were believed to be more powerful than others. Yet the Iroquoians rejected all such forms of domination as a basis for their social organization. Violence and public exhibitions of authoritarian behavior were regarded as illegitimate and disruptive of the social fabric. Leaders had to win public approval by exhibiting self-restraint, wisdom, and generosity. The latter requirement linked political authority and economic redistribution.

Both in theory and in practice, goods were accumulated in Iroquoian society either for routine family use or for redistribution. Exchanges of food and exotic goods were essential features of public feasts, major building projects, life-cycle ceremonies, curing rituals, community and personal religious celebrations, ritual friendships, dispute settlement, and the conduct of diplomacy. There is no evidence that a barter system was used to distribute goods within Iroquoian societies. Ritual exchanges tended to even out disparities in the amount of goods possessed by different individuals, while enhancing the reputation of the donors and producers. If a longhouse burned down, the other families in the community competed with each other in compensating its inhabitants for their losses (JR 14:43–45). Likewise, after major military defeats, refugees were welcomed into neighboring tribes and supplied with food, clothing, and arable land until they were able once again to support themselves (JR 17:25–27).

The Iroquoians associated generosity with health and peace. It was believed that gifts could satisfy the hidden desires of people's souls and cure them of serious illness. Hence, giving presents was an essential part of individual and collective curing rituals (Wallace 1958). Likewise, trade and ritual exchanges were vital aspects of relations between neighboring tribes that were not at war with one another (McIlwain 1915:195). The concepts of property and theft were also only minimally emphasized in order to avoid their disruptive consequences. Carrying off goods that were left out of doors was not counted as theft, even if their owner was known (Sagard 1939:95; JR 38:271–73). Likewise, individuals using trade routes without the permission of their owner could have their goods seized by the owner and his or her relatives only if the journey was not yet over (JR 10:225). Finally, no one could legitimately use force to try to recover stolen goods within a village until peaceful efforts to reclaim them had failed (JR 38:267–71). On the other hand, repeated anti-social behavior, including selfishness of any sort, was interpreted as a lack of concern for community welfare and the health of others, which in turn was viewed as a manifestation of witchcraft (JR 19:85–87).

Iroquoian generosity was reinforced by powerful positive as well as negative sanctions, which influenced the behavior of chiefs no less than that of ordinary people. No one who was ungenerous had any claim to public esteem. Chiefs and their lineages had to work particularly hard to maintain their privileged position, and the exotic goods that chiefs accumulated as a result of their own efforts or their office had to be liberally distributed to maintain their prestige. Stingy individuals, including chiefs, became the objects of censorious gossip and risked being accused of witchcraft if their behavior was seen as endangering the welfare of the community or the health of their neighbors (cf. Macfarlane 1970). If a person was thought to have died because someone else had refused to satisfy a soul wish, his or her relatives might seek to retaliate by killing that person, either physically or through supernatural means (JR 30:21). Accusations of witchcraft could result in death only if the accused were so widely believed to have injured others that his or her kin either killed him themselves or no longer dared to defy public opinion by defending him (Trigger 1963:163–65). Nevertheless, even a single accusation or a rumor of witchcraft was sufficient to pressure reluctant individuals into being more generous.

Iroquoians also feared becoming the victims of witchcraft practiced consciously or unconsciously by people who envied them (JR 10:285). Hence, individuals who were unusually fortunate or successful at hunting, fishing, or trading took care to share what they had obtained with as many people as possible (JR 8:95). Chiefs gave away particularly treasured possessions both to enhance their reputations and to avoid becoming victims of witchcraft. One Huron chief gave his prized European cat, which he had carried by canoe all the way from Quebec, to a woman who dreamed that she could be cured only by owning it (Sagard 1939:118–19). While chiefly office allowed a man to mobilize support for feasts and gift-giving and enhanced his ability to influence the behavior of others, such support could only continue if a chief lived up to Iroquoian ideals of generosity. This in turn required a chief and his supporters to work hard to acquire the means to enhance his reputation (JR 55:55–57).

The political significance of generosity, must further be qualified in terms of how the Iroquoians defined leadership. The principal functions of chiefs were to act as spokesmen for their respective groups and to coordinate activities within and between these groups. To do this, they had to consult continually with their constituents. Orders were never given to individuals and would have been fiercely resisted as a threat to their personal integrity and independence (Wallace 1958:246). Households and clan segments likewise rejected any interference in their affairs by outsiders. Such interventions quickly led to the break-up of large communities, with the offended groups establishing themselves elsewhere (JR 5:255; 8:105; Sagard 1939:92). Even murders had to be settled by transferring presents as compensation between clan segments, villages, or tribes, since the duty of clan segments to protect their members meant that no punishment could be inflicted directly on the murderer (Trigger 1963:159–61). Under these conditions, all political activity was a process of achieving consensus and no one was bound to support a policy against his or her will (Champlain 1922–36, 3:157–58). When public opinion overwhelmingly favored a particular course of action, those who still opposed it withdrew into silent opposition.

Less clearly defined situations gave rise to the factionalism that characterized much Iroquoian political behavior. Within tribes and communities, rival parties or cliques would evolve, usually along clan or clan segment lines, that respectively favored war or peace with a particular neighboring group (Richter 1983). Chiefs of the peace faction often quietly maintained good relations with the "enemy" even during

137

wartime, which led Jesuit missionaries to describe them as traitors to their own people (JR 33:233). For example, opposing factions that cut across all of the Huron tribes during the 1640s favored mutually exclusive alliances with the French and the Iroquois. Many adherents of the latter party were among the first to join the Iroquois after they had dispersed the Huron in 1649 (Trigger 1976:721–50; 738–84). Within the Iroquois tribes, opposing factions promoted alliances with the French and the Dutch (or later the English). Among the Mohawk, beginning as early as the 1640s, the moiety made up of the Turtle and Wolf clans favored peace with the French, while the Bears sought to ally themselves with traders at Albany so that they could attack the French and their Indian allies (JR 8:300; 31:117). Among the Onondaga the leader of the Bear clan was the chief promoter of an alliance with the French (Webb 1984:251–302). Policy differences within the Iroquois confederacy were sometimes so strong that member tribes attacked one another, although the main purpose of the league was to prevent such conflicts (JR 43:99–103; 44:149–51). The French interpreted factionalism as devious intrigues that increased the flexibility of Iroquoian responses to their changing political fortunes, and hence promoted their common interests (Blair 1911–12, 2:44). Yet it also exposed Iroquoian groups to political maneuvers by their enemies that divided them and weakened their ability to resist foreign aggression. Factionalism seems to have been one of the means by which the Iroquoians resisted not only arbitrary authority, but also public opinion as a coercive force in their collective lives.

Among the Iroquoians, we observe the opposite of what is found in state societies. Individuals cultivated prestige, goodwill, and a sense of indebtedness on the part of others that enhanced their powers of persuasion. No one, however, had the inherent authority to command another person to obey. Iroquoian societies were constructed as metaphorical extensions of kinship to form clan segments, communities, tribes, and confederacies, but no higher level had the right to interfere in the internal affairs of a lower one. An apparent exception to this rule related to the heinous crime of witchcraft, but even suspected witches could be executed by the community only when their own clan segments and lineages were unprepared to come to their defense. At most this gave chiefs as a group the authority to control rare individuals whom everyone, including their own kin, was prepared to recognize as a threat to society (Trigger 1963:165).

Iroquoian political activities far more often were characterized by factionalism, which asserted the continuing political independence of constituent groups that were drawn together in ever more precarious alliances built one upon the other. While chiefs and councils were essential to coordinate the affairs of these groups, no lower-level entity was prepared, or found itself required, to surrender its decision-making powers to any individual or higher-level group. While chiefs and their lineages could cultivate influence by means of their generosity, public opinion, operating through gossip and accusations of witchcraft, effectively curbed the abuse of power and defended the sharing ethic that was fundamental to Iroquoian culture.

The changes that did or did not occur in Iroquoian culture following European contact shed light on the ability of their institutions to resist transformation by state-organized societies. Many anthropologists have speculated that both matrilineal social organization and social equality were seriously undermined by the fur trade, as the Iroquoian men who carried on this trade sought to retain increasing amounts of goods for their own use, and to pass their gains on to their sons (Smith 1970; Hayden 1976). It has also been argued that men used the fur trade mainly to obtain goods that were of use and interest to themselves (Latta 1971:130–31). Yet among the Iroquois and other Iroquoian groups that practiced individual burial, iron axes almost invariably have been found buried with women, who must have used them to cut firewood (Wray and Schoff 1953:58; Kenyon 1982). This calls into question the assumption that the axes were used primarily by men to clear forests. It is also well documented that matrilineal principles continued to govern residence patterns, clan membership, and election to chiefly office, and that female children were still preferred to male ones (Trigger 1978). Iroquoian men seem to have been absent from their villages, trading and waging war, for longer periods during the seventeenth century than they had been previously, thus creating a situation where women became even more responsible for running the everyday affairs of their communities (Anderson 1985). Similar situations elsewhere have reinforced rather than weakened matrilineal institutions (Helms 1970).

It is also clear that traditional checks on the accumulation of wealth continued to function during the seventeenth century. Although in theory the discoverer of a new trade route had the exclusive right to control and profit from it, within five years all of the Huron peace chiefs possessed the authority to regulate trade with the French. The leading

chief of the Arendarhonon, the Huron tribe to which the man who had
begun this trade belonged, was recognized as the principal Huron ally of
the French, but most of the trade was carried on by the Attignawantan,
the largest of the Huron tribes and the one that had already been most
closely allied with northern hunter-gatherers in prehistoric times (Trigger 1976:286–92). Individual Huron traders also do not appear to have
utilized wealth derived from the fur trade to challenge the role played by
the chiefs of their clan segments. Instead they shared their exotic goods
with them so that these chiefs could continue to play their traditional
role in Iroquoian society (cf. Hayden 1976). Hence, new wealth did not
undermine the traditional social organization of these societies or lead
to an explosion of status rivalry as it is supposed to have done among the
native peoples of the Northwest Coast (Trigger 1984c). The fur trade
enhanced rather than undermined the capacity of traditional chiefs to
obtain and redistribute exotic goods.

A few Huron traders are recorded as having converted to Christianity
to avoid having to participate in traditional redistributive rituals (JR
23:129). They relied upon Christianity and their alliance with the
French to protect them against the political and supernatural consequences of their antisocial behavior; their behavior provided Hurons
with another reason to equate Christianity with witchcraft (JR 30:19–
21). Yet few Hurons became Christians for this reason, and many
converts continued to distribute surplus goods to both Christians and
non-Christians, although no longer within the context of traditional
religious rituals (JR 30:77–79). This information gives us reason to
believe that those who converted in order to be more acquisitive were
"deviants," such as would have existed in Iroquoian cultures at any time
but who normally would not have dared to reveal themselves. What is
significant is how few Iroquoians reneged on their social obligations at
this time (Binford 1983:220).

There is also no solid evidence of increased social stratification. The
Five Nations Iroquois, in an effort to maintain a population repeatedly
decimated by European epidemics after 1633, incorporated thousands
of prisoners of war into their society (JR 41:133; 51:128, 187). These
prisoners were adopted into Iroquois families or as entire extended
families into clan segments. Some were even allowed to live in their
own villages (JR 54:81). As had traditionally been done in the past,
prisoners adopted into families were initially required to work long and
hard for their captors, and if they proved unsatisfactory for any reason

140

they could be killed (Adams 1961:69; JR 43:295, 303; 49:107). The Jesuit missionaries who visited the Iroquois in the 1650s and 1660s frequently described these captives as slaves, and some recent commentators have viewed them as constituting a servile stratum in Iroquois society (Webb 1984:254). Yet, while absorbing such large numbers of prisoners posed special problems and even dangers for the Iroquois, the status of these prisoners quickly appears to have been determined by traditional kinship categories. Some prisoners adopted into chiefly lineages soon became chiefs themselves (JR 42:57), while after a few years an Iroquois chief was described as being dominated and "abused" by two Huron women he had adopted to replace his dead sisters (JR 62:61–63). Within one or two generations thousands of prisoners had come to regard themselves as Iroquois, and were socially and culturally indistinguishable from their captors.

A final question that is important for distinguishing Iroquoian practice from ideals is the extent to which individuals were able to remove goods from redistributive cycles and define them as personal possessions. While we cannot give a definitive answer, there is little evidence that seventeenth-century chiefs or traders and their families lived better or dressed more lavishly than did other Iroquoians. While the Hurons were reported to have encouraged their children to marry into "prominent families," it is significant that the chief characteristic that continued to be sought in a prospective groom was that he could prove himself to be a good warrior and provider of food (Sagard 1939:123–24).

The Jesuits reported that in the 1630s Huron chiefs were being referred to in a novel fashion as "big stones," "elders," and "stay-at-homes," the implication being that as a result of the fur trade they were able to profit from intertribal trade without having to leave home (JR 10:231–33). They also stated that in the redistribution of presents that accompanied the Feast of the Dead that was celebrated at Ossossane in 1636, Huron chiefs secretly appropriated large numbers of beaver pelts for their own use (JR 10:303–305). All of this sounds as if these chiefs were profiting from the fur trade. Yet the Jesuits do not appear to have had any precise idea at that time about how redistributions were carried out, nor is it made clear whether the chiefs involved retained the wealth they acquired for their own use or for redistribution at a later date. Jesuit discussions of changes in Huron society were deeply colored by their commitment to a degenerationist scheme of history, which saw native

141

people in the absence of Christianity falling ever more deeply into sin and depravity. Their comments on the declining morality of chiefs may be nothing more than a reflection of this doctrine. Archaeological data from the historical Huron Warminster site suggest that some extended families and some nuclear families within longhouses possessed (or at least lost or abandoned) more European goods than others (Tyyska 1968). This impression is not confirmed at the Fonger site (Warrick 1984:90). Until more is known about how goods were abandoned in Iroquoian sites (von Gernet 1982), or what phases of a redistributive cycle may be represented, it is dangerous to draw too many conclusions about access to exotic goods in Iroquoian daily life from archaeological evidence.

The principal archaeologically attested form of conspicuous consumption was the burial of exotic goods with the dead, a practice that was of great religious antiquity in North America, although it is evidenced only to a limited degree among the Iroquoians prior to European contact. The Hurons redistributed large amounts of furs and exotic goods both at the burials and the communal reburials of their dead. Yet relatively few non-perishable goods made their way into their historical ossuaries along with individual burials. The fur linings, copper kettles, large marine shells, and layers of corn meal appear to have been placed in these graves as communal offerings (Kidd 1953). On the other hand, considerable amounts of goods were buried in individual Neutral and Iroquois graves, making them a favorite target of looters since the late seventeenth century. It is not known, however, to what extent these goods were the personal possessions of the dead or tokens of esteem placed there by friends and relatives. It is probably safe to conclude that some Iroquoians had significantly more access to exotic goods than did others. Yet at present it is not clear to what extent the retention of such goods correlated with hereditary or achieved social status or was governed by other considerations.

Nevertheless a strong emphasis on redistribution lasted as long as the traditional Iroquoian religion which provided its ideological basis. Among the Iroquois such beliefs survived until an advanced state of economic, political, and religious integration with European colonial culture was achieved in the eighteenth century. The Handsome Lake religion was both a reaction against and a continuation of this process (Wallace 1969). Iroquoian leaders have continued until the present to follow the behavior of seventeenth-century chiefs, such as Garakontie, whose power was based on an ability to mold public opinion, and factionalism has remained a prominent feature of Iroquoian political life.

CONCLUSIONS

There are clearly many possibilities for differing interpretations of Iroquoian social organization in late prehistoric times as well as in the seventeenth century, especially with regard to how egalitarian or hierarchical it was. Roles were differentiated according to sex, age, and individual prestige. In particular, older people and those respected for various skills were listened to with more attention than were others. Major political offices were hereditary in specific lineages, and these offices conferred special prominence on the members of such lineages. In spite of this, Iroquoian societies had powerful built-in mechanisms of resistance that prevented the domination and exploitation of one individual or group by another. Chiefs functioned as mediators and coordinators, but did not have the right or power to impose their will on others. Their effectiveness depended on their prestige, which was determined by their reputations for wisdom, fairness, and generosity and their ability to avoid the appearance of being dictatorial. Chiefs and their supporters also had to work hard in order to be able to give away more than they received from others. Selfishness and acquisitiveness were penalized by negative gossip and could lead either to accusations of witchcraft or to misers thinking that they had become the victims of witchcraft practiced by those they had offended. This behavior was correlated with a world view that identified generosity, reciprocity, and cooperation with the life-giving forces that maintained the cosmos. Arbitrariness and acquisitiveness were equated with witchcraft, death, and disorder.

We do not know to what extent traditional Iroquoian ideals were realized in the seventeenth century. There must always have been misers and individuals with autocratic tendencies; otherwise Iroquoian society would not have developed mechanisms for controlling them that, in their own way, were as elaborate and coercive as the repressive institutions of state societies that protect private property and assure the obedience of individuals to those with authority over them. There may have been increasing acquisitions of private property as a result of the fur trade, and this would have involved a weakening of Iroquoian ideals.

Yet ideals can only be violated so far and still survive. There is convincing evidence that a sharing ethic remained strong throughout the seventeenth century, while consensual leadership and factionalism lasted even longer, despite the massive dislocation of Iroquoian life resulting from disease, warfare, loss of land, absorption into a European world economy, resettlement in communities composed of more than one native group, and subjection to European political control. Moreover, despite the massive wars waged by the Iroquois they continued in traditional style to incorporate defeated groups such as the Huron into their own kinship networks. They did not try to turn defeated enemies into tribute-paying subjects or a servile stratum within their own society. Nothing indicates the survival of the egalitarian principles of Iroquoian societies more clearly than this fact.

The semi-sedentary nature of Iroquoian and Tupinamba cultures, which was related to the practice of swidden agriculture, may have created less concern with property and its protection than developed among the more sedentary Pueblo Indians of the southwestern United States or among Northwest Coast collectors with their permanent base camps, geographically circumscribed natural resources, and elaborate material culture. While redistribution remained important on the Northwest Coast, these groups, usually consisting of communities of only a few hundred people, clearly exhibited a much higher level of concern with property, rank, and the exploitation of labor (including hereditary slavery) than did the Iroquoians. Tribal societies based on swidden agriculture may constitute an important subset of prestate societies that is of great interest for investigating the relationship between power, property, and equality, a study pioneered by Edmund Leach (1954) in his *Political Systems of Highland Burma*. Their relatively low overall population densities, lack of investment in long-term assets, and easy mobility may have facilitated the maintenance of economic equality well beyond the point where such equality gave way under many other economic regimes. Ultimately, an upper limit was imposed on the size of such systems by the inability of consensus to maintain even the limited order needed to make their overall political organization function, and by the inability of gossip and witch-fears to maintain economic equality in opposition to growing community size and decision-making requirements.

What is most important to recognize, however, is that whatever their differences, small-scale societies are not merely egalitarian by default,

144

or groups that have failed to "assign and focus . . . power" (Krader 1968:61). Instead, at least some of them appear to possess powerful and well-integrated mechanisms to defend equality that must be eliminated if hierarchical organizations are to develop. One of the challenges facing evolutionary anthropologists is therefore to understand the processes involved in the eventual destruction of the behavioral patterns that maintained equality in small-scale societies.

NOTE

A much shortened version of this chapter was read at the American Society for Ethnohistory annual meeting in Charleston, South Carolina, on November 8, 1986 and a longer one at the University of Victoria, British Columbia, on February 13, 1987, while I was a Lansdowne Visitor in the Department of Anthropology. I wish to thank those attending these talks, especially Professors Leland Donald, Peter Baskerville, and D. K. Richter, for their comments. I also wish to thank the students in my 1986 Settlement Archaeology Seminar at McGill University, and in particular Robert MacDonald, for an opportunity to discuss in detail issues raised in this chapter, and Dena Dincauze and Robert Hasenstab for sending me copies of their unpublished papers. Interpretations of Huron society and history made in this chapter are documented more fully in Trigger (1976, 1985).

6

One path to the heights: negotiating political inequality in the Sausa of Peru

CHRISTINE A. HASTORF

University of Minnesota

Understanding the origin of hereditary inequality in nonhierarchical societies has been one of the thorniest issues in archaeology (Flannery 1972:402). The difficulty arises because this cultural transformation, although eventually displayed in material culture, is initially generated by ideological transformations of cultural conceptions, social interactions, and power. Until recently, archaeologists have sought the causes of change by looking at economic results, especially in terms of resource access and production (Steward and Faron 1959; Service 1962; Fried 1967), rather than by looking at the continuing political nature of the change that deals with power, group relationships, and conflict (Oberg 1955; Carniero 1970; Helms 1979; and more recently Miller and Tilley 1984; Rowlands 1987b). Archaeologists have also tended to focus on "initial kicks" or critical relationships. The onset of political inequality, however, entails the continuous shifting of many unequal relationships. When major political transformations occur, identities and tasks are reassigned and boundaries are realigned. What becomes important, then, is to understand how these relations produce material evidence of political rank in the archaeological record.

THE ONSET OF INEQUALITY

In this chapter, I deal with only a small part of increasing inequality in prehistory. I attempt to identify the multivariate dimensions involved in such a shift and the importance of negotiation in these relations, including the two sides of negotiation: consensus and conflict. This discussion may not offer a crisp new explanatory model, but it leads us toward a better understanding of how individuals decided to give up, were forced to cede, or unconsciously lost their autonomy to a minority of their group.

I separate the onset of political inequality and ranking from economic production and, by extension, I decouple political inequality from wealth inequality. Social and political strategies are the nexuses of change from egalitarian to hierarchical organizations. At the onset, such strategies may or may not trigger changes in economic production that can be detected in the archaeological record.

In 1984 Feinman and Neitzel dealt a blow to the typological correlations of specific cultural traits with the onset of political rank in prestate societies. Investigating the traditional archaeological prime movers that were postulated to lead to political complexity, they found no universal links between rank and kin structure, agriculture, population, trade, surplus production, warfare, or storage. Further, their study implies that in all sedentary societies, asymmetrical social relations are continually being created, maintained, and destroyed. Asymmetry, however, does not always lead to an empowered political hierarchy.

I begin by defining *political rank* and *inequality* by what they are and what they are not. I define political rank using portions of definitions by Weber (1968) and Fried (1967:109): Formal political inequality in a population is operating when certain people claim (a) power over others' decisions about labor, access to production, resources, or circulation of certain goods, (b) influence on behaviors and communications between members of the group, or (c) authority over information and special knowledge. These acts of power tend to be in the public sphere and affect the group by defining political boundaries. Ultimately this power entails control (coercion) and service (obligation), although one can be used to mask the other. Further, political positions are limited, so there is not a position of influence available for everyone who would like one.

An important distinction is that political inequality is different from wealth inequality. Wealth differences do not have to correlate with

147

political rank and power over group decisions, although they often do once authority is legitimized. Some societies with intensive agriculture and clear wealth differences, such as the Ifugao of the Philippines, do not show formal political stratification (Conklin 1980).

This distinction can be extended: Differences in competence and production in resource use create economic inequalities, but do not always equate to rank in the political sphere. Economic inequality (differential ownership of goods, specific control over resources, etc.) is often considered a prominent aspect of political development (Brumfiel and Earle 1987).

One reason I separate economics from political power here is the social scale on which I am focusing: the *onset* of political hierarchy and the exercise of power in those relationships. At this stage, leaders are more concerned with symbols of power, opinion changing, and the negotiations of their social position (often giving out as much as they take in), rather than with control of economics. That is, they are engaged in appropriating social legitimation rather than material power. Rowland's (1987) recent paper on Cameroon chiefdoms illustrates such a split between wealth and authority: The chief gained more wealth than the lineage leaders because his men were in charge of defense. Thus, he claimed authority to participate in the slave trade, whereas the lineage leaders represented the pure moral order and could not join in slave trading. Further, at an early stage such leaders do not always have the power to control production. In larger and more complex groups, social inequality was linked to material inequality as we see in Bronze Age Europe, the Aztecs of Mexico, or the Chimor of Peru.

As Fallers (1973) points out, inequalities should be investigated in their cultural context if we are to understand their real roles. In different societies, different contexts dominate the social, political, and economic realms. The question is not "When do unequal relations develop?" but "When do unequal relations develop *into political rank?*" Why does a group institutionalize unequal access to power and to material goods?

Traditionally, social stratification was said to arise as kin-based senior lineages or clans took over control of certain resources, restricting access to them when resources became scarce because of a degraded environment, encroaching neighbors, or increased population density (Eggan 1950). The hallmarks of stratification are intensification of agriculture (Wittfogel 1957; Boserup 1965), specialized production leading to

148

surpluses that financed elite activities (Sanders and Price 1968; Brumfiel 1976; Earle 1978), and control of critical exchange networks (Johnson 1973; Rathje 1971; Helms 1979). Do these causes explain the onset of political ranking? I would argue that none of them is sufficient to cause long-term political differences, although they all contribute to them.

How, then, can we understand the creation and escalation of asymmetrical relations? When do any of these relations become the foundations for more permanent inequalities and political stratification seen in chiefdoms and states? How is inequality made acceptable in a group? Which historical conditions are built on? Why do people choose to give up their autonomy, and for what?

Service (1962), building on Durkheim's (1963 [1895]) holistic model, sees the trade-off of lost autonomy for economic organization as the most effective choice when a group needs to organize redistribution of goods and services. He claims that as groups became large, daily activities became harder to complete, and everyone agreed to specialize, lowering the per capita workload by allowing a leader to manage the network of exchange. Carniero (1970, 1981:64) takes another perspective. He sees the giving up of autonomy as a result of coercion by one group over another, not as a set of voluntary acts. For him the onset of permanent inequalities has a political basis resulting from villages joining together "under duress," perhaps not in the face of open warfare, but under a threat of warfare.

I think both consensus and conflict were involved at the onset of political development, in both the ideological and the physical realms. Incipient leaders could have suggested (and probably believed) that the group would benefit by organizing labor, managing resources, and uniting certain forces with others. Power to make decisions is not always coercive. Members might gain stability (or at least survival advantages) from such organization. Throughout the transformation, loss of individual decision-making power and realignments of people's beliefs might also provoke conflict within the group. Fundamentally, political hierarchy marks a shift from *power to organize* to *power over the organization*. This power may be conditioned by the economic base, but it is not just an effect of the economics (Giddens 1979; Foucault 1984; Miller and Tilley 1984:8–13).

Through debate and reassessment of situations, whether real or imagined, people change the perceptions of their needs and desires. Social and political boundaries are redefined. This change can occur

149

because new problems or constraints exist, because one opinion becomes more persuasive or latent, or because real force is brandished. New perceived needs create an array of positions, such as water managers, ritual leaders, war leaders, or trade negotiators (Johnson's sequential hierarchy [1982]). New asymmetries in one domain may lead to dominance over other matters simply as unintended consequences, without calling into question a new claim to power. This sequence can lead to the centralization of positions, or simultaneous hierarchy (Johnson 1982). Often these restructurings of power are questioned, and resistance works to disband the consolidation of positions (see Trigger, this volume).

Giddens (1979) has pointed out that in all relationships, conflicting interests are trying to find a balance while trying to deny the conflict. These interests operate at all social levels and axes: individual, family, neighborhood, and age cohorts. All decisions, including those of the dominant ruling group, must be negotiated between people with different interests. Even in the case of political domination, each party, whether it is a household or a community, will consider what it will gain and what it will give up as each decision is being negotiated. These negotiations are difficult to see in the archaeological record, because the negotiators trade in intangibles (position in society, personal autonomy, mores, social goals) and in conditions of existence (traditions, subsistence needs, stability, security, or even personal aggrandizement).

In the following sections of this chapter I address the role of exchange, surplus production, and specialization in the evolution of political systems and the origin of political inequality. Although I do not believe that these factors are prime movers in the *onset* of political inequality, each affects the economic conditions that can augment inequality. Exchange, surplus production, and specialization can become the locus of change in the social negotiations, and have been considered to be intimately involved in the complexity process in certain cultures (Sanders 1956; Wright 1969; Rathje 1971, 1972; Gledhill 1978; Earle 1987).

To illuminate the roles of these processes in the evolution of political inequality, I concentrate on one archaeological example where political ranking evolved, the Sausa of Peru. Archaeological data on the Sausa, a group that practiced intensive agriculture and herding, were collected in the Upper Mantaro Valley of the central Peruvian highlands. The data show evidence of political rank toward the end of the primary Sausa

150

occupation. At that time the group was not a complex chiefdom (Earle 1978) but more like Carniero's minimal chiefdom (1981:47). Despite the suggestion that interaction and complex trading systems formed the basis of the Andean economy (Murra 1980 [1965]), there is no strong archaeological evidence of intensive long-distance trade or overt external political influence on the Sausa before the Inca conquest. Although one cannot discount outside influences entirely, the evidence presents a picture of an ethnic polity becoming politically stratified more or less independently.

Much has been written about the importance of surplus production in political hierarchy. Mobilization of goods is especially critical for support of the leaders, once they are in power. Like Sahlins, however, I question the link between a chieftainship and surplus production. The two can affect each other: "leadership continually generates domestic surplus. The development of rank . . . becomes . . . the development of the productive forces" (Sahlins 1972:140), but surplus is relative and must be viewed as such to exist. I suggest that intensive agricultural production did not lead to the development of political rank in the Upper Mantaro Valley. Exchange, a common indicator of political asymmetry, seems to be implicated in the onset of political inequality among the Sausa in some ways; in others, exchange appears unrelated to political position. Specialization often demarcates subsets of a population asymmetrically. If specialization is linked to production, then, like surplus production, its economic impact is important in maintaining inequality but not in generating it.

With these couplings and decouplings in mind, how do exchange and production function in the emergence of political inequality? They are intertwined and have an historical link to political inequality. Marx (1971 [1867]) argued that control over production and reproduction was political power. Meillassoux (1981) notes that power in agricultural societies is based on access to and exchange of women: those who controlled women controlled reproduction. By controlling reproduction, they controlled production through access to labor. In the Marxist tradition, production has been considered a core ingredient in societal change. More recent research has suggested that control of production alone is not sufficient for political power to be maintained, that manipulation of circulation and exchange of goods are also necessary (Earle 1978; Gledhill 1978; Rowlands 1980). Whether or not these economic conditions are sufficient to create a political hierarchy seems

151

to hinge on the changing conceptual system (perceived needs) of the population and the pressures on the system in production and exchange.

EXCHANGE

In this section I examine two fundamentally different types of exchange. Each has a different place in society and a different role in politics. The first I label local (intra-group) exchange. The second is exogenous exchange, undertaken for prestige, often over long distances.

The local, domestic form is reciprocal, that is, relatively equal among partners. Essential goods are exchanged, as well as ritual and symbolic "non-utilitarian" goods. Essential goods include critical resources that cannot be produced in every household or must be traded for, such as salt, ceramics, lithic raw materials, food, and certain types of knowledge. They can also be goods that are scarce or of great cultural value. Women (and therefore labor) can thus be considered essential trade items. In certain cases, such as highland New Guinea, exchange networks and trading partners are developed and socially maintained to keep these goods moving.

The most straightforward form of exchange is what Sahlins (1972:194) called balanced reciprocity, in which identical or equivalent goods are returned without delay. There is, however, more often an aspect of delayed debt. Some scholars believe that the delay masks an inequality that is inherent in exchange (Bender 1985a). For example, marriage exchange alliances (that is, exchanging a woman for a woman) are seen as potentially developing formal inequality between larger and smaller exchange groups (Gledhill 1978). Others see this type of exchange as a guarantee of leveling between partners (e.g. Gregory 1980). Although exchange can cause social friction, it also benefits people and obliges them to interact. So long as individuals do not control the goods, services, and opinions of others, exchange remains nonhierarchical.

Also essential to exchange are the less "necessary" items, primitive valuables (Dalton 1977:197). Although these goods (shells, certain ceramics, feathers, decorations, metals, special stones, special knowledge, etc.) may be considered essential by the communities exchanging them, they can also be seen as goods needed to keep the exchange system going, to ensure that the network is maintained and critical goods keep arriving (Rappaport 1967, in Wright and Zeder 1977). A critical

152

component of this insurance value is the social network that is maintained through exchange to retain alliances, allowing the group to obtain women, goods, and information and to call on allies in times of need (Braun and Plog 1982).

Another aspect of exchange, one that is harder to see in the archaeological record, is the symbolic, ritual side that is linked to social prestige. Ritual exchange is an important ingredient in social relations. The rituals themselves join people together in a cohesive event based on general sharing, often of food. For highland New Guinea, Strathern (1971) makes a distinction between trade for goods and exchange for creating friends and maintaining relations. He notes that the two are intricately entwined, but that they can have different outcomes in the distribution of goods. Especially among politically autonomous groups, exchange associated with periodic rituals is important in maintaining stable relations between groups. It demonstrates participation in the system and generates position as well. Loss of participation and position means loss of the group's social boundary and, therefore, its social existence.

In general, the overall function of this first type of exchange is to maintain intergroup relationships, to perpetuate the system, and to gain access to needed goods. This type of exchange system usually does not allow for the accumulation of wealth. Wealth must go out again to purchase social position in the status competition (Strathern 1971; Gregory 1980). What can be gained is prestige. The big-men entrepreneurs of highland New Guinea never end up with noticeable wealth, but they *do* gain recognition and position within their group as well as in other neighboring groups (Rappaport 1967, in Wright and Zeder 1977; Strathern 1971; Meggitt 1972). They gain a voice in decision-making and provide a locus for negotiation.

This local exchange has been called *gifts-to-men* by Gregory (1980), where gifts are the form of exchange. As long as the exchange network is gifts-to-men, the exchange cycles between groups are not inflationary, but eventually pay back each participant involved (Gregory 1980:638). Strathern (1971) makes the same point by noting that in a series of New Guinean pork exchanges, the returns are actually only a small increment larger than the previous gift; it is the increment (not the gift plus the increment, as some have suggested) that becomes the debt owed in the next gift returned.

This domain of exchange can be called political because it maintains

153

the social system and its alliances, but it is not sufficient to transform the political structure itself. That is, within the exchange relationship there are mechanisms to curb inflation of the exchange. More complex social organizations (new controls on certain raw materials, labor, or knowledge, changed access to surplus production, or new forms of interaction) must be involved before local exchange is a motivating force in political change.

Of a different political nature is the "prestige," inter-regional, or long-distance exchange system. Prestige exchange is not linked to the onset of political rank, but to the *extension* of power in an already differentiated society. Although it can include utilitarian items, it tends to have a more overt political purpose and to deal in exotic, symbolic goods (Upham 1982). The distances and costs involved are greater than in local exchange (Drennan 1984a), and often the mechanisms for the exchange are more complex. Travel to a distant land is costly, perhaps dangerous; alliances with far-away polities are risky to maintain. The items traded and received are usually of high value (gold, textiles, metals, sea shell, symbols, etc.), adding to the price of the interaction (Helms 1979; Drennan 1984b). The costs of prestige exchange must be supported by surplus production (Brumfiel and Earle 1987).

Monopolies of external trade can reinforce internal control within a group (Ekholm 1972; Rathje 1972). Elites exchange with elites, creating new wealth items. Because these goods are often symbolic, beautiful, and exotic, it is easier in this exchange system to identify prestige goods from other artifacts. Special styles and objects are often found in very specific locations associated with political or religious centers. By owning foreign objects and styles, leaders can visibly set themselves apart, legitimizing their sacred and special role in society, as we see in the highlands surrounding the Valley of Oaxaca or in the chiefdoms of Panama (Flannery 1968; Helms 1979).

This uneven distribution occurs during the Peruvian Formative in Chavinoid motifs of the central Andes (Rowe 1962; Patterson 1971; Burger 1978; Pozorski and Pozorski 1987). The motifs blend several symbolic traditions from the eastern Amazon jungle and the arid western coast, forming a complex iconography that was found at ceremonial centers on the coast and in the Andes. The distribution of this style, however, is patchy. The Chavin complex's exact origin is still unclear, but what *is* clear is the political nature of this very religious art. Foreign images were selected actively by leaders who could use them to

154

their advantage. In addition, there is no evidence of conquest or overarching political domination accompanying the distribution of such images. This is not to say that the different "elites" were not in some kind of competition. Warrior and captive motifs are common in the Peruvian Formative material. Goods with these motifs take on meaning at many levels, including the symbolic and the political. They could be given away to allies, and they were also used to display elite separateness at home. Prestige derived from these gifts, and the introduction of new rituals and esoteric, sacred knowledge into the Formative groups enhanced the ability to control resources. The power of the elite solidified because of the indebtedness incurred by the recipients of the gifts (Ekholm 1972).

This discussion of prestige power is not new in the anthropological literature. Such power has always been associated with politically stratified societies. It implies that surplus production was controlled by those who participated in this form of exchange system (hence the title "prestige exchange"). Drennan (1984a) has remarked that some of this trade can be undertaken for economic reasons, but foremost was the legitimation of control.

All societies participate in some sort of exchange (Bender 1985a), and they always value some "non-utilitarian" items. Strict functionalists call goods that are not essential to survival "non-utilitarian," but I do not think that is what the people who value them would call them. Is extra food production considered basic subsistence, or is it surplus? Calorically it is extra, but not if one considers the need to bank food for calories in the future (this is an important form of risk reduction [Braun and Plog 1982]). Groups, especially small-scale groups, are often eager to produce a bit extra for feasts, exchange, or insurance against environmental risk. This extra produce is not monopolized or transformed into goods, as is the surplus described in the prestige exchange system; hence it plays a different role.

SURPLUS PRODUCTION

A discussion of exchange must necessarily include a consideration of production because material exchanged must be produced, whether it is for a feast or for bride price. Subsistence production is the base of all societies, but this is not the level of production at which a group normally operates (see Upham, this volume). People, except those in the most precarious circumstances, always produce some extra. Archaeologists have tried to identify caloric baselines to determine what is required for a group (Jochim 1976; Earle and Christenson 1980; Keene 1981). Production beyond the minimum for survival could be called risk reduction or *social produce*, but it is not strictly surplus. The same can be said for craft production: some is produced for daily survival and some for exchange. How do we identify and separate surplus from "necessary" production?

In archaeology a portion of production, whether argricultural or craft, has been labeled surplus when nonlocal items are found in the archaeological record (Saitta and Keene 1985:3; this volume). That is, surplus is identified only when there is evidence of exchange. This is an incomplete definition of surplus, because it omits what was actually produced. Because base caloric needs do not give a true picture of subsistence production and equivalent produce for exotic trade items is not a definition of surplus, I suggest adopting a political orientation for a definition of surplus.

Surplus produce can be defined as material that is taken away from its producers and converted to goods or support for political uses (appropriated surplus). When goods are used by the producers for themselves, they should not be called surplus, even if they are exchanged. In this way the definition of surplus becomes directly related to political stratification. A group can obtain exotic goods without "surplus" production or elite control over production. The form of entry into the exchange system and the distribution of goods will be different when goods are funneled through people who control distribution. This dichotomy is stated slightly differently in Gregory's (1980:626) discussion of gifts. He distinguishes gifts-to-men from gifts-to-god (Mauss 1967). Gifts-to-men are exchanged between people on an equal basis, and both parties get something roughly equivalent to what they gave. Gifts-to-god, on the other hand, leave the system by destruction (e.g., potlatch coppers [Boas 1966]), in buried caches (Bradley 1982), in burials (Parker Pearson 1984), or by alienating goods from the producers but not giving anything concrete back (as in tribute masked by religious connotations [Earle 1978; Helms 1979]).

Removal of goods is often masked by a religious cloak, neutralizing the arbitrary system of removal by justifying it as a universal law for all humans (Giddens 1979). Such appropriation has been labeled negative reciprocity and can be associated not just with surplus, but also with

156

unequal inter-regional trade (Sahlins 1972:191). This phenomenon is discussed by Earle (1978); he notes that a prestige economy produces for the elite, who do not give back an equivalent share to the populace. In his Hawaiian example, extraction of goods and food is the mechanism for maintaining political stratification. In this way, surplus accentuates inequality.

PRODUCTIVE SPECIALIZATION

There are at least two ways to view the onset of specialization. Netting (this volume) argues that craft specialization and accompanying exchange for food can be initiated by individuals as insurance risk management when they cannot produce sufficient sustenance themselves. This bottom-up model can generate independent specialists without controlled distribution. Alternatively, specialization can emanate from the top, where political and economic differentiation develops first, and then stimulates the initiation of craft specialization (Trigger 1974; Tosi 1984; Brumfiel and Earle 1987). This pattern leads to the creation of attached specialists. Both models focus on craft specialization; neither case creates rank out of specialization.

Traditionally, productive specialization has been defined as the production of a commodity or service that is exchanged for some other commodity. Craft specialization is a special case. Specialists and generalists can produce similar items, but products are more systematically produced by specialists, who invest more time and streamline the production process (van der Leeuw 1976). By exchanging with others, independent specialists obtain necessities that they do not or cannot produce. They are not controlled by any person, but by the general demand of the group (Earle 1981). Specialization requires cooperation between participants, but also includes competition between producers.

Products are more controlled in their production and distribution when the producers are affiliated with an individual or an institution. These specialists tend to produce wealth and luxury goods that are different from those of the independent producers (Costin 1986:331). Such items are used by the leaders to maintain allegiances and as emblems of inequality. Production is localized and is often associated with elite compounds. Distribution, too, is restricted, mainly to elite areas and to selected people in the community. This form of specialization does not occur until elites (patrons) solidify their political positions

157

and can support the producers. Hence, it is not involved in the initial creation of stratification.

I suggest this kind of specialization is the form that provides the structure to allow political specialists to develop who might create a simultaneous political hierarchy under certain conditions. Depending on a group's particular circumstances, specialist positions can either expand in power and dominate other realms of society or they can collapse from unorganizable tensions. This dampening of hierarchy or resistance to leaders is continuous in nonstate societies. To prevent collapse in the centralization of power, there must be a successful outlet for continued dominance. Building on existing cultural structures, specialization can extend into realms such as production, control of raw material extraction, distribution, administration, adjudication, ritual, and/or military organization for endemic warfare. In this way specialization is integral to political development. Administrative and decision-making specialists are able to direct the ideology of the populace while addressing cultural needs. Leaders as part-time or full-time managers can begin to control by organizing people. Larger and denser populations tend to require organizers whether the populace desires them or not.

Tensions that accompany large populations in dense settlements can lead to managerial specialization or to fissioning (Johnson 1973). In fact, the question of why a group stops fissioning while it is still growing becomes very important. As settlements grow in population for whatever reason, especially if they grow quickly, production unit costs increase (Gamble 1982; Hastorf 1983). This "cost escalation" with intensification can increase the likelihood of restricted access to important resources and tighter monitoring of them. As these productive resources are brought under ownership, intensification and specialization begin to develop around the restricted items. This increased control can be used by land managers (be they clan leaders or village heads) to reinforce and expand the power vested in them. At the same time that specialization, exchange, and intensification increase within and between groups, fear associated with the loss of goods (from warfare) also increases. People become more competitive and protective the more they have to lose.

Specialization, surplus production, and exchange are complex economic forces, but by themselves they stimulate formal inequality in only a few cases. Rather more important in the onset of rank is political

158

involvement or intervention in these domains. Exactly when such involvement begins to operate in a significant way depends on environmental potentials, scale of the social system, traditions of production, and social relations. Unraveling this complex of political development and economic change almost requires that it be studied in specific cultural examples. Although cultural processes can be discussed in a general way, I choose here to view one archaeological example to explain how economic change and political change can be fundamentally decoupled. I use the Andean Sausa's economic and political history to complete this task.

AN ARCHAEOLOGICAL EXAMPLE

The Wanka of central Peru have been the focus of investigation by the Upper Mantaro Archaeological Research Project since 1977 (Earle et al. 1980; Earle et al. 1987). Previous research on the Wanka was done mainly by Ramiro Matos and Jeffery Parsons (1978). We are interested in the economic and political changes within the northern population of the valley, today called the Sausa.

The ancestors of the Sausa have lived in the Upper Mantaro Valley in the central Andes, about 250 km. east of Lima, for more than 2,000 years. Environmental diversity is not just a typical characterization of the Andes; it dictates the economics and cultural history of its residents. Frost, rainfall, and topography constrain the production of crops and animals today, just as they did throughout prehistory. The study region is approximately 20 by 20 km., bounded naturally by high peaks and plateaus with elevations ranging from 3,300 to 4,200 m. (Figure 6.1). Small valleys cleave steep rocky hills and higher rolling plateaus that rise east and west up to the craggy snow-covered peaks of the Andean Cordillera. The study region is bounded on three sides by the high, nonarable *puna*, a treeless, windswept plateau that extends up to the Cordilleran peaks.

The Sausa live in and use four main environmental zones: the valley lands, the hillsides, the rolling upland plateau, and the higher *puna* plateau. These are also land-use zones, separated by different temperatures, soils, and moisture. Dry farming dominates in all zones, but irrigation does occur in the valleys and hillsides near springs and streams. Today, as it did in the past, the region produces the two staple crops of the Andes, maize (*Zea mays*) and potatoes (*Solanum spp.*), as

159

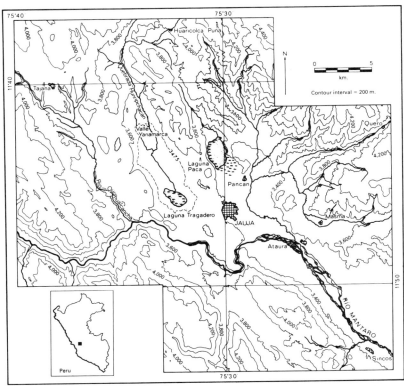

Figure 6.1   The Upper Mantaro Archaeological Research
Project study area. Drawn by Patrick Finnerty.

well as several other crops. The valleys and lower hillsides can produce
maize up to 3,600 m., and tubers grow up to 4,100 m. (see Hastorf
[1983, chapter 3] for details on the crop geographies in these
microzones). The Sausa herded camelids (llama [*Llama glama*], and
alpaca [*Llama pacos*]) throughout the whole region, permanently in the
puna and periodically among the fallow fields of the arable zones. The
people therefore lived in a relatively rich region that provided different
production opportunities in different zones. Of special note is the
proximity of these zones to each other. A small shift in residence places a
group in a different production zone.

People have been residing in this setting (which has not changed
much over the last two millennia) since the Early Horizon (800 B.C.).
Although archaeological investigation of the earliest human occupation

160

in the region is incomplete, it is thought that when the hunter-gatherer population moved permanently off the *puna* into the highland Andean valleys, they did so to take advantage of the diverse resources, eventually focusing on the arable land. (Legumes were harvested at least 6,000 years ago. Although we have very little evidence of the domestication of the potato, it is thought that the potato was not domesticated until 2000–3000 B.C. in southern Peru and northern Chile. Maize had been cultivated on the coast at least from 2300 B.C., but the varieties adapted to the elevations in the Mantaro region probably developed after that date.) The thirteen sites found dating to the Formative period in the 1986 survey (Earle in Hastorf et al. 1986) are located slightly off the valley floors near springs, with easy access to upland grasslands and low slope farmlands.

By the beginning of the Early Intermediate Period (E.I.P., 200 B.C.), the archaeological evidence suggests that small farming/herding hamlets were scattered on the hillsides and across the valley lands. For approximately a thousand years the region's population grew gradually and new villages were built. Although few sites from this time period have been excavated, the evidence suggests that the inhabitants were taking advantage of plant and animal resources in the local environment. Of sixty-four sites surveyed and tentatively dated to this phase, the average site size is 4.4 ha. Site dating based on the ceramic seriation shows that new sites were forming while earlier settlements continued to be occupied. This evidence of site fissioning suggests a pattern of cultural redundancy and growth without systemic cultural change (Graber 1984).

The overwhelming sense in each hamlet is of local self-sufficiency. Simple crafts, mostly pottery and stone tools, were produced from local raw materials. Exchange occurred, but at a nonescalatory level. From excavations, we know that Sausa tools included projectile points, small mortars and pestles, and a range of scraping tools (Russell in Hastorf et al. 1986). The ceramic finds include simple storage jars, grain-toasting jars, and serving bowls made in a wide variety of pastes and tempers. Such bowls were made in a few colors using simple design styles.

Of note are the ceramic figurines. In the earliest E.I.P. deposits, we have encountered human (often male) plank figures holding knives and trophy heads. This warrior image is the earliest identifiable symbol in the region. The motif ties into the Early Horizon Andean symbolism of human gods as warriors holding images of power and suggests that the

161

Sausa were linked with other Andean polities through a mutual use of this power image. Later in the E.I.P., on into the Middle Horizon, the plank figures are replaced by camelid figurines, many of which are smiling and very fat (pregnant?). Interpretation of these figurines is difficult, but abundance and fertility are the most obvious connotation. Camelid figurines do not occur in the later Wanka I phase. Sacrifices of six- to eight-month-old camelids (no butchering marks on their bones) were found throughout the excavated domestic areas. Lack of butchering marks suggests that the animals were buried without the meat being removed or consumed by the people (Sandefur 1987).

The botanical data indicate that potatoes, maize, and quinoa were the dominant crops at the lower elevation sites. Potatoes and quinoa were more prominent at the hillside sites, although all other crops occurred regularly. Faunal data show that the bones of domestic camelids are common; wild species occur less frequently. The ceramic assemblage includes basic serving bowls, cooking jars, and storage jars. Although the styles vary throughout the entire prehistoric sequence, the functional types do not (LeCount 1987). The most common ceramic style of this time, however, is widespread throughout the region, suggesting regular intersettlement interaction. Some copper items of local origin are found in burials, and obsidian is common. The distribution of obsidian (a long-distance trade item) does not suggest restricted exchange, as the pieces are mainly small points and chipping debris and seem to be dispersed without restriction.

The Middle Horizon (M.H., A.D. 600–1000) is named after a pan-Andean phase, although it is not chronologically equivalent to this phase in other areas of the highlands. Until the 1986 field season we were not able to distinguish materials dating to this phase from the E.I.P. In the central Andes, the Middle Horizon has been identified using the presence of intrusive Wari ceramics (Wari is a major polity to the south). Since we have found very few Wari artifacts in the Sausa region, we assigned these strata to the E.I.P. From the site survey and more detailed ceramic seriation, however, we now believe that sometime during the later part of the E.I.P. and the Middle Horizon the Sausa built some of their settlements upslope on the hillsides (sixteen out of fifty-five sites on the hillsides for the M.H. as compared to six out of sixty-four sites for the E.I.P.). The cause of this settlement shift has not been systematically researched, although defense appears to be the most likely preliminary explanation.

A trend toward sites located less on knolls (nine out of thirty-six sites) and more along valley edges is seen in the next phase, called Wanka I (ca. A.D. 900–1350). In general, Wanka I sites are slightly larger than the earlier ones. Of the thirty-six sites occupied during this time period, one-third were new. The houses excavated from this time period show a structural continuity with the earlier phases: stone foundations topped by adobe blocks built into circular structures and joined by a patio wall. What separates this phase from the earlier periods artifactually are new ceramic types with more stylistic variability, a change in agricultural production and processing tools, and lack of figurines. Evidence for agricultural intensification exists; production and exchange were active, but pottery appears to have more restricted distributions, suggesting low rates of interaction throughout the valley.

The ceramics on the Wanka I sites were made in new shapes with new colors and designs. Overall, the serving-bowl sizes increase, suggesting both large families and more frequent gatherings. Although figurines drop out, the motif continues as the large storage jars are decorated with embossed faces around the necks.

Evidence of agricultural intensification can be seen in the ground stone tools. The presence of the stone hoes suggests the development of new agricultural methods, perhaps more intensive cropping practices, different planting techniques (digging deeper in the soil), or the expansion of cultivation on to new soil types. In addition, a new form of grinding implement was used, a large flat rocker grinder (*batane*) that could process much more grain than the earlier mortars and pestles (Russell in Hastorf et al. 1986). New races of maize are evident in the botanical record. The isotopic analysis from short-necked cooking jar encrustations suggests increased maize boiling, possibly because of a dietary shift with increased emphasis on maize as well as potatoes as bulk carbohydrates (Hastorf and DeNiro 1985).

The mix of agricultural crops in the archaeological deposits, however, is basically the same as in earlier times with a slight increase of maize (Hastorf 1983:252). Camelids continued to be butchered and buried, but fewer wild species are found in the excavations (Sandefur in Hastorf et al. 1986). Compared to earlier levels, the frequency of worked bone tools in these deposits increases, suggesting more in-house processing of plants, wool, and hides. Local metals are present in the same quantity as during earlier periods. There is inconsequential evidence of long-distance trade in obsidian, although in the 1986 excavations we found one piece of *Spondylus* shell from Ecuador.

Wanka I evidence suggests a general intensification of local household activity and production with little outside trade, but an increase in local social interaction. We infer no pressure on resources, as settlements were located near prime agricultural and pasture land, there was no evidence of inter-site tension (defensive walls), and the few warrior symbols that existed earlier drop out of the assemblage.

In the last cultural phase of indigenous development, we see the artifactual evidence for what I am calling *incipient inequality* in the Sausa population. During this Wanka II phase (A.D. 1350–1460), which was curtailed by the Inca invasion, we have a marked change in many of the material correlates of behavior I have presented thus far. Production and exchange evidence from excavated households differs from the earlier phases. Evidence for increased production costs can be seen in all artifactual classes. In addition, the architectural data suggest new political differences within and between sites.

The geographic distribution of the population changed, with major population aggregation on to twenty-three Wanka II sites. The population moved into massive sites in defensive knolltop locations, overlooking the uplands and the valleys. The ratio of hillside/upland sites to valley sites went from 0.09 to 0.29 to 0.25 throughout the earlier periods, but for the Wanka II the ratio is 0.70. None of the Wanka II sites are located in the exposed flat lands of the valleys; all are in protected canyons or on hillside knolls. Given the earlier trend of agricultural intensification in the valleys and our empirical knowledge that uplands are less productive than the lower fields, we know that the switch could not have been driven simply by the need to increase production.

In the Wanka II period we see evidence of village fusion; villages that were previously separate joined with other villages. This population aggregation must have produced increased daily interaction, causing new strains on social relations between the residents. Everyone had to share the same local resources as well as to interact with greater numbers of people every day.

The site size alone suggests both a settlement hierarchy and a related political hierarchy. Whereas the largest sites in the Wanka I phase were 8–10 ha., with perhaps 1,000–2,000 people, two large Wanka II centers, Tunanmarca (23 ha.) and Hatunmarca (95 ha.), dominate the settlement system. From detailed architectural mapping, we have estimated the sites' populations to range from 10,000 to 16,600 for Hatunmarca and from 8,000 to 13,400 for Tunanmarca (Earle et al. 1987:11).

These two centers each had a constellation of smaller villages surrounding them, creating alliances. Affiliation with one of the larger centers is evident from the notably different ceramic frequencies in the two clusters of sites (LeBlanc 1981). This distribution suggests a restricted exchange network within each alliance. Clear spatial boundaries of artifact style distributions suggest competition between social groups (Bradley and Hodder 1979; Hodder 1979).

Increased internal tension and new forms of defense are inferred from the settlement construction. The sites' teetering position on the top of rocky limestone outcrops indicates that the locations were chosen for their defensibiliy, and one or two defensive walls encircle the habitation area of each knolltop site. These sites were quite well constructed from locally quarried and hewn limestone. The regularly occurring artifacts and hearths in household patios suggest a range of daily activities. The main difference between earlier patios and these later ones was the use of stone to construct the walls, where adobe brick had been used previously. Carbon dating substantiates that they were not simply retreats during time of war, but were occupied throughout the 110 years of the Wanka II period. Of particular interest are the few, highly fortified site entrances. They give a sense not only of keeping the enemy out, but also of monitoring the inhabitants' movements to and from the settlements.

Further suggestions of the importance of warfare among the Sausa come from ethnohistoric documents recounting interviews with five Wanka leaders in the early colonial period. The interviews contain specific questions about the pre-Inca period and its political organization (Toledo 1940 [1570]; LeBlanc 1981:335). Although the informants were reporting about the time of their great-grandfathers, their answers were surprisingly consistent. The historic Wanka leaders talked of *sinchicuna*, or war leaders. There was repeated emphasis on protection and defense of the community, with concrete statements about the ability of the *sinchi* to maintain power through success in war. The warriors, the informants reported, were the bravest Indians, who were chosen as "captains" to lead the Sausa into battle amongst themselves (Toledo 1940 [1570]:27). When victorious, the war leaders received the captured land and women. Exactly who the women were is unclear (but see Toledo (1940 [1570]:23, 31). This reward system suggests that the leaders had some ability to appropriate goods.

The Wanka informants implied that the choice of men as war leaders was based on effective personal action. Occasionally, when the son of a

165

sinchi demonstrated appropriate qualities, he could become the next leader (LeBlanc 1981:343). This report suggests that the positions were limited and contested, and that there was some desire to consolidate power. The documents also suggest that these leaders occasionally operated in internal political spheres, but that their authority was limited.

The information from these interviews, that leaders (and probably their followers) gained access to land and perhaps labor (women) through war, suggests that we should find differences in the agricultural products and artifactual frequencies linked with this political behavior (access to production and reproduction).

New political structures are suggested also by the specialized site organization at the two central settlements. These sites are unique not just because they are massive, forbidding fortresses, but because they had open public areas within their walls. Figure 6.2 shows the major walls of Tunanmarca. Notice the main division created by two walled-in unoccupied areas and two large central patios with several square structures attached. This new form of architectural space suggests the emergence of new public rituals that involved the entire community at one time. Moreover, the thousands of people crowded within the walls would have created a new social dynamic and would have required new forms of maintenance, keeping the peace, and providing new ways to solidify the population. Managerial positions would have become a necessity to maintain these cities.

From architectural study and subsequent excavation, we claim to identify status differences among the Wanka II habitations. The residential zones are divided up into walled patio enclaves that include

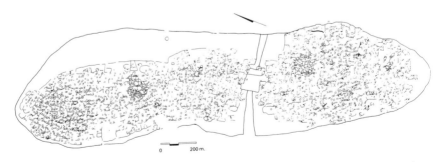

Figure 6.2   The site of Tunanmarca. Showing structure and settlement walls. Drawn by Glenn Russell.

166

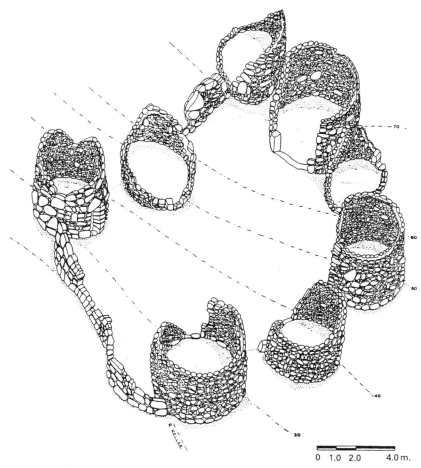

0   1.0 2.0   4.0 m.

Figure 6.3   An axiomatic to scale view of patio 7 = 2 at
Tunanmarca. Drawn by Robert Keller.

one or more circular structures surrounding an open space (figure 6.3).
We identified differences in construction among the stone houses and
in size among the enclosed patio spaces. Using the higher-quality
architecture, proximity to the central area, size of patio, and number of
circular structures, we predicted and identified the richer households,
and separated these from the patios of commoners. We assumed that
these larger and better-made houses were associated with wealth, and we
have labeled this group of households the *economic elite*. What was the

167

extent of the difference, how much wealth did they have, and was there any evidence for political power associated with it?

The previous Wanka I period displayed evidence of increased serving-bowl size that I linked to larger gatherings. These larger serving-bowls increase in density and in stylistic variety in the Wanka II phase. At both the household and the larger group level this evidence suggests increased social or ritual interaction. From the ceramics, we can tell that both ordinary and luxury items were produced and used on the sites. We found evidence of local exchange restricted within alliances, increased specialization, and differential access to certain types of wares. Ceramic specialization was inferred from the distribution of pottery wasters (malformed during firing: Costin 1986). Analysis of the wasters shows that certain ceramic types were produced only at the individual settlements. In the northern alliance group, for example, the center of Tunanmarca produced cooking pots, and a satellite, Umpamalca, produced serving-bowls and storage vessels. The waster distribution among the patios suggests that it was the commoners who actually produced most of the pottery. In this northern site cluster, all types of pottery were found at all of the sites (LeBlanc 1981).

The elite households had more ceramics per unit area, more varieties, more fancy types, more labor-intensive types, and more nonlocal ceramics. In addition, they also yielded more fragments of large jars, which we assume were used for storing crops and for producing *chicha*; a maize beer that was (and still is) essential for social gatherings, work parties, and rituals (Murra 1980[1965]).

Direct evidence of other wealth production exists but is slight. In the elite patios we found a greater concentration of spindle whorls used to spin wool (Costin 1984). From ethnohistoric accounts, we know that cloth was an important Andean wealth item, used to display and exchange status. The elite patios also yielded more evidence of metal production in ore, mold spill, and lugs (Earle 1987:74). The elite emphasis on producing status items, *chicha*, cloth, and metal, while trading for "utilitarian" goods, such as ceramics and blades, suggests they had an interest in activities beyond economics; that is, they were producing for prestige.

We found differing frequencies of artifacts between the two statuses, although the types of artifacts were the same. Although the elites had more of everything, especially the higher-quality ceramics, they did not control ceramic production. The commoner households also had the same range of products as the elites, just fewer of the more elaborate types. This finding suggests that independent specialists produced the pottery. Attached specialists, household members, or servants might have been working in the elite patios producing cloth or perhaps metal. At the time of abandonment (as far as our data show), however, these tasks were not monopolized by the elites.

We see the same pattern of restricted production and distribution in the stone tools. We found evidence of site-level specialization in blade production: dense presence of cores and primary debitage at Umpamalca. Although the initial production took place at this one site, used tools were found in every patio and site sampled (Russell in Earle et al. 1987). This discovery indicates not only that distribution was open, but that all households, including the elites, used lithic tools.

Evidence of prehistoric land-use techniques reveals the effect of the population aggregation in the Wanka II period. When the Sausa relocated into the uplands, they adopted new land-use strategies. The uplands are not as fertile as the valleys. In order to maintain adequate yields for the same population, it was necessary to work fields at longer distances and to develop intensive farming methods near the settlements. Evidence of an irrigation canal that carried water to the northern alliance sites can be traced across the landscape (Parsons 1978; Hastorf and Earle 1985). Stone-walled terraces are located in and near the settlements. These intensive strategies resulted in more expensive agriculture (more labor per unit area), but not necessarily more productive agriculture (the yield per unit area and the harvest security is lower in the uplands than in the valleys).

The Wanka II agricultural data reveal this same effect of relocation. There was a major shift in what crops were grown. For example, maize appears in 50 percent of all excavated Wanka I samples, but only 13 percent of the samples at the upland Wanka II sites contain maize. Potatoes are present in 25 percent of the Wanka I samples, but increase to 35 percent in Wanka II samples (Hastorf 1983:252). This reorientation of crop production can be explained by the shifts in site location. The arable land around Wanka I valley sites could accommodate all of the Andean crops, including maize. When the Sausa relocated to the knolls in the Wanka II period, the nearest arable land could not produce maize, but instead yielded potatoes, Andean tubers, quinoa, and lupine.

The aggregated Wanka II inhabitants would have had to travel farther to farm land that could produce maize, making that crop much more expensive and its production risky. Some Wanka II inhabitants probably had to trade for their maize. In fact, given the number of people at each site, most inhabitants would have had to travel farther than before for all agricultural production, making agriculture more costly. In addition, yields in the uplands were less reliable.

In botanical finds, striking contrasts between the elite and commoner patios exist. Overall, all crops are more dense in the elite samples. The greatest disparity, however, shows up in the frequency of maize. From the Wanka II patios, 43 percent of the elite samples contain maize, but only 12 percent of the commoner samples include it. Maize is traditionally a very important crop in the Andean world. Not only is it nutritious, but it is essential in ceremonial events, for maize beer. It is the crop that is especially sought in trade today; when it cannot be produced, it becomes a luxury trade good. The maize data from the Wanka II excavations provide clear evidence of differential access to maize-growing land or to the maize exchange network.

The elites either controlled the maize-growing lands, received maize as "gifts," or had greater access to the exchange networks with the southern Mantaro Valley residents who were growing the crop. We know that one high-quality ceramic type, andesite ware, came from the southern Mantaro Valley (Costin 1986:487). Elite patios have twice as much andesite ware as commoner patios. Maize could have been traded into the elite households along with or in the andesite jars.

As in the earlier periods, the Wanka II domestic animal bone data are dominated by llama and alpaca, with guinea pig and domestic dog rarely present. The elite patios have denser frequencies of bone than the commoner patios. Much less wild bone is present than in the earlier occupation levels (Sandefur in Earle et al. 1987). The upland locations, however, placed the populations closer to the camelid grazing lands, and meat may have increased in the diet as a result. Stable isotope analysis completed on Wanka II human skeletons, however, does not suggest that meat was a dominant part of their diet.

In summary, the Wanka II data show the result of economic, social, and political change. Change is most evident in material distributions, settlement and architectural organization, and the creation and elaboration of managerial positions. It is still not known if the economic elite were the political (war) or the managerial leaders, or if there was a sequential hierarchy with a series of positions during the Wanka II times.

Evidence suggests that the basic household unit remained the same, as did subsistence production strategies. Some households did amass more goods than others and mustered a labor force to build larger compounds and produce certain goods. The new economic elites did not monopolize products, however. They simply had more goods, perhaps because they had larger, more industrious families.

We see the onset of specialized production and distribution of certain items: specialized architectural space, new forms of agricultural production, new exchange patterns, new rituals, and new forms of decision-making. The decision-making evidence is clearest between settlements within the alliances. We know that the restructuring of daily life produced new constraints and expenses. Increased settlement sizes and associated increase in interactions surely created new institutions for group cohesion and intergroup negotiation. This inference is supported by evidence of new public space and increased ritual activity.

Using military threats and people's need for protection, the war leaders probably transformed their power to organize military actions into power over social relations. To convince people of the benefits of the more costly upland habitation, political leaders first had to convince villages to join into large social units, and then to organize work parties to build new towns. As a decision-making body, these leaders were not totally specialized. Sausa leaders of one alliance, for example, did not have the political or military power to take over the competing alliance. A leader could have gained greater wealth through military leadership first by amassing booty and second through the acquisition of increased decision-making power. Restructuring decision-making positions could have allowed the leaders to accumulate goods and women, whereas previously they would have had to trade for these goods. Through such channels the political elite could have become an economic elite.

Evidence of links between the economic elites and political power now must be sought. The evidence of intra-alliance exchange supports the inference of increased group cohesion and identity. Interalliance trade suggests social and prestige exchange, but does not include highly specialized, beautiful, symbol-laden goods. Interregional trade was negligible, and although it is evidenced by the presence of some exotic goods, it is extremely rare. This kind of exchange was not a common strategy in use by the elite for status maintenance.

We know that cloth and ceramics were important trade items throughout Andean prehistory, carrying important symbolic messages in places like Paracas and Chavin. Since virtually no cloth was preserved in the Sausa sites, we may never learn what symbols were brought in or created by the Sausa to link the inequality of the economic elite with political actions. If, however, we assume that the iconography was transferred on to ceramic vessels, as it was in many other cultures, then the Sausa did not have a very large array of politically meaningful iconographic symbols. The only symbols to occur on the latter ceramics are appliquéd faces on andesite trade ware from the southern part of the Mantaro Valley (most prevalent in the elite patios), and modeled animal faces on the Sausa-made Wanka Redware.

Given the ideology of hierarchy in Andean religion and the political structures that existed throughout the Andes on the eve of the Spanish conquest, we might expect a predisposition toward social ranking (Hastorf n.d.). The ease of the Inca conquest of Andean groups is often attributed to stratification systems already in place among the conquered groups. The Sausa data suggest that various status positions were coming into existence sometime during the Middle Horizon and the Late Intermediate Period. The elaboration of these statuses occurs by the end of the Late Intermediate Period; leadership positions existed when the Inca arrived from the south.

DISCUSSION

Although societal change is a continuum of negotiation, resistance, and consensus, there are still social transformations that can be labeled as radical. The problem for archaeologists is, of course, to identify such changes in the archaeological record. Certain cultural conditions are considered to be critical for political change. Many of these conditions have been "decoupled" in this chapter (and in the rest of the volume), yet some traits remain indicators of political change.

The Sausa were not a formally stratified society, but there was political inequality as I have defined it. There were also wealth differences. Yet the spectrum of social differences does not seem to have been localized in one ruling body. The Sausa fall between the cracks of traditional definitions for small-scale and complex societies (as defined by Service 1962; Fried 1967; Earle 1978; Johnson and Earle 1987). These "cracks" are exactly the places where political systems evolve from a communal mode. Among the pre-Inca Sausa, formal hierarchy was in the process of being negotiated.

How did the new organization develop? What were the diachronic trends in its formation? In the E.I.P., M.H., and Wanka I periods, the unit of production and consumption was the household, and social interaction (including trade) was between households. Loose alliances were probably operating and crosscutting the villages as they do in traditional Andean life today (Bastien 1978). In subsistence, agricultural production increased with the addition of new tools and new technologies that opened new lands. Through time, herding decreased in importance. There is no concrete evidence of resource stress in the Wanka I period, yet tensions could have been growing over specific localized resources, such as intensively used valley-drained fields.

The move to higher elevations was not a step toward increased productivity and cost efficiency. The valley fields, springs, and clay sources were more distant from all of the new sites. The move to defensive heights suggests that there was a need for more security in a rapidly changing social situation. The ethnohistoric evidence states that war leaders became important to organize defense. At some point, the social situation became so unstable and insecure that settlements joined together and moved on to the knoll sites. The emerging leaders organized the populace, either by consensus or coercion, to abandon their homes and build new, congested cities. Individual freedom and local productivity were traded for increased group size, increased specialization, defensive settlements, and new leaders.

The Sausa data suggest that three issues were important in the decision to move: (a) there was a perceived fear of attack, (b) there was acceptance of the need to join with other communities to work against these threats, and (c) there was a need to maintain social divisions among the populace. In this situation a larger population meant more security for all, but more power for a few. Once this social compromise was made, changes in access to goods, production, and specialization occurred as unintended consequences for the group, but also perhaps as planned schemes for the leaders. Coercion, warfare, and social stress were the motives for action. It appears that the underlying causes were not simple economic constraints, such as insufficient agricultural production from the accessible land, as discussed by Carniero (1970), but were based on the changing social and political dynamics of the Sausa.

What constitutes political rank in the Sausa case? Not common possession of exotic and luxury trade items leading to iconographic or ideological legitimation of the elite. Nor does Sausa political rank mean control over production. Every household produced, consumed, and traded for its needs. All households practiced intensive agriculture, shown not just by the crops present, but also by increased density of agricultural tools in the households.

Political differentiation existed in the power to make intra- and intersettlement decisions, affecting literally tens of thousands of people. Leaders' distinct organizational skills and positions might have allowed them to accumulate more and better goods. Elite access to more labor or goods might have grown out of old social norms: communal agriculture, labor exchange for food, payment for conducting group rituals, and required exchange when a trading partner arrived. Although they may not have controlled production, leaders could have negotiated exchanges of goods for management or played off these traditional structures to gain extra labor in their fields or homes. In Wanka I or the early stages of Wanka II, wealth differences might not have been as significant to political leaders as having followers who allowed the leaders to make decisions for the group. Material accumulation, although extant, was still in negotiation and not monopolized.

Not stressed in this argument but certainly influencing the developments was the wider Andean scene. During Wanka I and II times, sociopolitical regulations among Andean groups were chaotic. Older power relations were breaking down and new ones forming. This atmosphere might have made the Sausa more uneasy, pushing them to join forces when earlier they did not sense a need to do so.

I believe the development of political hierarchy occurred when households, out of fear, gave up their individual autonomy in order to gain household security through heightened group solidarity (increased ethnic identity). This change could have been accomplished though manipulation of the threat of war. It does not rest on agricultural intensification, craft specialization, or the control of trade. If there had been such a need, large central settlements could have been located conveniently on valley floors, as they are today. Nor does there seem to be a social structural need for stratification. The centralization of power in the Sausa was probably less than one might expect in settlements of more than 10,000 people.

Although the Sausa are just one case, their history spans an important period of cultural change. It seems more plausible that the potential shift I have described was instigated from internal dynamics between factions using existing Andean ideologies and identities. Warfare and

174

stratification, for example, existed in such ideologies. We know war motifs had been produced and large states had been present to the east and south of the Sausa. As the consensus shifted toward the need for protection, several different "histories" could have been manipulated. Once this process became part of the sociopolitical makeup of the group, it could be legitimized in religious domains, as we see in the ranking of Andean mountain gods (*Wamanis*). These gods received gifts much as local leaders did in exchange for protection and integration (Silverblatt 1987).

I agree with Carniero (1981) that the threat of destruction by other humans and the need for stability are important factors in internal political change. But these are social issues that must be mediated in the cultural sphere. The economic shift may have begun simply as gifts to the spokesperson/war leader/ritual leader for work. But with the transformation the gifts became a kind of escalating salary. Specialized activities can be mechanisms for growth of the system and for maintenance of politically stratified positions.

The emergence of political rank is complex. It seems to include both integration and conflict, gain and loss. The goal of incipient leaders is to convince the group of the advantages to be gained by changing their own habits and uniting forces. The initial gains and losses, however, do not remain stable. As the consequences of change unfold, many unexpected results evolve, leading to formal inequality.

For this change to occur, a society does not need have a certain type of kin structure, nor do leaders initially have to extract surplus from the population. Eventually, however, they will begin to retain extracted produce. Many different combinations of conditions and cultural dispositions can exist in the world. Although each group's path of political change will manifest itself differently, all groups will react to instability and competition, the outcome of which will form the basic patterns for survival we see in the patchy material record of human history, including exchange, production, and specialization.

NOTE

I would like to thank Steadman Upham and the School of American Research for inviting me to participate in the seminar on the evolution of political systems. The field work to collect the material reported on was conducted by the Upper Mantaro Archaeological Research Project, directed by Timothy Earle, Terence D'Altroy, and Christine Hastorf, although many others were also involved. It was funded in part by the National Science Foundation (grant number BNS 82–03723), with additional support from the College of Liberal Arts at the University of Minnesota.

I would also like to thank the Center for Advanced Study in the Behavioral Sciences, which provided the opportunity to write (funded in part by BNS 84–11738). The staff provided assistance in many ways, especially Kathleen Much with her editing. Bob Netting, Jane Atkinson, Bruce Trigger, Stephen Plog, and Ian Hodder provided useful discussion and comment on the ideas presented in the chapter.

7

Agriculture, sedentism, and environment in the evolution of political systems

STEPHEN PLOG

University of Virginia

In this chapter I address the process of sedentism and the evolution of sociopolitical complexity as they relate to structure and change in the physical environment. More specifically, Upham (chapter 1, this volume) has posed the question "Does the natural environment condition, limit, or select for the kinds of social responses that result in emergent multi-community political systems, or are factors of social production and technology more important determining variables in political evolution after the adoption of sedentary horticultural lifestyles?" In its most general sense, this question has been a focus of anthropological research since the time of Franz Boas, and has continued as a topic of interest in the writings of Julian Steward, Leslie White, and Marvin Harris. It is also a question that has persisted largely because of those who have taken an extreme position, arguing either that the natural environment totally determines or, conversely, is irrelevant to processes of social and political development. If we reject these extremes, and I think most of us would, the first part of the above question must be answered affirmatively: The environment *does* play a part in selecting social responses that result in changes in political systems. Without amplification, however, such an answer could be considered little more than a reassertion of environmental "possibilism," a point of view often characterized by ambiguous statements about the relationship between the natural environment and the structure of sociocultural systems.

These statements of environmental possibilism have both advantages and disadvantages. On the one hand, they tell us little about prior conditions or about the specific reasons why subsequent social or political developments occur. For those interested in prime movers, the identification of specific causal factors, this deficiency presents a serious problem. On the other hand, such statements point us away from the pursuit of sometimes questionable generalities that are applicable to all human societies, and toward the examination of processes of change in similar groups of societies. The latter direction is the one I take in this chapter. Through a discussion of environmental and cultural change associated with the adoption of sedentary horticultural lifestyles in a few areas of the New World, I focus on the latter part of Upham's question – the relative importance of the natural environment, social production, and technology.

While I evaluate the role of the natural environment and outline some of the factors that may have been important in subsequent political development, I argue that if one acknowledges the complexity of human behavior and, in particular, utilizes models of open rather than closed systems, then conclusions concerning the relative import-ance of particular factors will vary from case to case.

Many anthropologists with an ecological or systems perspective have criticized the search for prime movers (e.g., Flannery 1972:23–24). I suggest that the systems models often employed virtually force us to isolate such factors when we develop explanatory proposals. The frequently accepted view of the cultural system as a homeostatic entity regulated by various negative feedback processes, in particular, has required us to look *outside* the system for forces of change. And when we look outside, the constant fluctuations in the natural environment are the most obvious and easily identifiable potential sources of change. Thus, the explicit (or often inexplicit) use of homeostatic models has led to an overemphasis on the importance of the natural environment in cultural change; the environment is the archaeologist's *deus ex machina*.

While these comments may echo similar criticisms made by struc-tural or Marxist archaeologists, I am not trying either to endorse those perspectives or to argue that the natural environment is unimportant.

178

The recent contributions of the structuralists and Marxists have significantly enhanced our understanding of important "internal" relationships and processes, aspects of prehistoric human behavior that have been underemphasized, but those relationships and processes should be viewed in interaction with the natural environment. In the discussions below, I am thus advocating a systemic framework, not a systems theory. This framework is open rather than closed, recognizes the possibility of both internal and external forces of change and, therefore, requires no *a priori* assumptions about the priority of environment, technology, or social relationships.

In addition to these issues about particular causal variables, I think it is important to note that there are also methodological problems that hinder our discussions of causation. That is, it is difficult, if not impossible, in most archaeological studies to characterize relationships between variables (e.g., environmental change and trade activity) so precisely that one can identify causation and thus determine whether social or environmental factors were primary. This difficulty results from at least two factors. One is the complexity of cultural systems referred to above, a complexity that even with so-called "simple" hunting and gathering societies requires that our research focus on only certain components of the system while others are ignored or underemphasized. An additional problem consistently encountered when one attempts to identify causation is that our chronological control is so imprecise that when examining the relationships between two or more variables it is not possible to determine which of the variables changed first. Statements of causation, of prime movers, also result from ignoring that oft-repeated refrain "correlation is not causation." I argue that this is the case even in the American Southwest, an area sometimes referred to as the archaeological "Garden of Eden" because of the chronological precision presumed to result from the application of dendrochronology.

Despite these qualifications, I attempt in the remainder of the chapter to identify some of the environmental–cultural relationships associated with sedentism that have been important in the evolution of political complexity. I have organized my discussion of these issues into four sections: (a) a general consideration of the environment in models of sedentism, with emphasis on the concept of risk, (b) an outline of similarities in the archaeological record of two areas where sedentary villages developed, (c) an interpretation of data that emphasizes the

179

relationship of risk and such factors as surplus, sharing, ownership, and ritual behavior, and (d) a brief examination of the implications of change in these factors for sociopolitical development after sedentism.

THE "ENVIRONMENT" AND SEDENTISM

While suggesting that the difficulty of determining causation is significant, the above statements indicate that I regard characteristics of the physical environment as important in understanding the evolution of prehistoric societies. To address Upham's question explicitly, the natural environment does select for social responses in the sense that a given cultural system must extract enough energy and nutrients for the population to survive. The significance of such a statement depends, however, on answers to several related questions. What, for example, is the frequency with which food provisioning problems occur? To what extent are such problems caused by environmental change, and to what extent are they a product of cultural factors such as fluctuating ratios of consumers to producers, or other changes in the demographic structure of the group that may be related to rules regarding marriage and procreation? Similarly, the extent to which food provisioning problems will select for different organizational forms or rules depends on the degree to which those forms vary in their ability to manage the extraction of resources. Although this is a question that many have posed (e.g., Sahlins 1972:101–48), it is also one with few concrete answers. Thus, the *degree* to which the natural environment causes particular social responses is an empirical question that we may attempt to answer for particular regions and particular time periods.

The impact of the physical environment on sociopolitical evolution in all likelihood varied significantly from one area to another, from one time period to another, and from one level of sociopolitical complexity to another. When examining the importance of the physical environment in processes of political development, I think it is important to distinguish between sociopolitical changes that accompanied sedentism and those that occurred afterward. ("Sedentism" is a word that most of us use in an ambiguous manner because it is difficult to define precisely. I use it to refer to groups in which all major segments of the population – infant, adolescent, and adults as well as males and females – use facilities and structures within a village during all seasons of the year. I

180

say "use" rather than "reside" because I regard agricultural populations that construct farm houses during the agricultural season as sedentary.)

Some attempts to understand the initial period of sedentism in arid regions of the world have emphasized the relationships between "risk" and various types of social arrangements (e.g., Wiessner 1977:368–82, 1982; Braun and Plog 1982; Cashdan 1985), a concept that I will discuss below in more detail. Although sedentism and significant dependence on agriculture are not necessarily interdependent in all areas of the world, they appear to be so in the areas to be considered in this chapter; sedentary villages were not characteristic of periods when most resources were either hunted or gathered. For that reason, "risk," sedentism, and agriculture will be considered together.

Following Winterhalder (1986:8), risk can be defined as "the probability of falling below a fixed minimum requirement." One type of risk, the probability of inadequate food supplies, is in part a function of variance in local resource productivity, which has at least two important dimensions (Hegmon 1986): (a) temporal variation, differences in the availability of resources during different seasons or years (Winterhalder's intraforager variability) and (b) spatial variation, differences in the availability of resources from one place to another (Winterhalder's interforager variability). Risk clearly can be affected by spatial and temporal variation in such environmental parameters as temperature, precipitation, and soil fertility. Recent studies (Hegmon 1985, 1986; Winterhalder 1986) demonstrate, however, that social, economic, and ritual arrangements also have significant impacts on resource variation and, therefore, risk. Assessments of risk must include consideration of variation not only in climate, but also in such factors as the relationship of consumers to producers, methods of land inheritance, and economic or ritual relationships that affect resource-sharing. In addition, the concept of risk can be expanded beyond variation in subsistence resources to include demographic fluctuations in sex ratios, the length and intensity of periods of individual disability and conflict (Wiessner 1982:64), the effectiveness of societal mechanisms for reducing such conflicts, or the problems in maintaining trading networks and trading partners.

Many discussions suggest that the relationship between sedentism and dependence on agriculture resulted from both increases in the productivity of those domesticated resources when compared to the

181

natural vegetation that they replaced, and increases in the spatial predictability of resources. Such explanations of sedentism therefore focus on the evolution of characteristics of cultigens that increase productivity (e.g., cob length [Kirby 1973]) or drought resistance, on the technology that allowed those cultigens to be processed and stored, on favorable climatic changes (increased precipitation or water tables), and on such factors as population growth that would have "selected" for more productive economic systems (e.g., Cordell 1984:182–89).

What these explanations have been unable to account for, however, is the time lag in many regions between the appearance of productive forms of cultigens on the one hand and significant dependence on agriculture and sedentism on the other hand. In most areas of the New World, the technology necessary to process and store cultigens efficiently was present in combination with periods of favorable climatic conditions and productive varieties of cultigens well before sedentism and agricultural dependence evolved. Such technoeconomic and techno-environmental explanations have thus failed to account for the initial development of sedentary villages based on an agricultural economy.

I suggest that this failure results from an overemphasis on what agriculture provides and an underemphasis on the problems it creates. At the same time that agriculture increases productivity, it also increases productive variation and risk, both spatially and temporally. The increased variation is not simply a product of the direct relationship between the mean and the variance (i.e., a variable [such as productivity] with a higher mean will also have a higher variance). Rather, the coefficient of variation (standard deviation/mean) for annual production is also likely to be higher because agriculture simplifies natural ecosystems and replaces native plants that are adapted to the local environment with plants indigenous to different environmental zones (Ford 1984:129–30). As a result, increases in productive variation, and therefore in the risk of agricultural failure, were likely even in the initial stages of sedentism and agriculture. These increases may have been reinforced as population increased, ratios and relationships of consumers and producers were modified, group mobility declined, and more marginal zones were settled. In addition, the social changes that I argue were a necessary part of the transition to sedentism also increased risks in a variety of ways.

For highland Mesoamerica and the Southwest, I suggest that the major issues regarding agriculture and sedentism are not when and how

182

productive varieties of cultigens developed, but why sedentism was selected for and how populations could survive the increased variation in resources and increased social risks that accompanied dependence on agriculture and reduced mobility. Given the preexisting sociocultural system during the periods of hunting and gathering and greater mobility (a system likely characterized by "collective ownership of the means of production," access to all the "forces of production," the right of "reciprocal access to resources of others," little emphasis on accumulation, and "total sharing or generalized reciprocity within the camp" [Leacock and Lee 1982:8–9]), new social mechanisms were needed to reduce the growing risk of insufficient resources. And along with these social mechanisms, which included new views of territoriality, resource ownership, and accumulation, came a new ideology and cosmology that supported the changing views of social relationships. That is, the establishment of sedentary villages with agricultural economies not only required technological or ecological changes, but also necessitated a "social and religious revolution" that had important implications for subsequent sociopolitical developments.

Rigid environmental explanations have ignored or underemphasized the latter changes, while structural approaches often disregard the technoecological context. The necessity of change in both domains, however, must be considered to achieve adequate explanation of the time lag referred to above. Without concomitant changes in technology, economy, and critical sociocultural parameters, significant dependence on cultigens will be selected against. With associated changes in such factors, sociocultural evolution appears to have crossed a critical threshold, a threshold beyond which there were much greater possibilities (and probabilities) for increasingly complex organizational forms. While the concept of the communal mode of production as elaborated by Lee (this volume) explicitly postulates the possibility of similar thresholds at increasing levels of complexity, a weakness of the concept is that it encompasses both hunting and gathering and agricultural societies within the "communal mode," and thus obscures important sociocultural variation by compressing them into a single concept. In order to understand the evolution of political complexity, we must explicate and explain the variation, not conceal it.

THE ARCHAEOLOGICAL DATA

Before discussing how increases in political complexity may have evolved from sedentism and dependence on agriculture, I describe characteristics of the archaeological records of highland Mesoamerica and the American Southwest that suggest some striking parallels in sociocultural change in those areas. My discussion focuses on those regions simply because they are the areas I know best, not because I believe they are more or less important. I make no pretense about controlling the literature of other areas to the extent that I would argue for cross cultural processes. The discussion does, however, focus on some of the same data that Flannery (1972) has emphasized in his comparison of villages in Mesoamerica and the Near East, and the reader is referred to that seminal article for additional information.

Corresponding types of social, economic, and religious change accompanying sedentism and agriculture in the Southwest and in highland Mesoamerica are suggested by similarities in several aspects of the archaeological records of those regions. Those parallels include the following patterns of change:

1. *An increase in the volume of storage facilities and an increasing association of those facilities with individual residences as part of formalized village plans.* In highland Mesoamerica, the storage facilities were bell-shaped pits that became a regular feature of household clusters, clusters that also included rectangular houses with 18–24m.^{2} of floor area, ovens outside the houses, burials in shallow graves, and, to a lesser extent, refuse middens (Winter 1976:27–29). Individual settlements generally consisted of several house clusters, each cluster separated by 20–40 m. (Winter 1976:25). These would appear to have been the residences of individual households or extended families.

In the Southwest, villages of sedentary agriculturists had above-ground, masonry storage structures attached to either masonry or jacal habitation structures. Early examples have been called "unit pueblos" or "Prudden units," and usually consisted of a surface masonry structure divided into several rectangular rooms, a semisubterranean kiva, and a refuse area. These three components are most often oriented along a north–south axis (Prudden 1903; Gorman and Childs 1981:154). The small numbers of habitation rooms also suggest that each unit was occupied by a few households or extended families, and only one or two

184

units characterize most settlements. The types of communal arrangements and activities that Keene and Saitta (this volume) described for
the twelfth and thirteenth centuries in the Zuni area are therefore not
characteristic of all time periods or geographic regions in the Southwest
and do not appear to have been present during the initial establishment
of sedentary agricultural villages. The later development of such
communal arrangements does, however, raise important questions
about the tensions and conflicts those relationships could have created,
as Saitta and Keene argue.

In contrast to the characteristics of early sedentary villages, southwestern settlements that preceded sedentism are more similar to a type
that Flannery (1972:30) has termed "circular hut compounds." Such
sites are characterized by circular structures, frequently arranged in an
oval pattern, and by food storage that is shared by all occupants and
usually located in open, visible areas in a cleared compound (Flannery
1972:30–31). The site of Shabik'eschee, a pithouse village in Chaco
Canyon in northwestern New Mexico occupied between A.D. 500 and
700, is an example of the latter type. Originally excavated by Roberts
(1929) and recently studied again by Wills and Windes (1986),
Shabik'eschee is a large settlement of perhaps sixty-eight pit structures
and probably an equally large number of extramural storage pits.
Although some storage pits were associated with individual dwellings,
the large number of external storage structures suggests a different type
of storage system from that occurring during more recent prehistoric or
historic times (Wills and Windes 1986:4–5, 23–24):

The typical ethnographic Puebloan approach to storage involves large rooms or
portions of rooms which are cool and dry . . . In the case of corn, portions of the
stored crop are removed daily to be processed and consumed. The small cists or
bins typical of Shabik'eschee Village represent a very different kind of storage
strategy from the ethnographic model. Partially preserved examples of cists
from rockshelter sites indicate that the cists were probably sealed . . . at the top,
rather than open for easy access . . . Each bin at Shabik'eschee is isolated from
others and separate from individual houses; in other words, each storage facility
is a distinct entity occupying a public place.

It thus appears that at least in the Southwest, one process associated
with sedentism based on agriculture was a transition from primarily
public storage to primarily private storage, from a concept of communal
ownership of resources to belief in more circumscribed ownership.

2.   *The more regular appearance of formalized cemetery areas or,*

minimally, rules regarding where burials are placed. The former are characteristic of the American Southwest, where the well-defined trash zones that appear with unit pueblos already appear to have become sacred places. In Mesoamerica, cemeteries exist at some sites and are characterized by standard burial positions (Whalen 1976:78; Flannery and Marcus 1976b:382). In other instances, rules stipulate burial in shallow pits or deep-storage pits within 10 m. of a house suggesting "that the buried individuals were probably occupants of the nearest house" (Winter 1976:29). Burials have certainly been found in both regions from periods prior to sedentism. Such burials, however, are not only less abundant, but also are not always associated with major settlements, appearing to have been placed in a less patterned manner within sites.

3. *Significant increases in the frequency of ceremonial structures or "public buildings."* Although ritual structures or areas also are known from the periods preceding sedentism, they were constructed at a small proportion of settlements. With sedentism, ritual structures became a regular feature of the formalized plan characterizing most habitation sites (Flannery 1972:38; Flannery and Marcus 1976b:220). Steward (1937) has suggested a consistent ratio of habitation to ritual structures in the northern Southwest of approximately 6:1 during the initial periods of sedentism, and a large percentage of sites in both areas have a relatively restricted size range from 1 to 10–12 households (Prudden 1903; Plog 1974:96; Marcus 1976:89). In both Mesoamerica and the Southwest, the early "public buildings" or ceremonial structures were modified versions of habitation structures, were located in portions of the sites where they would be visible and accessible, and were standardized (Flannery and Marcus 1976a:220). Although the Mesoamerican structures were surface buildings while the Southwestern equivalent were subterranean, I suggest this has more to do with the type of habitation structures from which the public buildings evolved than with the visibility of the activities (*contra* Johnson 1984:9).

4. *Significant increases in both local and long-distance exchange.* Ceramic vessels, obsidian, marine shell, and magnetite were among the resources that moved through Mesoamerican trade networks. In the Southwest, turquoise, copper bells, marine shell, pottery, and obsidian were exchanged. While movement of such "exotic" goods as marine shell and turquoise has been recognized since initial archaeological research in both areas, the diversity and abundance of other types of

trade goods, particularly more "domestic" or "utilitarian" items, has been documented only recently. In both areas, much remains to be learned about many of the important parameters of these exchange systems, particularly the complexity of the organizational ties the mechanisms of exchange, and the degree of temporal variation in the magnitude of the exchange (e.g., Upham 1982; Drennan 1984a and 1984b; Plog 1986a). Nevertheless, it is clear that the magnitude of exchange among sedentary villagers was far greater than that among earlier, more mobile populations.

5. *Changes in stylistic patterns.* Early periods are characterized by artifact styles distributed over large geographic areas (yellow or white pottery with incised designs in Mesoamerica, black-on-white pottery with simple decorative motifs in the Southwest), and such strong patterns of association between attributes that types are relatively easy to define (Plog 1987:16). These distributions are replaced by style zones that are smaller in geographic extent, and by variable styles with weaker patterns of association between attributes, making type definition and identification difficult (Plog 1987:16–21). This change can be interpreted as a transition from "isochrestic" variation to symbolic variation (Sackett 1985; Wiessner 1985; Plog 1987; see also Upham, this volume). The former type of variation is "acquired by rote learning and imitation and is employed automatically," functioning "to make life predictable and orderly" (Wiessner 1985:160–61). The latter type of variation is a more active tool for conveying messages of social identity (Wiessner 1985). Such communication mechanisms appear to have been used increasingly with the establishment of sedentary agricultural villages.

6. *Significant population increases causing major alterations in the social environment.* Population increases in all likelihood were caused by some of the changes outlined above. Storage and exchange, for example, may have reduced seasonal variation in resource availability, leading to higher or more constant fertility levels. Higher fertility levels increased the possibility of periods of rapid population growth (Binford and Chasko 1976:70; Wilmsen 1979, 1982) comparable to those that occur in many regions as sedentary villages are established. Alternative food preparation techniques that were selected as stored corn became a larger part of the diet (corn had to be boiled in containers to extract the full nutritional benefit [Ford 1968]) may also have increased the availability of foods suitable for weaning children and therefore reduced

187

the impact of lactation on fertility levels (Lee 1979:329–30; Binford and Chasko 1976:138). Several factors, including the contribution that young children can make to agriculture (Ford 1974; Wiessner 1977:376–77), the nature of the female role in agriculture and food preparation (Blanton 1975:122; Binford and Chasko 1976:139; Howell 1976:37), and the political and economic advantages of high growth rates as competition for resources increases (Bates and Lees 1979:283) may also have caused individual social units to choose larger family sizes.

SEDENTISM AND SOCIAL CHANGE

Although the above similarities in the archaeological records of the northern American Southwest and highland Mesoamerica likely occurred for several reasons, I suggest they are associated with increased risks, both economic and social, that accompanied dependence on agriculture, increased sedentism, and reduced mobility. With reductions in temporal variation in resource availability resulting from more storage, and with the increased fertility levels that were probably associated, groups may have increased in number and expanded at the expense of other populations utilizing different adaptive strategies. The social changes suggested by the above data also may have reduced risks in several ways, and in all likelihood were as important, if not more important, than technological changes like increased storage. (At the same time, boundedness and sedentism created new risks – the relationships are circular, not linear – that were important in the subsequent evolution of the system, as discussed below.)

Several researchers have proposed that a set of interrelated changes in various aspects of social relationships (local, regional, and interregional) are associated with sedentism. Steward (1937) and Eggan (1950:128), among others, have hypothesized the development of formalized social units, possibly lineages, in the Southwest during this period, and Flannery (1972:29) has made a similar proposal for Mesoamerica. Supporting evidence that is often cited includes the development of formalized cemeteries as well as the ratio of habitation rooms to kivas. In regard to cemeteries, Flannery (1972c:29) has argued that

the placing of permanent, nucleated communities on or near localized areas of strategic resources probably changed group ideology from one of weak territoriality to the pattern of a small, defended core area versus a large,

188

undefended periphery, further emphasized in concepts of descent. In this regard, we should perhaps not be surprised to find burials under house floors or in adjacent courtyards, as in Early Formative Mesoamerica; repositories for multiple secondary burials, as in both regions; or the saving of ancestors' skulls, as in the Near East.

From this point of view, the increasing appearance of cemeteries and formalized burial rules with sedentism is indicative of more bounded social units that were attempting to mark and legitimate their claim to particular parcels of land.

Focusing on other types of settlement data from the Southwest, Steward also postulated the development of "more clear-cut social units," arguing that

it is difficult to reconcile the division of the early villages into small house clusters with any other social unit than a unilateral lineage or band. Each house cluster is so large that it must have sheltered several families (Steward 1927:163, 167).

In both the "small house" unit and the much larger villages, the kiva–house ratio continues to be one to five or six (Steward 1927:163–64).

A recent simulation study by Hegmon (1985), based on Hopi environmental, demographic, and agricultural information, supports the likelihood that some type of formal, well-defined social unit of limited size would evolve with increasing dependence on agriculture. Hegmon (1985:53, 57) found that if there is no sharing of agricultural surplus among all households in a simulated community of between two and twenty families, only 44 percent would survive after twenty years, largely because "independent households often could not recover from a bad year in which their storage buffer was depleted." Surprisingly, that survival rate is little different if there is complete sharing among households such that all agricultural resources are averaged out among families; 50 percent of the families survive after twenty years. Therefore,

complete sharing within groups buffers individual households from both positive and negative extremes (in resource availability). A household is protected against the chance of having an unusually low yield, but it also loses the benefits of having an unusually high yield. The result is a survival rate for groups that is scarcely higher than that for individual households

and

It appears that the advantage a household gains by having a low yield

189

supplemented by the group is outweighed by the disadvantage of the household being pulled down with the group (Hegmon 1985:54, 55).

These results thus suggest that intergroup sharing – with limitations on who must share and how much must be shared – might produce a higher long-term survival rate. Hegmon therefore also modeled a form of restricted sharing in which households only share surplus production. In this instance the survival rate of households increased considerably, to an average of 60 percent. There also are increases in the survival rate as the number of households sharing resources increases to between six and eight, but minimal change occurs with further increases in households (Hegmon 1985:60–63). Winterhalder's (1986:17) recent study of foragers produced a similar conclusion: While resource variation decreases with increases in group size, "the major part of the risk reduction occurs at small [group sizes] . . . and 80% of the potential risk reduction can be gained by only six foragers." Hegmon (1986:34) therefore argues that if only sharing is considered, there is little advantage gained from increasing group size above six, but no significant disadvantages result either. When other factors related to the flow of information and capacity for information processing are considered, however, the studies of Johnson (1978, 1982) suggest that problems in information processing and problem-solving do arise as group size rises above five or six. The result may be difficulties in achieving efficient resource distributions or in resolving disputes. With further increases in the number of groups or components to be integrated, additional organization or control mechanisms must therefore be added to ensure efficient functioning of the system.

Archaeologists working in the Southwest and elsewhere (Flannery and Marcus 1976b:206) have often suggested that the observed increase in ritual behavior in sedentary villages is related to increased sharing of goods or information and, on the basis of the above data, I concur. That is, some characteristics of early sedentary villages result from (a) the development of a more restricted form of sharing, producing a smaller, more formalized social group composed of a limited number of households that limits risk while increasing the probability of group survival, and (b) a new level or form of information processing that evolves from previously existing ritual organizations. Many have argued that such organizations have always had an important role in information gathering and processing, even in hunting and gathering systems. The result is the pattern that Steward (1937) identified long ago: the consistent association of one ceremonial structure, a "public building," with a limited number of habitation structures.

Too little work has been done to determine if or when such control mechanisms ever developed in the Southwest, although data presently available suggest they did in a few regions. Steward's (1937) early and provocative analysis of room to kiva ratios has often been cited as one that supports that possibility. After room to kiva ratios that average 6:1 from approximately A.D. 700 to 1100, Steward found that the ratio increased to 14:1 between A.D. 1100 and 1300 and to 100:1 between A.D. 1300 and 1500 (Steward 1937; Plog 1974:122). In contrast, more recent analysis based on larger amounts of data than were available to Steward indicate not only considerable spatial variation in such ratios, but also little change in most regions before and after A.D. 1100 (Most and Jones 1983:14). (Keene and Saitta [this volume] also have discussed problems in defining ritual or communal structures, and the impact such problems can have on the measurement of room to kiva ratios.) The lack of change in the ratio over time could be regarded as supporting the contention of Whiteley (1985:369–70) that, even during historic times, families or lineage segments were the fundamental social units in Hopi society that owned land and controlled ceremonies, an argument that is also consistent with the results of Hegmon's simulation. A much wider range of data must be considered, however, before conclusions are drawn about the presence or absence of higher-level controls or integration (e.g., Plog 1974:126–27; Upham 1980; Wilcox and Sternberg 1983; Lightfoot 1984).

In addition to changes in social organization on a local scale, changes that appear to have developed on the regional level in association with increasing sedentism also are important (Braun and Plog 1982; Hantman 1983:281–82, 1984; Madden 1984). Trends identified in several areas of the world include a transition from open, undifferentiated social networks to networks that are more localized and discrete with complex patterns of cooperation and competition. Madden (1984:194), for example, suggests that the advantage of open networks will decline as "distance between groups in a region decreases to the point where there is much overlapping of exploitation territories and competition for finite resources." As such changes occur, they will select for the symbolic,

191

social identity functions of stylistic variation (Steward 1937:160; Hodder 1979; Braun and Plog 1982:510–11; Hantman 1983:41–42; Madden 1984:194).

As more discrete social networks develop, however, social boundaries become

expensive to maintain both with respect to risks incurred in limiting the range and flexibility of linkages and because of the time and energy necessary for boundary maintenance. We may assume that in many cases there would be not only a continuation of certain social alliances across these imposed barriers (although on a more limited and structured scale), but also a development or an elaboration of formalized and probably extensive communication and exchange linkages of other sorts (such as trading connections and political alliances) to offset the economic risks incurred by putting limits on the social network (Madden 1984:194; see also Hantman 1983).

Thus, Hantman (1984:179) suggests that southwestern groups, while defining boundaries with their immediate neighbors, still maintained exchange alliances with spatially more distant groups residing in environmentally distinct zones.

Although many have emphasized that exchange ties (whether within or between groups) build social ties, Foster (1977:3) has suggested that exchange, particularly involving utilitarian items, "does not itself promote social solidarity or stability, but rather is fundamentally a dissociative, conflict relation which must be carefully regulated" (see also Sahlins 1972:188–91; Braun and Plog 1982:511). Particularly when hunting and gathering as well as agricultural societies occur in the same locales, the possibility of exploitative exchange ties, what Schneider (1975) has called "unbalanced exchange," is increased. Exchange activity therefore may be regulated by embedding it in a larger ritual context. "Ritualization gives trading behavior an affective dimension and in many cases provides supernatural sanctions" (Foster 1977:12–16) that may reduce conflicts and obscure the many inequalities that can develop in exchange. This proposal may thus explain why data from both the Southwest and highland Mesoamerica (Flannery, Marcus, and Kowalewski 1981:65–68; Stark 1981:368–69; Plog 1986b:313–14; Toll 1985:404–06) show a strong association between the ubiquity of public buildings and the growth of regional exchange systems.

In combination with the characteristics of individual settlements summarized earlier, I suggest these changes in regional organization are the central elements of a social transformation associated with increasing sedentism. Along with concomitant changes in economy and technology, these processes moved groups past a major cultural evolutionary threshold and led to the rapid expansion of villages of sedentary agriculturists. To summarize this proposal, I am suggesting that some of the characteristics of the archaeological record during periods when sedentary communities were established resulted from: (a) the development of a more restricted form of sharing, producing a smaller, more formalized social group composed of a limited number of households, (b) an associated change from public storage of resources to private storage areas associated with individual habitation units and an increasing probability of land and resource ownership by smaller social units, (c) the evolution of a group ideology consistent with increased territoriality and symbolized by formal cemeteries and stylistic patterns, (d) increases in ritual behavior that are associated with increased potential for social conflict as exchange activity increases, (e) more complex regional ties and the possible need for an increased capacity for information management and processing, and (f) more "vested interests" in the new social relationships and cosmology. The result is the pattern that Steward (1937) and others identified long ago: the consistent association of a ceremonial structure or "public building" with a limited number of habitation structures, storage rooms, and formal cemeteries, and a greater concern for expressing group identity through distinctive styles. I also propose that these or similar types of changes were necessary to reduce the greater degree of risk, both social and economic, in agriculturally dependent societies in highland Mesoamerica and the Southwest, and that it is the complex nature of these changes that explains the time lag between the appearance of productive cultigens and significant dependence on agriculture.

ENVIRONMENT AND THE DEVELOPMENT OF POLITICAL SYSTEMS

Once villages of sedentary agriculturists became common in the prehistoric Southwest and highland Mesoamerica, what were the factors that determined sociopolitical development during subsequent periods? An interesting difference between archaeological studies of Mesoamerica and the Southwest is that the physical environment is continually emphasized in studies of the latter area, while it receives much less attention in studies of the former. One could argue that this differential emphasis is a product of the more marginal natural environment in the Southwest in contrast to Mesoamerica, where agricultural conditions are generally more favorable. While this perception may be one part of the explanation, I suggest that it also results from at least two other factors.

First, the differential emphasis on the environment follows from the biases and assumptions that we bring to studies in different regions (Upham 1982), particularly in regard to the likely spatial scale of social systems in each region. Although Mesoamerican archaeologists have little difficulty postulating and supporting relationships between distant highland and coastal regions, even during periods when sedentary villages first appeared, those of us studying the Southwest have often had a narrower, more localized focus. Some general patterns of culture change (e.g., trends in population and exchange) are strikingly similar across broad areas of the northern Southwest, even between such seemingly different areas as Chaco Canyon in northwestern New Mexico, where many pueblos have hundreds of rooms, and sections of northeastern Arizona where villages usually have fewer than ten structures. Given our common assumption that the geographical scale of prehistoric social systems in the Southwest was limited, however, there is little else but region-wide climatic fluctuations that could have caused such a phenomenon as contemporaneous demographic fluctuations in different regions (e.g., Euler et al. 1979:1098). It is therefore not surprising that it is climatic change that almost all southwestern archaeologists end up talking about as the primary cause of culture change.

A second reason for the emphasis on environment in the Southwest is, not surprisingly, the quality of the information that has been generated from dendroclimatological studies. In no other area of the world do we have paleoenvironmental data comparable to those that have been generated from southwestern tree-ring studies. When discussing issues of causation or relationships, however, those fine-grained reconstructions based on decadic intervals must be compared with much less precise reconstructions of culture history that tend to smooth out rates of changes and obscure short-term fluctuations (Plog 1974; Plog and Hantman 1987; see also Upham, this volume). In such cases, it is *always* possible to find some type of climatic fluctuation that is roughly contemporaneous with any given episodes of culture change.

A case study

To what extent, then, can we actually demonstrate that environmental change was a major factor in sociopolitical development? An excellent case study is found in the period from approximately A.D. 850 to 1150 in the northern Southwest, a period following the establishment of sedentary, agricultural villages when most syntheses indicate that regional population density grew continually and rapidly and village size increased significantly in some areas. There is also increasing evidence of greater sociopolitical complexity, at least until A.D. 1120–1150, when many of these trends were reversed and parts of the region were abandoned. Consistent with the above discussion, favorable climatic change has been the most frequently cited stimulus for population increases, and unfavorable changes in climatic parameters are commonly argued to be responsible for the reductions in sociopolitical complexity in the twelfth century. Major articles in *Science* (Euler et al. 1979) and *American Antiquity* (Dean et al. 1985) exemplify this approach.

With recent improvements in the precision of our culture historical reconstructions for a few parts of the region, however, it has become possible to examine the relationship between cultural and environmental change using similar measurement scales. For a small study area in northeastern Arizona, Hantman and I (Plog and Hantman 1986, 1987) analyzed frequencies of ceramic design attributes on tree-ring-dated sites and were able to seriate sites on an absolute scale (*absolute seriation* as defined by Braun [1985]) rather than on a relative basis. Estimates of demographic change for ten-year intervals could then be generated for comparison with dendroclimatic records. That comparison indicated that (a) the depopulation of the area began well before the periods of decreased moisture usually cited as causal, and (b) rates of population change through the period in question are poorly correlated (none was statistically significant at the 0.10 level) with the various dendroclimatic indices emphasized in recent studies (Euler et al. 1979; Dean et al. 1985). Density-dependent relationships between population growth and dendroclimatic fluctuations were also examined and received no statistical support. Analyses of data from the Dolores region of southwestern Colorado from the period in question has resulted in similar conclusions (Schlanger 1985:211–12).

Similarly, some aspects of other proposed relationships between

195

environmental and cultural change should be modified given these data. Braun and I (1982:515; see also Dean et al. 1985:548) have suggested that variation in exchange intensity was probably related to variations in local productive uncertainty. *After* the development of sedentary villages, however, correlations between exchange intensity and local and regional dendroclimatic fluctuations ($r = -0.27$ and $p > 0.10$ for lithic raw material exchange and $r = 0.04$ and $p > 0.10$ for the exchange of red and orange ware ceramic vessels), or between exchange intensity and local population density are low and statistically insignificant. Whatever is causing the variation in exchange intensity, it does not appear to be the climatic factors emphasized in recent discussions. Nevertheless, there was a substantial increase in exchange intensity between the pre- and post-sedentism periods, supporting hypothesized relationships between initial increases in exchange intensity and higher risks associated with agriculture. Schlanger (1985:222) also found a better relationship between climatic variation and population change during periods prior to sedentism.

CONCLUSION

Such results emphasize the fact that relationships between culture and nature are complex and particular types of environmental changes may have different impacts with different socioeconomic arrangements. It seems clear that the role of the environment has been overemphasized and new models of culture change must be developed. Although that effort is beyond the scope of this chapter, I propose that the construction of such models should begin with a consideration of the social changes that accompanied sedentism and agriculture. Those social changes were important not only because they were a necessary part of the transition to agricultural villages, but also because they created the necessary variation for subsequent sociopolitical processes. As Flannery (1972:49) has suggested, "the success of village society may have been a prerequisite for further political evolution." Given some of the sociocultural changes suggested by the parallels between archaeological data from the Southwest and highland Mesoamerica, significant variation may have been produced in several dimensions of those societies:

1. *Higher potential surpluses produced by both the greater productivity of agricultural systems and expanded storage facilities.* As Saitta and

196

Keene (this volume) have argued, we must study not only where surpluses are stored, but whether and how they are extracted from producers. While surpluses can be stored to minimize productive variation, they can also be manipulated for political purposes and used to support the development of either horizontal or vertical administrative specialization. Such specialization appears to be associated with the development of ascribed social status (e. g., Johnson 1978:101). Johnson (1984:3), among others, has argued that "ancient complex societies, as modern ones, were built upon surplus." In turn, the extraction and distribution of surplus can create tensions that must be adjudicated by new socioreligious relationships and concepts (Keene and Saitta, this volume).

2. *The potential for a larger labor pool and therefore for surplus labor that can also be exploited.* Again, Johnson (1984:6) suggests that "elites tend to hunger for things other than food. Most importantly, they are also noted consumers of labor." This "hunger" may lead elites to provide incentives for families to have more children, providing an additional factor that may have fueled population increases.

3. *Significantly altered ratios of people to land as a result of population increases.* Whether or not carrying capacity was ever approached, settlement of new areas was required. At the same time, increasing emphasis on farming reduces the total amount of productive land available (Flannery 1969:24). As a result, variation in the productive potential of land held by different social groups would have been amplified, and this trend could have been exacerbated by the development of farming strategies that focused on even smaller and less numerous environmental zones (Flannery 1969:24). Thus, Flannery (1969:24) argues that "this kind of differential access to strategic resources, including the means of production, is at the heart of 'ranked' or 'stratified' societies."

4. *Increased elaboration and complexity of ritual knowledge, increasing the possibility for differential access to that knowledge.* As Upham (1982) and Whiteley (1986:70) have argued for Pueblo societies, access to ritual knowledge "in practice amounts to access to political power." Adams (1956:228), among many others, has noted that early political leaders in regions of the world where complex societies ultimately developed appear to have evolved from individuals closely connected

197

with religious leadership and knowledge: "to judge from the placing and content of tombs and representational art, individual status differences were largely derived from, or at least closely connected with, leadership in the temples."

5. *The evolution of personal wealth, with less sharing of some goods.* Flannery (1972:40, 48) notes that ethnographically there is little disparity in wealth among social units in circular compounds while differences in wealth appear early in villages. Consistent with this observation is Hegmon's (1986:35) conclusion that "restricted sharing results in post-distribution variation among social units and thus involves some inequality." For these reasons, we see social arrangements such as that among the Hopi, where "the lowest ranking households in a clan, or clans in a village, are forced to leave the village in bad economic times, but the clan or village survives" (Hegmon 1985:69–70; see also Connelly 1979:549–50). Similarly, Whiteley (1985) has recently criticized ethnographic models of the Hopi that emphasize clan or lineage control of land and has argued that (a) most Hopi land is individually owned, (b) what have been called "clan lands" are actually controlled by the family or lineage segment that controls clan ceremonies, and (c) the clan as a corporate unit exists only at an ideological level as a means of expressing group identity. With individual, rather than corporate ownership, the potential for differences between individuals is increased.

6. *More personal disputes, in part because of the trend identified in (5) above, creating social conflict that must be adjudicated.* Many studies have noted the importance of mobility in conflict resolution in hunting and gathering societies. That is, if various social or ritual mechanisms for resolving disputes fail, the conflicts can be avoided (though not necessarily resolved) by one of the parties simply leaving. As population densities increase and social boundaries become better defined and less permeable, this method of conflict resolution becomes less feasible. Other mechanisms are needed, and such selective pressures may favor the evolution of leaders who have the ability to mediate such problems.

7. *Increased needs for organization and regulation as the intensity of exchange activity, particularly regional alliances, increased.* Many discussions of the possible importance of both long-distance and local exchange or specialization in the evolution of complex societies have

198

emphasized this issue. Such proposals could be regarded as one example of a variety of factors that could increase information-processing needs, and thus select for new regulatory institutions with increased control and power.

It should be clear that these "social" changes cannot be separated from aspects of the physical environment and that it is possible for changes in the natural environment to amplify any of the above disparities. Long periods of favorable environmental conditions, for example, might increase the amount of available surpluses that could be manipulated by political leaders. Nevertheless, both theoretical and empirical studies of the prehistoric Southwest, where environmental factors are often said to be more important because of the marginal nature of agriculture, have revealed the importance of regional and interregional social, political, and economic relationships (Saitta 1983:823; see also Upham 1982; Hantman 1983; Plog 1983; Wilcox and Sternberg 1983; Toll 1985; LeBlanc 1986; Plog 1986a, 1986b). Evidence thus suggests that multivariate explanations of political development in sedentary societies must include such factors as risk, surplus, sharing, alliance formation, and conflict resolution. In addition, we must not only consider the relationship of these factors to the structure of local networks, but also must examine how they affect the articulation of those networks and the growth of regional political systems.

PART III

Marxist views of political change

8
Politics and surplus flow in prehistoric communal societies

DEAN J. SAITTA

University of Denver

and

ARTHUR S. KEENE

University of Massachusetts

The writing of this chapter was initiated in the field, where one of us (Keene) was living on an Israeli kibbutz. The kibbutz is a moderate-sized agro-industrial community within which social labor is communally appropriated and where a strong ideology of social equality prevails. The kibbutz as an institution has severed the link between the labor a person performs and the reward she/he receives. One works according to one's ability and receives according to one's needs. Kibbutzim comprise 3 percent of the national population, and produce 60 percent of the nation's agriculture and 8 percent of its industrial output. Kibbutzim often outcompete more conventional enterprises in national and world markets, especially in the production of agricultural produce and technology, plastics, and chemicals.

What does the kibbutz have to do with this volume? For us, there are three points of significance. Foremost among these is that the existence of the kibbutz throws a wrench into conventional social evolutionary typologies. Though large (some numbering up to 2,000 people), kibbutzim are relatively non-hierarchical and egalitarian. Though actively integrated into a competitive global economy, kibbutzim are communally run. Though possessing a complex technical division of labor, differential compensation is virtually nonexistent. With its

203

juxtaposition of categories and processes typically held in opposition, the kibbutz has forced us to confront the limits of what is (and was) possible where the organization of human social forms is concerned. It has forced us to rethink the utility of many assumptions and generalizations that inform contemporary archaeological thought. We have had to consider turning our ideas inside out, thereby opening up the past to new and perhaps unconventional interpretations.

Second, kibbutz life underscores the effects of analyses at different scales. Relationships on the kibbutz are not constant or uniform on a day-to-day basis. Inequalities continually arise and are mediated in a variety of ways over the course of days, months, or years. These inequalities are situational and transitory rather than institutional. Struggles over what constitutes equality, what is tolerable and intolerable, are continual. Kibbutz society is in a constant state of becoming, of self-definition and redefinition. The tendency for archaeologists, particularly within the evolutionist paradigm, to treat culture or society as a fully integrated, seamless object of analysis (e.g., Brown and Price 1985) masks these important tensions and struggles and disguises significant variation within the generic categories we call egalitarian and non-egalitarian society. It consequently prevents us from confronting the self-productive capacity of society and the role of human agency and intentionality in social change.

Finally, interaction with other observers of kibbutz life has demonstrated how the "facts" of kibbutz existence can support many different conclusions about the success of this social arrangement. The kibbutz is a controversial institution, especially within Israel. Whereas we see the kibbutz as communal, egalitarian, lacking in class divisions, and successful, others have argued that it is unequal, has well-established social classes, and is a relative failure in terms of adhering to its original ideals. To some, the kibbutz is unequal because it contains a rather rigid sexual division of labor. It is bourgeois because it has acquired, for all of its members, the creature comforts of a consumer society such as swimming pools, televisions, and air conditioners. It is not socialist because it actively participates in the world capitalist system by buying and selling on the world market. It is a failure because its members now live in modest comfort, compared to the spartan existence of the early pioneers.

The status of the kibbutz is, of course, a complex debate, but it has everything to do with the focus of this volume. People understand the world in different ways. They mold their observations to conform to their own experiences, to the way they expect the world to be ordered. The terms equality, commune, exploitation, and hierarchy are emotionally and politically laden, evoking the same kinds of strong responses as terms like fascism, sexism, communism, capitalism, and slavery. As investigators of the world, then, we must consider not only the extent to which we are talking about the same thing, but the extent to which the categories we use constrain our imagination and thus our conclusions about what is real and possible in past or present.

The kibbutz is irksome because it is not easily explicable with models of organizational variation in use today. Indeed, some typologists have gone so far as to isolate kibbutzim as "intentional" as opposed to "natural" communities, thereby excluding them from the realm of anthropological generalization (cf. Greenwood 1985; Keene 1986). Social forms in the past are emerging as similarly problematic, as material evidence for organizational variation in prehistory accumulates. In this chapter, we will elaborate a framework which we feel can be uniquely productive for illuminating some of the dynamics responsible for producing this variation. We will accomplish this task within the scope of the volume's topic by elaborating an historical materialist approach to the question of political organization and change in small-scale societies. Our concern is to link political dynamics to economic processes of surplus extraction and distribution. We believe that the relationships between power and surplus flow at all ranges of societal complexity are many and varied, and that the task of exposing such variation has barely begun.

Impeding such exposition are notions about what constitutes "simplicity" and "complexity" in social forms. Consider, for example, the following set of terms: hierarchy, power, prestige, aggrandizement, inequality, tribute. These terms have traditionally been regarded as closely related correlates of complexity in human society (e.g., Flannery 1972; McGuire 1983; Brown and Price 1985). The literature on complexity manifests a tendency to use these terms interchangeably, in the bargain confusing hierarchy with inequality and conflating necessary conditions with causes (e.g., while surplus or large populations are necessary to sustain tributary systems, they do not necessarily require or promote such systems). This conflation has given us a rather coarse-grained analysis of the processes by which social organizational changes in general, and in "complex" systems in particular, develop. Our aim in this chapter is to begin to question some of these linkages, so as to prepare the ground for new organizational models.

We must note at the outset that, in contrast to other authors, we are not concerned here with a particular political development, be it the emergence of differential access to resources, decision-making hierarchies, mechanisms for maintaining economic inequality, or direct, coercive rule. Rather, we are concerned with the *interaction* between political and nonpolitical walks of social life and how the archaeological record can be used to explore these interactions. We believe that our ability to distinguish between several conceivable outcomes in a specific case will be greatly enhanced if the complexity and potential variability of these interactions is appreciated.

We begin by sketching the epistemological foundations of our approach, as these guide our reformulation of social theory. Next, we outline historical materialist concepts of society and social change and justify this orientation by noting some problems with alternative conceptualizations. We then outline a theory of "communal" social forms which highlights surplus flow and its structural position in society, and illustrate what this theory comes to in an archaeological context using data from the American Southwest. We close by underscoring the advantages of our approach for studying political development in small-scale societies.

A THEORY OF KNOWLEDGE

While much energy is devoted in our profession to the refinement of methods and the clarification of facts, relatively less attention is given to epistemological issues: what theory *is*, and how equally coherent theoretical alternatives can be evaluated. In this section we offer a brief summary of our particular epistemological position as a way to clarify and contextualize the theoretical formulation which follows.

The theory of knowledge to which we subscribe is one best described as *dialectical*. This epistemology draws from the philosophies of a diverse group of thinkers, the most sweeping and systematic of which has been articulated by Althusser (1974). Resnick and Wolff (1982, 1987) have been particularly successful in clarifying a dialectical epistemology, and what follows is greatly indebted to their recent review and reformulation of the work of Althusser and others working within a broadly defined dialectical tradition.

A dialectical epistemology implies a particular conception of the relationship between "thought" and "experience" (i.e., "reality"). Specifically, it understands that relationship as reflexive or intereffective: thought structures experience, and vice versa. For a dialectical epistemology, what people experience (i.e., what they accept as the "facts" of their social existence and historical past) is conditioned by prior beliefs about what the world is like, how it is organized, and how it changes. These beliefs are shaped by a variety of cognitive and noncognitive (i.e., personal, professional, social) factors. Althusser used the term *overdetermination* to describe the myriad influences affecting the knowledge process. Just as thinking is overdetermined (i.e., affected by more than one factor) by experience, so too is experience overdetermined by thinking, inasmuch as thought informs the strategies and policies people use to cope with and participate in the world around them.

A dialectical epistemology thus views knowledge as a *construction*, with concepts representing the building-blocks or raw materials of such constructions. A key implication of this position is that no uniquely correct or "true" way of knowing exists. Rather, truth is conceived as relative to the respective processes of thought which produce it. What a thinker determines to be the truth of existence depends upon the particular way she/he experiences the world through concepts, theories, and methods. People select different facts of experience to scrutinize and relate, and have different ways of producing, defining, ordering, testing, and reworking the concepts which give such facts meaning. For a dialectical epistemology, knowledge of the world is fully conventional and situational (Scholte 1981). It is constructed in conformity with particular sets of fundamental beliefs and presuppositions, and is fully dependent upon the time, place, and social position of the thinker.

This understanding of the knowledge process has traditionally represented a minority position in Western thought and continues in that role today. Epistemologies that sharply contrast with a dialectical view underpin the bulk of Western science. Within archaeology, for example, the dominant epistemology is a positivist one which, *contra* dialectics, maintains the possibility of acquiring truly "objective" knowledge of experience and of establishing absolute criteria for evaluating different knowledge claims. For positivism, the objective truth of experience lies outside thought, in the former's myriad observable facts. These facts simultaneously serve as the object for, and measure of,

207

thought. Knowledge acquisition for positivism is, accordingly, about *discovery* rather than construction: different theories of the world are evaluated against a presumed theory-independent, empirical "factuality" and, depending on their ability to square with that factuality, are eternally categorized as true or false (Harvey [1973]; for recent archaeological discussion of the regulative ideals of positivist epistemology see Schiffer [1981]; Binford [1982]; Watson, LeBlanc, and Redman [1984]).

Versions of dialectical and positivist epistemology have long been at odds within the history of thought, over complex issues of justification and evaluation (Keat and Urry [1981] consider this confrontation in social science generally, Gibbon [1984] in archaeology specifically). Full consideration of these issues falls outside the scope of this chapter. Suffice it to note that the evaluation of competing arguments and theories is not excluded from a dialectical epistemology (Tibbetts 1986; Saitta 1987a), nor does a dialectical epistemology deny the importance of empirical inquiry. Rather, it recognizes the relationship between theoretical and empirical work to be a profoundly overdetermined one, having far-reaching consequences for thought and society. An awareness of, and active interest in, this overdetermined relationship is what underlies a dialectical approach to paradigm growth and evaluation. In the next section, we review the key assumptions and concepts that anchor our interaction with the empirical world.

CONCEPTS OF SOCIETY AND SOCIAL CHANGE

Every research strategy in anthropology is anchored by a set of organizing principles considered applicable to the study of all societies. Historical materialism is no different from other research strategies in this respect. It maintains and continually reworks a particular set of guiding assumptions and analytical principles. The origins of these ideas lie in the work of Marx, with whose "ghost" social scientists have maintained a continuing (if usually implicit) dialogue over the past century (Wolf 1982a:20; Bloch 1983:124–40).

There is much disagreement and debate in historical materialism over just how Marx is to be read and his ideas utilized. Historical materialism is a continually changing position in the social sciences, and the last two decades have witnessed particularly intense examinations and reformulations of Marxian theory. These debates have centered on the relative contributions of economic "base" and ideological "superstructure" to social change, the role of agents in sequences of change, and other issues. We are unable to review these debates here. We note, however, that out of these debates we have distilled the following five guiding assumptions:

1.   It is human labor that secures and reproduces successful human interaction with the environment. Through specific and historically variable sets of social relations, human labor is deployed along with tools, skills, organization, and knowledge ("information") to wrest energy from the environment. This labor is conceived to be of two kinds. Necessary labor is the amount of labor required to reproduce the laborer in an immediate, personal sense. It is that portion which is directly consumed by the producer. Above this amount, individuals perform surplus labor which unites them into a productive, inter-dependent whole. Extracted surplus labor is conceivably targeted toward many ends. These include replacement of the tools and other factors of production used up in the extractive process, production of subsistence reserves to protect against accidents and environmental perturbations, care of unproductive and infirm individuals, meeting of administrative overhead, satisfaction of common social needs as in ritual and ceremony, and so on (Wolf 1966; Cook 1977). The amounts of both kinds of labor performed in society are not fixed quantities in any given society or at any particular time. Rather, they are fully socially determined and vary with historical and environmental circumstances (Hindess and Hirst 1975; Friedman 1979; Cook 1977).

2.   The nature of human interaction with the environment is irreducibly social. The way humans are organized socially governs the way they transform nature, and nature thus transformed affects, in turn, the architecture of human social organization (Wolf 1982a:73–74). Stated differently, what is extracted from nature, the way it is extracted, and how the resulting product is distributed are processes which are all socially mediated. They take place in and through culturally designated entities (family, commune, firm, etc.), and are reproduced by symbolic and ideological means (Godelier 1978:406; Rowlands 1982:167; Bender 1985a:53).

3.   A certain amount of social differentiation necessarily attends the

mobilization and allocation of surplus labor. Such differentiation stems from the fact that any economic process of appropriating surplus labor requires that a whole host of other economic and noneconomic processes (specifically, processes regulating the exercise of power, access to property, exchange, etc.) also be in place to support that appropriation. To the extent that reproduction of these processes depends upon the allocation of at least some surplus to agents who participate in them, distinctions may be drawn between people who extract and receive social surplus. These distinctions exist alongside, but are not necessarily congruent with, social distinctions established by relations of power, property, and exchange.

4.   In light of the differential placement of individuals vis-à-vis the surplus labor process and processes of power, property, and exchange, all manner of conflicts and struggles are conceivable over such matters as the form in which surplus labor is extracted, the amounts of necessary and surplus labor performed in society, the amounts of surplus allocated or shared out, and surplus labor's various conditions of extraction. Such conflicts and struggles are in turn seen to unite individuals sharing similar (though again, not necessarily congruent) interests in a variety of alliances and coalitions that stand against other such alliances and coalitions. The individuals participating in these alliances pursue strategies aimed at reproducing or realizing change in the organization of human production.

5.   In contrast to traditional and many contemporary forms of evolutionist thought in anthropology (especially those invoking some form of "stage theory"), historical materialism accepts that nothing is predetermined or guaranteed with regard to how or in what direction a particular society will develop or evolve. No "laws of motion" can be constructed for the transformation of one kind of society into another; rather, social change is understood to be contingent upon the particular tensions, conflicts, and impulses produced in societies as a consequence of the complex social dynamics that constitute them. For the theorist interested in labor extraction and allocation, relevant developments include, among others, change in the socially determined amounts of necessary and surplus labor produced in society, change in the way a particular form of surplus extraction is secured by the political, economic, and cultural conditions with which it coexists, and change in the

social prevalence of one or another form of surplus extraction, if more than one way of extracting surplus exists in society.

For historical materialism, then, questions about political change are considered against the backdrop of surplus labor flow. Stated differently, surplus flow serves as an "entry point" (one of many that are conceivable) for examining political change. With this approach, questions about political change invite inquiry into the formal mechanisms of surplus labor appropriation and allocation existing in society, how these arrangements relate to (i.e., are sustained and compromised by) political processes, and what social tensions and conflicts are in evidence as a result (Saitta and Keene 1985). Such analysis produces not only an understanding of the overdetermined nature of particular episodes of political change, but also insights of general interest concerning the ways political and economic processes interact in human social life.

A JUSTIFICATION

Why have we adopted this labor-theoretic approach to political analysis, especially given the significant "middle-range" problems associated with operationalizing the concept of surplus and with distinguishing from each other changes in the amount, mechanisms, and conditions of surplus production in society? We do so because we believe contemporary Marxian and non-Marxian theories of political evolution are themselves too narrowly "political" in emphasis. Although we cannot elaborate a full critique here (see Saitta 1987b), this political bias is apparent in the centrality accorded concepts of "power" and "domination" in Marxian models of social structure (e.g., Miller and Tilley 1984; Spriggs 1984), and in the emphasis on "decision-making" and "information management" in non-Marxian approaches (Plog and Upham 1983; Lightfoot 1984). This political bias has a number of limiting theoretical effects. First, it masks patterns of variation by encouraging strict conceptual oppositions between "leaders" and "followers," "dominant" and "dependent" producers, and "elite" and "nonelite" segments of society. By their nature these categories allow little room for imagining alternative social positions, patterns of differentiation, and alliance. Further, these oppositions all too often coincide with, and help sustain, strict correspondences between political practices and economic and cultural practices. Thus, for example, in many current models elites exercise power and authority as they simultaneously extract surplus production and exert ideological hegemony. This view allows little opportunity for exploring the conceivably much more problematic articulation of political and nonpolitical processes in small-scale societies.

The overriding political interest of contemporary social theory has a second significant effect where the matter of change in small-scale societies is concerned. The theories of development produced by current approaches have a certain teleological quality: change turns on the working out of built-in drives to political competition and expansion which ultimately push societies to absolute limits established by the environment, or occurs by default as leaders reach an upper limit in their ability to manage increases in the volume of interactions and exchanges occurring over time (e.g., Friedman and Rowlands 1987; Kristiansen 1982; Upham 1982; Lightfoot 1984). Lost in such theories is a sense of the always contingent, mediated nature of social relations and the overdetermined nature of historical development (Gledhill 1981; Saitta 1987b).

We believe the need exists for an approach to political life in small-scale societies in which received generalizations about the internal logic of these societies are relaxed, assumed correspondences between different variable states are broken, and greater latitude for imagining different logics (that is, different combinations or "mixes" of political, economic, and cultural relations) is introduced. We believe that a labor-theoretic approach can fill this need. The surplus labor process is by and large a blindspot in Marxian and non-Marxian approaches in archaeology. Even where surplus flow is explicitly considered, the focus is on how *already extracted* surpluses are used to secure social existence (and, more specifically, on how they are channeled into political alliance relations or relations of "social reproduction"), rather than on the extraction process itself: the precise form surplus extraction takes, how this form is sustained by distributions of surplus, and how surplus extraction is specifically overdetermined by a variety of other social processes.

In short, current approaches to social life in small-scale societies tend to treat surplus production as an effect of, or reducible to, political power relations. By reaffirming the overdetermined relationship between political and economic processes in society, we invite alternative understandings of society and social change. In the next two sections we outline and empirically elaborate a model of "communal" society that illustrates the productivity of this approach.

ON THE SPECIFICITY OF THE COMMUNAL FORMATION

We use the term "communal society" to describe our object of study because it addresses the form of labor extraction in these societies with greater specificity than does the term "small-scale." We avoid alternative terms like "kin-ordered" (Wolf 1982a), "nonhierarchical" (Braun and Plog 1982), "middle range" (Feinman and Neitzel 1984), and the more traditional categories of "egalitarian" and "tribal" for the same reason. We also prefer the term communal because it can accommodate a broader range of behaviors and variable combinations. For example, communal relations of surplus appropriation are not necessarily incompatible with political hierarchy, as the case of the kibbutz illustrates. Here, hierarchy may at times be critical to the maintenance of the commune (see also Blasi 1986). To preclude such a combination is unnecessarily to restrict our imagination of alternative organizational possibilities for prehistoric societies.

There are many connotations attached to the term communal society (Berthoud and Sabelli 1979). We define communal social formations as organizational arrangements in which the social surplus labor performed by direct producers is appropriated by a collective body which *includes* those producers (Amariglio 1984:5). Under communal forms of surplus appropriation, extractors of surplus labor are, simultaneously, performers of surplus labor. The social group as a whole (the commune) serves as the presupposition for all productive activity. Access to necessary factors of production is guaranteed to all members, and all members participate in determining the division between necessary and surplus labor.

We emphasize that our concept of communal formation does not refer to a single organizational entity. Communal relations of production do not preclude the possibility of significant variation in the political, economic, and cultural means by which these relations are secured. The notion of communal appropriation does not imply organizational "simplicity," perfect equality of access to means of production, or a situation in which the production and distribution of surplus occurs without account. For example, it is not inconceivable for

213

some communal relations to involve technical divisions of labor involving specialized production of strategic use-values (e.g., subsistence items, tools, containers, etc.), extended social divisions of labor based on forms of socially regulated *unequal* access to various strategic factors of production, and centralized forms of economic redistribution, political planning, and dispute mediation. Moreover, we can imagine certain conditions of communal production entitling some communal agents to shares of extracted surplus without their necessarily having to participate in communal relations of production as performers of surplus labor.

Such arrangements establish a complex social dynamic within even the "simplest" of communal societies concerning how, and how much, surplus is produced and allocated. Recall that such dynamics are always understood to be conditioned by specific sets of ecological and historical circumstances. Thus we can go no further in elaborating our model of communal sociopolitical dynamics without turning to the archaeological record for specific case material. We discuss such material in the next section.

A SOUTHWESTERN CASE STUDY

Our case material comes from the American Southwest, where archaeological research is currently undergoing an exciting period of development (Cordell 1984a). In recent years, much received wisdom about the prehistoric past has undergone reevaluation. Questions about the level of organizational "complexity" attained by prehistoric social forms in the area have been raised anew. Debates have emerged between those emphasizing the egalitarian nature of past societies (Graves et al. 1982) and those emphasizing their nonegalitarian, hierarchical character (Upham 1982; Lightfoot 1984).

Room for a third class of models is created, however, if we accept that the existence of political hierarchy *necessarily* implies very little about its wider institutional context and articulations. On this understanding, it is possible to construct models of Southwestern polities which allow for political complexity but which also preserve ideas about egalitarianism and communalism. We offer here a historical materialist model of the ancient Pueblos as communal societies, one which distinguishes surplus flow from the exercise of power. In this framework, "empowered" political agents are ultimately *subsumed* to the commune, receiving

214

communally extracted shares of surplus as compensation for performing a variety of political, economic, and cultural functions necessary for reproducing communal relations of production. These functions include determining productive needs, regulating flows of strategic use-values, and arranging ceremonies (one could cast a similar interpretation of the Iroquoian situation: see Trigger, this volume). The social positions of these political agents are many and varied and, further, thoroughly problematic. These agents are continually "squeezed" in different ways by the structure of communal social life. They struggle with each other and with the commune over the amounts of surplus produced and distributed in society and over the precise way these surplus flows are secured by various other social relations (e.g., by the way labor is divided, work coordinated, resources distributed, production planned, ceremonies organized, etc.). Out of these dynamics come impulses to social development conceivably having little to do with the testing of technoenvironmental limits to economic intensification as in a Marxian model, or "scalar" limits to effective decision-making for managing the social order as in non-Marxian models of change.

The existence of the "commune" as a fundamental presupposition for Puebloan social life, and the subsumption and problematic position of elites within the communal social structure, is suggested by ethnographic, ethnohistoric, and archaeological data (Saitta 1987b:87–95). Variation in the latter seems particularly well disposed for further expanding our understanding of diverse patterns of communal political organization and change in the past. This variation takes the form of evidence for local forms of specialization in the production and exchange of ceramic and stone manufactures (Plog 1980; Longacre 1966; DeGarmo 1976; Robertson 1983); intra-settlement differentiation in household size and storage capacity (Lightfoot 1984); and the discontinuous distribution of "exotic" non-local and labor-intensive items across samples of contemporaneous settlements and households within settlements (Upham 1982; Lightfoot 1984).

One of us (Saitta 1987b) has examined data from several prehistoric settlements in the Zuni area (figure 8.1) to show what an examination of this kind of evidence from a labor-theoretic perspective might provide. Limitations of space preclude a detailed exposition of the specific data and bridging arguments used to tie those data to a theory of communal formations. Suffice it to say that analytical emphasis focused on aspects of the prehistoric "built environment" (architectural relationships and

215

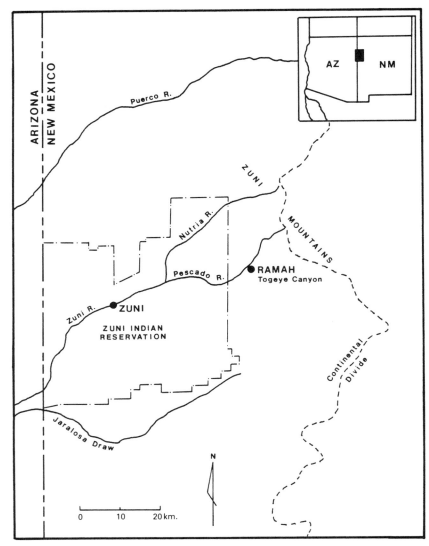

Figure 8.1 The Zuni area.

patterns of space use), using fairly traditional lines of investigation (room-set patterns, ratios of nonresidential to residential built space, and the structure of spatial "sequencing" [Saile 1977]).

The subject of this inquiry was a group of settlements in Togeye

Canyon, New Mexico, located just off the eastern edge of the Zuni Indian Reservation. These settlements date to the late twelfth and early thirteenth centuries. This is a time period of great organizational flux, if not social "upheaval" in the Zuni area (Anyon et al. 1983). Stuart and Gauthier (1984:131) characterize the period as a "calamitous" one marked by the fragmentation of earlier Chacoan-San Juan Basin social networks, substantial population redistributions to higher elevations, and a restructuring of regional settlement and trading patterns in the form of an "upland economic network." Thus we might expect material patterns on the local level to suggest tensions and struggles relating to the reformalization of social boundaries and the principles used to extract and distribute communal labor (Handsman 1985).

While we are still far from reaching a fully satisfying resolution of how groups were organized in Togeye Canyon, why the area was eventually abandoned in the mid thirteenth century, and what long-term political change in the Zuni area involved, preliminary examination of the Togeye data from a labor-theoretic perspective does provide a productive basis for addressing these issues. As understood through our approach, the Zuni data suggest an unlikely combination of features for at least some prehistoric communal societies in the area. This organizational structure involves a delicate, tenuous balance between social subgroup autonomy and interdependence. Briefly, room-set analysis at the largest settlement considered, the 150-room Pettit Site (figure 8.2), discloses a number of different institutional "sites" at which communal relations in Togeye Canyon were transacted. The most basic of such entities is reflected in the persistent association of a single habitation room with (usually) one storage room. These basic organizational units are in turn grouped into larger blocks of rooms, which may represent distinct descent groupings. In most cases, one or more roomblocks can be associated with a single ceremonial room or kiva, which are widely assumed to be indicative of wider, non-lineage-based integrative ties (Steward 1937; Hill 1970).

This "modular" arrangement of architectural units is typical of Puebloan settlements. It suggests the presence in Togeye Canyon of small social units akin to "households" whose productive activities were embedded in, and overdetermined by, institutional relationships of wider scope involving both lineage and nonlineage processes. The ratio of kivas to secular rooms at the Pettit Site is on the order of 1:23, suggesting a relatively high degree of social integration (Steward 1937).

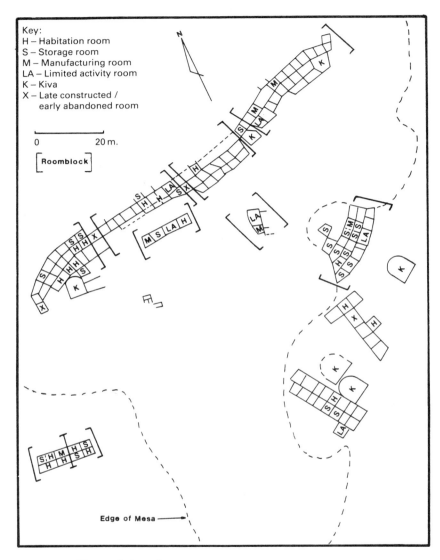

Figure 8.2   The Pettit Site.

However, the existence in roomblocks of what we term "limited activity" rooms renders this interpretation problematic. These rooms contain architectural features reminiscent of kivas and are suggestive of the "clanhouses" described by some Puebloan ethnographers. It is interesting that when these rooms are figured along with kivas into the computation of nonresidential to residential room ratios, the ratio increases to about 1:6. To us, and adapting arguments advanced by Johnson (1978, 1982), this ratio suggests that those social entities likely possessing the effective capacity to set means of production in motion (our descent groupings) retained a certain amount of socioeconomic autonomy. Further, the fact that many limited activity rooms show evidence of having been remodeled from earlier habitation rooms suggests the establishment, from time to time, of potentially *competing* spheres of socioceremonial integration within the settlement. Evidence for the active maintenance of social boundaries between adjacent roomblocks (e.g., abandoned rooms with secondary debris throughout their fill precisely bracket several of the roomblocks at the site) also buttresses this interpretation.

While our inquiry hints at the relative autonomy of sub-village social groups, at the same time it suggests some significant intergroup dependence in basic productive ventures. Intrasite variation in room size and artifact content suggests the existence of a distinct set of manufacturing rooms for ceramic containers and for stone and bone tools. These rooms are differentially distributed among blocks of rooms. We take this differential distribution as suggesting a measure of lineage or lineage subgroup specialization in the production of strategic use-values. The notion of specialization we have in mind is taken from Cross (1983), in which the production of certain use-values is limited to a small percentage of individuals in a group or to a number of groups within a larger polity. On this view, specialization does not imply market relations, a social class division, or the necessary withdrawal of specialized craftspersons from subsistence production. Rather, it only suggests that the subsistence package of primary producers depended upon the realization of necessary labor in the form of use-values produced elsewhere in an extended division of labor.

This situation could also imply, however, the existence of a set of political agents who received subsumed shares of surplus labor as compensation for regulating the circulation of raw materials and finished products, determining levels of social need, and in general negotiating a balance between the lineage and nonlineage processes shaping the commune. Such subsumed shares might have been realized in the form of work parties that tended "elite" gardens, maintained their houses, or prepared their food (Titiev 1944; Upham

1982). Clues to the existence and complexity of such institutional arrangements in archaeological contexts can be detected by combining information on the number of distinct levels of social integration in a society with information on the different kinds and amounts of nonresidential space in use. The relevant bridging arguments are found in McGuire (1983:127), who understands the resulting "heterogeneity index" as quantifying the distribution of a population between residence groups and institutions. The heterogeneity index of 9.70 produced for Togeye Canyon (for further discussion see Saitta [1987b:185–87]) approaches those generated by McGuire for peak developmental periods in the Hohokam culture of southern Arizona (10.01) and the Casas Grandes culture of northwestern Chihuahua (12.67), periods when "complex" sociopolitical structures helped regulate high population densities, the production and distribution of craft items, and a range of activities associated with irrigation agriculture (LeBlanc 1986; Minnis 1984).

If we allow for the plausibility of this complex communal arrangement (one admitting high residence-group autonomy in the conduct of jural and socioceremonial matters, significant residence-group interaction and interdependence in productive activities, and a relatively complex subsumed political structure involving a number of different agents who regulated the productive activity of subcorporate task groups, the distribution of strategic use-values, and labor across residence groupings), then we have an extremely fertile basis for theorizing an array of social tensions and struggles capable of transforming the communal formation from within. Any number of organizational loci where these dynamics can be played out are conceivable. For example, tensions and struggles are imaginable within descent groups concerning access to strategic use-values that are produced by individuals or sets of individuals, but to which other corporate members have sanctioned claims (see Sacks [1979:117] for further elaboration of this point). This dynamic can lead to alliances being struck *across* descent groupings *between* subcorporate units charged with specialized production of strategic use-values. Individuals in such alliances would, as a consequence, be forced to struggle with competing social identities and positions, inasmuch as they would understand their labor both in relation to overall social labor and in relation to the extended, lineage-based division of labor. We can also imagine tensions erupting between primary producers and subsumed recipients of surplus labor over the

Table 8.1. *Space utilization at the Pettit Site*

Type of space	Total amount of space (m^2)
Habitation	424.95
Storage	283.11
Manufacturing	90.59
Limited activity	137.18
Kiva	124.90

Table 8.2. *Activity indices for the Pettit Site*

Index	Value
Manufacturing	0.21
Storage	0.67
Kiva[a]	0.62

[a]Includes limited activity rooms and kivas.

division between necessary and surplus labor, as this affects the share realizable by the latter. Finally, struggles are imaginable among subsumed communal agents over shares of communally appropriated surplus, as well as at the level of individual subsumed recipients who, like primary producers, are faced with conflicting corporate and noncorporate allegiances and interests. Together, these dynamics would present severe obstacles to the oft-assumed easy "decomposability" of small-scale societies along kin lines (e.g., Sahlins 1972 [1965]; Braun and Plog 1982; McGuire 1983).

Preliminary data from Togeye Canyon is in hand which justify further research in this direction (tables 8.1 and 8.2). These data are in the form of measures of per capita storage and ceremonial space, achieved by dividing the amount of space given to each kind of functional activity at a settlement by the total amount of habitation space (after Lightfoot 1984:94–96). If we allow that storage can represent an important allocation of communal surplus labor in part for the support of various subsumed functionaries, then we might expect indices of per capita storage space to be relatively high where complex communal political structures exist. Similarly, if we allow that ceremonial space can represent an arena where lineage and nonlineage claims on surplus labor are asserted, negotiated, and resolved, then we might expect indices of per capita kiva space also to be relatively high where struggles over surplus flow abound.

Storage and kiva indices as determined for the Pettit Site (see discussion in Saitta [1987b:187–89]) are both much higher than those generated for similarly sized and dated sites in eastern Arizona that have been interpreted as seats of political power (Lightfoot 1984). Given no evidence for population pressure on available resources (i.e., arable land) in the Zuni area at this time (Kintigh 1984), we believe our storage index warrants the inference that this production was motivated to fill communal social rather than biological needs. We do not, however, see these needs as stemming from the existence of expansionist political structures as Lightfoot claims for his situation, as there are no obvious indicators of variation in house size, control of storage facilities, or differential mortuary treatment in Togeye Canyon. Nor do we see our high kiva index as warranting the inference that kivas were serving an enhanced redistributive function under conditions of subsistence stress as is commonly assumed (Plog 1974; see Dean et al. 1985 for a critique of this assumption on empirical grounds). Rather, an interpretation emphasizing the kiva's role as a locus of negotiation and struggle over the competing economic and political interests of relatively auto-nomous kin-groupings seems equally plausible. Data on room remodel-ing (mentioned above) and one instance where kivas have been constructed back-to-back have yet to be fully analyzed, but our sense is that this evidence will provide additional instructive clues to the nature of communal struggle over surplus flow in Togeye Canyon.

The ultimate impact of these tensions and struggles on Zuni area political organization is not yet clear. The Pettit Site and contemporary settlements were abandoned in the mid thirteenth century, the regional population consolidating into much larger Pueblos like Pueblo de los Muertos at El Morro (Watson et al. 1980), and the Kluckhohn Site in Togeye Canyon (Kintigh 1985). We need better control of time at sites like Pettit, as well as more analyses to complement those discussed above in order to determine what regional political organization was tending toward just prior to population nucleation. Lee (this volume) implies that the communal mode is abandoned neither readily nor easily. It is conceivable that communities like Pettit were on the verge of developing noncommunal relations of surplus extraction, and that abandonment was a form of resistance to impulses in this direction. Obviously, not only do we need to fine-tune our analysis of sites like

Pettit, but we must also explicate the political organization of the later, nucleated communities in order to clarify the developmental forces at work and their outcomes.

Probing available data with different schematic variants of a communal model of socioeconomic integration would help in this investigative process. For example, we can ask how different degrees of subsumed agent involvement in communal relations of surplus extraction (as communal performers *and* recipients of surplus) and their participation in external exchange relations might have propelled the communal organization in different directions. We can ask what effects different degrees of continuity in the occupancy of subsumed social positions (e.g., permanent occupancy versus some form of rotated occupancy) might have had on the communal structure. Other organizational features worthy of consideration include the character of producer participation in decision-making (whether direct or through representatives), and variation in the balance written between pooled and privatized appropriation of surplus. We might expect each of these different combinations of features to be beset with its own contradictions and developmental tendencies.

CONCLUSION

We have argued in this chapter for an approach to political development in small-scale societies which puts issues of surplus flow on the analytical agenda. By treating surplus flow as more than just an effect or reflection of power relations, we are able to theorize a wider range of organizational variants, impulses to social change, and developmental outcomes than if we simply reduce economics to politics. We have many examples of simple/acephalous and complex/chiefly societies already in hand, but are experiencing a shortage of social forms conceivably falling between these extremes. We are of the opinion that such social variation awaits our grasp, pending further development of theory capable of penetrating it.

While the specific model of communal integration presented here is in need of refinement, its deployment in the context of the American Southwest casts some doubt on the "simple and egalitarian" paradigm that has long informed interpretations of prehistoric social life in the area. Our formulation raises similar doubts about the "complex and hierarchical" paradigm, in that we have shown how some of the same data used to support notions of political ranking and economic exploitation in the Southwest can be used to support quite a different model of prehistoric interpersonal relations. Continued effort at refinement stands to enrich our understanding not only of the ancient Pueblos, but of all those societies forming the traditional subject-matter of anthropology.

NOTE

We thank Maura Keene and Yaakov Altman for their comments on a previous draft of this chapter. Special thanks to the participants in the Advanced Seminar for a rigorous cross-examination, and to Steadman Upham for his support, criticisms, and encouragement throughout the project.

9
Primitive communism and the origin of social inequality

RICHARD B. LEE

University of Toronto

How did social inequality come into being? Some argue that it has always been present, that it represents an inevitable and natural state of affairs. Therefore, inequality as a social phenomenon does not require explanation. Others, from Rousseau to the present, believe that the causes of social inequality cry out for explanation. One way to approach this seeming paradox is to explore the concept of primitive communism, or the communal mode of production – the notion that there was a period of human history before the rise of the state during which private property was unknown and inequalities of wealth and power were minimal. Many anthropologists would undoubtedly accept the broad validity of this notion, judging from its prevalence in introductory textbooks. Yet few would be prepared to explore the implications of this acceptance, and fewer still would be prepared to embrace the rubric of primitive communism.

Primitive communism is a simple concept, yet the very words evoke uneasiness and embarrassment, containing two of the most loaded terms in Western ideology. Yet that fact doesn't explain why the concept is an embarrassment to so many who profess Marxism. Nevertheless, I will argue that without the concept of a communal mode of production, an attempt to account for the development of social complexity in

225

prehistoric sedentary societies is doomed to mystification and failure. The very title of the seminar on which this book is based, "The Development of Political Systems in Prehistoric Sedentary Societies," was designed to sidestep the issue of social inequality. For that matter, even the issue of social complexity is not directly addressed. Is there a theoretical possibility of a complex society without inequality? Or a hierarchical society without complexity?[1] No doubt there is, but in practice the very criteria we employ archaeologically to determine social complexity (differential burials, presence of imported and/or luxury goods, house types, settlement hierarchies) are in fact indices of social inequality.

This chapter is divided into four parts. First, I attempt to formulate a theory of social change that can be applied with equal facility to state and nonstate, to communal and hierarchical societies. Second, I explore the concept of primitive communism to determine what it does and does not mean. Third, I develop an argument for the origin of social inequality (and social complexity) from a communal baseline, and finally, I seek to comprehend communalism's underlying dynamic.

A METHODOLOGICAL NOTE

As for most Marxists, for me the concepts of mode and relations of production are central, but unlike many Marxists I have been acutely aware of the absence in Marxist thought of a theory of historical dynamics in preclass societies.[2] Marx and Engels wrote before the appearance of anthropology as a discipline, and their works offer few guidelines for the analysis of simpler societies, a lacuna epitomized by the fateful opening lines of the Communist Manifesto: "The history of all hitherto existing societies is the history of class struggle." Although Engels amended that formulation,[3] it was left to later scholars – Luxemburg, Kautsky, Leacock, Diamond, Godelier, and especially Cabral – to correct and amplify the relevance of Marxist theory for all societies and not just class-divided ones.

The goal shared by all materialist theories of social change is to account for directional change, without recourse to vitalist, essentialist, racialist, metaphysical, or other teleological forms of explanation. The basic starting-point of any Marxist analysis of the concrete is the concept of *mode of production*, "an articulated combination of relations and forces of production, structured by the dominance of relations of production" (Hindess and Hirst 1975:190–11). Central to mode of production has been the analytical division of the totality of social life into the economic base or infrastructure, and all the remainder (variously defined), the superstructure. What the mode of production concept does, simply and brilliantly, is to plug the property relation (or the "property connection," as Marx would say), an aspect of the superstructure, into the economic base or culture core. To put it another way, it puts politics into the economic base, and it defines a mode of articulation between base and superstructure.

Politics, ideology, religious beliefs, and culture have been variously attributed by Marxists to infrastructure or superstructure, and much debate has raged over their placement. Much of this continuing debate is rendered beside the point when we turn to the concept of *social reproduction*. Social reproduction resolves the base–superstructure debate by showing that ideology functions as both base *and* superstructure through the medium of relations of production and reproduction. In *Lenin and Philosophy*, Althusser drew attention to Marx's comment in 1868 that "every child knows that a social formation which did not reproduce the conditions of production at the same time as it produced would not last a year" (1971:247). At least three analytically distinct forms of behavior need to be considered under the rubric of social reproduction: (a) the reproduction of labor power, (b) the reproduction of life, and (c) the reproduction of the conditions of production.[4]

In a capitalist mode of production, *reproduction of labor power* occurs on a daily and generational basis. Daily reproduction of labor power involves the provision of food, clothing, rest, and emotional support for the workers, the task of restoring their depleted capacity for work, while generational reproduction of labor power involves child rearing and child care, the work involved in producing the next generation of workers.

Biological reproduction (the reproduction of life) is the aspect we usually think of when we use the term reproduction. It is closely related to generational reproduction of labor power. Engels emphasized the twofold character of his and Marx's theoretical framework. Biological reproduction, "the production of human beings," was regarded as being of equal import to production of the means of subsistence as crucial determining factors in history (see, for example, Engels (1972 [1884]:71–72).

The reproduction of the conditions of production in its strict sense can refer to the reproduction of the instruments of labor: tools, factories,

227

roads, banks, and other preconditions for the continuation of production. But it quickly becomes clear that the concept must necessarily expand to include a much broader field: schools, churches, hospitals, and governments. In fact the entire economic infrastructure and the political and ideological superstructure of society can be regarded as constituting conditions necessary for the continuation of production. Thus, this third element in the concept of social reproduction extends it to cover a very broad field of social life indeed.

Social reproduction is or could be *the* central concept in social theory. All social processes can be viewed as forms of social reproduction. This definition of social reproduction makes it virtually coterminous with the concept of *culture*. I would argue that social reproduction offers more analytical leverage than the culture concept. Culture has a static quality, like a map or blueprint. Social reproduction is dynamic: forms of social life and of meaning constantly reproducing themselves through the acts of people. Further, large-scale social change, as we shall see, always manifests itself initially as a crisis in social reproduction.

Now we have to consider the following question: If social formations are strictly in the business of reproducing themselves, how, then, does change occur? The answer is, and this is a crucial point, it doesn't, at least not always. If environmental and demographic conditions are stable, it is possible and indeed probable for social formations to reproduce themselves with relatively little *directional* change for long periods. The layout of some !Kung San camps in the 1960s appear indistinguishable from later Stone Age living sites of five hundred years ago. Twentieth-century agricultural settlements in parts of southwest Asia look remarkably similar to their counterparts in the second millennium B.C.[5]

Such conditions probably obtained much of the time in some parts of the world. Life went on, social formations were reproduced, and the life of the children was very much like the life of their parents. But stability of conditions doesn't always obtain. Populations grow, environments degrade, peoples impinge on their neighbors, technologies evolve: all of these processes create pressures for directional change. And at points in history the cumulative pressures for change become so intense that radically different social/technological forms may emerge. The origin of the state was one of these; the earlier agricultural revolution was another. Our task is to specify the conditions for stability or change, and in the case of the latter to understand the different kinds and magnitudes.

REPRODUCTION, CHANGE, AND EVOLUTION

The totality of social processes can be usefully considered under three headings: social reproduction, social change, and social evolution. These terms are commonplace in anthropological discourse; my task here is to assign to each a much more restricted meaning.

Social reproduction, as we have seen, is the reproduction of social life and institutions on a daily, annual, and generational basis. It includes biological, social, and ideological components. *Social change* involves expansion of life *within* a mode of production. Directional change, involving the exploration of the possibilities of a given mode of production, takes many forms, including expansion of production, increase of the scale of society, geographic radiation of a people or a mode of life and its adaptation to new local environments, and, of course, the development of social complexity. Change can be expressed in an increased diversity of life ways, of customs, of religious ideas, based on a single mode of production; and it may include involution, a movement towards increasing intricacies in production, in social forms (e.g., kinship), and/or ideological content.

The initial causes of social change are likewise numerous: population growth is among the most important; environmental variation, drift, and isolation play roles as well. Such broad forces, however, tell us little about what kind of change will occur. The response to population growth might include outcomes as varied as increased warfare, infanticide, emigration, or expansion of production. About all one can say at this point is that such broad forces do act as a motor for some sort of change. About the only outcome that is precluded is the maintenance of social reproduction without any directional shift (i.e., the maintenance of the status quo).

The problem addressed in this volume makes us particularly interested in the development of structural dynamics, internally generated motors of change such as intergroup conflict, social inequality and stratification, and sexual antagonism. The dialectical method allows us

229

to search for and discover the locus of contradiction in a given social formation; it allows us to predict the structural evolution of a social formation by a specification of the structure of contradictions.

At infrequent intervals in human history the combination of internal and external forces becomes too intense to be contained within a given mode of production. There follows, in Marx's view, a period of fairly rapid social change in which the whole structure of society is overturned. This third form of change is *social evolution*, the transformation from one mode of production to another. The transition from feudalism to capitalism is certainly the most intensively studied example of social evolution. But a smaller coterie of anthropologists and archaeologists have made the earlier but no less important transformations, the neolithic revolution and the origin of the state, their particular province of research.[6]

In one important respect, contemporary theories of social evolution in precapitalist societies are curiously deficient: in specifying the dialectic of change between old and new. The emergence of a new mode of production is not simply a question of new technical achievements or even of radically new forms of organization, though both are involved. *It also involves the systematic dismantling and destruction piece by piece of the old societal forms.* This does not happen overnight, and for periods of time old and new modes of production coexist in an uneasy stalemate. At times, older social forms may persist for centuries alongside and encapsulated by newly dominant ones.

Although the new relations of production achieve dominance, they do not succeed in completely eliminating the old from the social formation. This intertwining of old and new is particularly apparent when we turn to the communal mode of production, the oldest and least understood of the five modes of production (Communal, Asiatic, Ancient, Feudal, Capitalist, as defined by Marx). *In fact, it could be argued that the contradiction between communal forms and emerging hierarchy has provided much of the energy for the social dynamic during long periods of human history (since 10,000 B.C.) prior to the development of classes.*

It is the phenomenon of persistence of communalism, and the long struggle between it and hierarchical modes in prehistoric (and historic) sedentary societies, that provides the rationale for the present chapter and offers a perspective that is often absent from the growing literature in social evolution which arises from ecological, demographic, or social-organizational starting-points.

PRIMITIVE COMMUNISM CONSIDERED

Primitive communism: This refers to the collective right to basic resources, the absence of hereditary status or authoritarian rule, and the egalitarian relationships that preceded exploitation and economic stratification in human history. Eleanor Leacock (1983:394).

Despite the emotional loading of the term, there is no great mystery about the phenomenon of primitive communism and the communal mode it describes. Before the rise of the state and the entrenchment of social inequality, people lived for millennia in small-scale, kin-based social groups, in which the core institutions of economic life included collective or common ownership of land and resources, generalized reciprocity in the distribution of food, and relatively egalitarian political relations. This basic pattern, with variations, has been observed in literally hundreds of nonstate societies, as described, for example, in Murdock's *Ethnographic Atlas* (1967). These societies, including bands, tribes, and some chiefdoms, have been known by a variety of names: savagery, nonstate, prestate, nonliterate, kin-based, primitive, in fact anything but communist. But the basic underlying principles of these social formations are the same. Something is there that demands explanation.

Prestate societies had no overriding political authority. Political power of any kind was weak. Decisions were made in a diffuse way, usually democratically, by consensus, by elders, by family groups, and by a variety of other means. There was no private property in land; land was held in common, or collectively (e.g., by all or by kin groups); rarely was it held by individuals. Production was for use rather than for exchange. There were no markets, no currency. Where exchange existed, it was based on sharing and reciprocity. The law of hospitality was strong; more than that, it was inviolable. There were strong sanctions against wealth accumulation. Leaders existed, but where they existed they were redistributors, not accumulators. The main bases for the status distinctions which did exist included age, gender, and locality. The whole population retained access to the means of produc-

231

tion and reproduction. As Marx put it, "it was a community of owners who also worked." There was no division into economic classes.

Lest I portray too rosy a picture, I hasten to add that some prestate societies did have the germs of inequality and did have chiefs, ranked lineages, wealth differences, and slavery. The Northwest Coast Indians are an example, and many societies in North America, Africa, and Polynesia followed this pattern. There are hundreds of other societies, however, including the bulk of the foraging societies, where these institutions were absent or only present to a small degree. And even these chiefly and ranked societies had by no means abandoned all the institutions of communalism. Many continued to hold land in common and to practice reciprocal economic relations. Therefore, I will designate such societies semicommunal.

Another misconception about primitive communism is that preclass societies were peaceful. As the Iroquois, Tiv, Nuer, and other societies demonstrate, communal organization is by no means incompatible with warfare. Yet even the "fierce" Yanomamo held land and resources in common.

Rather than accept the proposition that this remarkable clustering of traits is coincidental, historical materialism argues that there exists a core of culture in primitive society that is intimately linked to mode of production. It is much longer lived, has a much deeper time-depth, than our own Western capitalist culture. Historical materialism further argues that this culture core is communal: the collective right to basic resources and the egalitarian political culture. By any dictionary definition of communism, our ancestors were communist.

MORGAN AND THE EVIDENCE

It was neither Marx nor Engels, nor Fourier nor Saint-Simon, who can be regarded as the principal architect of primitive communism. That honor belongs to a Rochester ethnologist and staunch member of the bourgeoisie, Lewis Henry Morgan. In *Houses and House-Life of the American Aborigines*, Morgan devoted over a hundred pages to the conceptualization and documentation of primitive communism, calling it "communism in living" (1965 [1881]).

Morgan introduced the concept almost diffidently, as an extension of the law of hospitality. Noting the universal presence in aboriginal

232

America of the obligatory custom of offering hospitality to visitors, Morgan sought to elucidate its central core.

The law of hospitality as administered by the American aborigines tended to the final equalization of subsistence. Hunger and destitution could not exist at one end of an Indian village or in one section of an encampment while plenty prevailed elsewhere in the same village or encampment (ibid., p. 61).

How did the system of communism in living arise? In a strikingly modern form of argument, Morgan derived the institution from the ecological and social constraints of the mode of life of savagery and barbarism, from what Marxists would call the low level of development of the productive forces.

Communism in living had its origin in the necessities of the family, which, prior to the Later Period of barbarism, was too weak in organization to face alone the struggle of life . . . Wherever the gentile organization prevailed, several families, related by kin, united as a rule in a common household and made a common stock of the provisions acquired by fishing and hunting, and by the cultivation of maize and plants. To a very great extent communism in living was a necessary result of the condition of the Indian tribes. It entered into their plan of life and determined the character of their houses. In effect it was a union of effort to procure subsistence, which was the vital and commanding concern of life. The desire for individual accumulation had not been aroused in their minds to any sensible extent (ibid., p. 63).

The notions of the law of hospitality and of communism in living were backed up by an overwhelming array of ethnohistoric data. Morgan went as far back as the fifteenth-century journals of Columbus's voyages to document his thesis for the earliest periods of European contact. Among his other sources were the journals of De Soto, Sir Walter Raleigh, Cortez, Pizzaro, Capt. John Smith, Marquette and Joliet, Lewis and Clark, and many others.

Most anthropologists in the early part of this century, while not necessarily accepting his use of the terms, did accept Morgan's thesis of communism in living, adding the proviso that while land and its resources were communally owned, movables (tools, weapons, cooking utensils, procured food, occasionally trees, etc.) could be owned individually. A few more or less random examples from the bookshelf of classic ethnographies will suffice.[7]

if a cabin of hungry [Iroquois] meets another whose provisions are not entirely exhausted, the latter share with the newcomers the little which remains to them

233

without waiting to be asked, although they expose themselves thereby to the same danger of perishing as those whom they help at their own expense so humanely and with such greatness of soul (Lafitau 1974 [1724]:61).

The economic life of the local [Andaman Islander] group, though in effect it approaches to a sort of communism, is yet based on the notion of private property. Land is the only thing that is owned in common [! R.B.L.] A man of one of the local groups of the coast may notice in the jungle a tree suitable for a canoe. He will tell the others that he has noticed such a tree, describing it and its whereabouts. Thenceforward, that tree is regarded as his property, and even if some years should elapse, and he has made no use of it, yet another man would not cut it down without first asking the owner to give him the tree (Radcliffe-Brown 1922:41).

In the abstract, there are desirable practices in the [North American] Indian way of life. He was not really a communist, but he was liberal with food. So long as he had food, he was expected to share it. That he did not always do it, we learn from legends, but since in these tales the one who concealed food always came to grief, there can be no doubt that to share it was the thing to do (Wissler 1966 [1940]:281).

A most important difference between the Plains Indians and the Tahitians concerns material property. Whereas in Tahiti a monarch could appropriate the possessions of a lesser man, on the Plains any comparable act was unthinkable. On the contrary, a great man could maintain his standards best by lavish generosity to the poor. Such liberality, next to a fine war record, was the basis for high standing. The Oglala had a society of chiefs enjoying superior prestige, but when a novice was admitted, he was urged to look after the poor, especially the widows and orphans (Lowie 1963 [1954]:124).

Among the Navajos certain things are "communal property," in which no individual or family has vested or exclusive rights. Water resources, timber areas, and patches of salt bush (which serve livestock in lieu of mineral salt) belong to all The People, and certain conventions are observed in regard to this type of property. It is not good form to cut wood within a mile or so of someone else's dwelling. One uses no other than his accustomed water hole except when that source fails or he goes on a journey. Attempts of some Navajos to emulate white practices with respect to wood and water rights are among the most bitterly resisted of all innovations (Kluckhohn and Leighton 1962:105–106).

In general it may be said that no one in a Nuer village starves unless all are starving (Evans-Pritchard 1951:132).

A number of contemporary authors make wide use of the concept of primitive communism, while showing a certain reluctance to use the term. Sahlins, in his "Sociology of Primitive Exchange" (1972 [1965]:185–275), attempted to bring together the evidence for what I have called primitive communism under the rubric of "generalized reciprocity." The latter concept, the giving of something without the immediate expectation of return, expresses an aspect of primitive communism in "social science-ese" and therefore in a way less threatening to hegemonic ideology. The basic import of both terms is, I believe, the same. Other contemporary restatements of Morgan's position can be found in the writings of Diamond (1974), Fried (1967), Leacock (1981), and Woodburn (1981). (Leacock and Diamond, in particular, have explored in their own work much of the ideological ground examined here, while Woodburn has given detailed attention to the substantive data. See also Testart [1985].)

ON THE ORIGINS OF SOCIAL INEQUALITY

Proceeding from the assumption of a primitive communal baseline in human history, I now attempt to "reproblematize" the central issue: the development of a political system in prehistoric societies of the middle range (i.e., beyond bands and before states).

Fundamental to the historical evolution of these societies is an increase in the scale of social systems. This increase raises two questions: (a) why does increase in scale lead to increase in the complexity of social orders, and (b), why does increase in complexity lead first to the straining, then the breaching, and eventually the destruction of reciprocal norms upon which primitive communism is founded? It is important to reformulate these questions so that the development of social inequalities is not reduced to a "natural" outgrowth, a realization of human possibilities.

At a point in the history of some primitive communal societies the fabric of social reproduction becomes threatened by growing contradictions. The breakdown of social reproduction is then accompanied by directional change toward a new mode of production. Social and sexual inequality have their beginnings as untoward consequences of changes in societal scale and in the levels and forms of production. Gradually in the course of social evolution, social inequality and its concomitant, economic exploitation, shift to central stage and become the core institution and one of the driving forces of historical change in class-based societies.

In attempting to account for this phenomenon, we must first recognize and deal with yet another major misconception about the nature of equality. Scholars who want to demonstrate the universality of social inequality use the following device. They take an impossibly high, abstract definition of equality and then sit back and show that "true" social equality is nowhere to be found.[8] But the fact is that perfect equality doesn't exist anywhere. It is a fact of life that human beings differ in their abilities: some are bright, some are stupid; some are strong, some are weak; some are charismatic and some are drones. What is significant is that some societies take these differences and minimize them, to the point of making them disappear, while other societies take the same basic material and magnify it. Still other societies (and this includes the great majority of class societies) describe differences between people as being enormous, even though they have no reference to actual differences on the ground. Thus, the upper classes of Britain were described as tall, handsome, intelligent, powerful, witty; the lower classes were described as brutish, stupid, and coarse. No attempt is made to align these judgments with the actual abilities of the people concerned. In other words, in dealing with the question of equality, we are dealing with an enormous cultural/ideological overlay. Some scholars have argued that even the !Kung San are not egalitarian, because even if they lack chiefs, they do have leaders. My response to such an assertion is that if one takes a definition of *perfect equality* as a standard, it will never be found. Some !Kung men *are* better hunters than others, for example, but the question is, do they parlay that into wealth, wives, or power? As I have shown in a variety of different contexts, they don't.

In the broadest terms, population growth has to be regarded as a starting-point in the analysis of directional social change.[9] Human numbers tend to grow, however slowly, and the growth of humankind has been a constant push over the millennia. Such growth has had the effect of upsetting equilibria between people and resources. Population pressure was generally not a problem for hunting and gathering humans; low fertility, infanticide, and outmigration prevented numbers from reaching critical levels in a given area (Cohen 1977; Spooner 1972).

During the late Paleolithic and Mesolithic this situation changed. Sedentary villages founded on a subsistence base of marine resources appear in the Old World and the New between 15,000 and 10,000 years ago. Here we see for the first time the appearance of the destabilizing conditions that have become almost pan-human by the present century (Cohen 1977; Binford 1968; Smith 1976).

However, between population growth and the growth of social

inequality, there are a number of intervening steps. Four general factors are crucial mediating variables: (a) an increase in population density, which leads to (b) a relative decrease in per capita resource availability, and therefore a decreased ease of subsistence, which leads to (c) an increase in societal scale and levels of production to meet increased demands, which in turn leads to (d) an increase in internal/external social tensions.[10] These directional changes tend to operate on fairly long time scales, at a pace that is imperceptible to an observer within a lifetime. As a result, it may be difficult to document this kind of change with ethnographic case material. And in this century these kinds of slow internal evolutionary changes have been almost everywhere preempted and obscured by the massive forces of Western imperialism.[11] Therefore, the model presented here delineates hypothetical trajectories for large-scale changes that we know occurred.

Let us begin by visualizing a population of 500 foragers or simple farmers organized communally, and divided into ten villages of 50 people. If populations increase and the area occupied remains the same, then more people will have to make do on less land per capita. This process implies two outcomes: (a) more "strangers" will be in intimate contact, and (b) people will have to intensify production (i.e., increase labor to make ends meet). Societal scale increases when more people live under the same cultural/linguistic jurisdiction. And if these changes are taking place on a regional basis, then the expanding peripheries of villages are eventually going to impinge on one another.

Foraging societies organized in bands can function very well in groups of 25–50 with economically active members working two to four hours a day. Simple farmers can be seen to operate along similar lines. Doubling the population to 100 begins to introduce logistical problems. Who is going to hunt and gather where? Where are the new fields to be located, and who will clear them? And even if these questions can be sorted out, the nature of the productive process requires that the economically active adults will have to work harder to maintain their dietary standard, either by travelling farther afield, in the case of hunters, or by the added work of clearing new fields, for the farmers. If the poulation doubles again, to 200 people, the group may rapidly be approaching the limits of their resources under a given technology. Added to this are the problems faced by foragers or farmers from one area expanding their range fourfold and coming into contact with similarly expanding neighbors.

Such processes put definite (though by no means impossible) demands upon the institutions of communal society. The injunctions on the sharing of food and the sharing of work to produce the food would carry the group for a time. Sharing levels out disparities in food supply. Interlocking kindreds allow for the equitable distribution of work and land. The germs of inequality arise, not from a breakdown of the sharing ethic, *but from an effort to make it work under altered circumstances.*

When the scale of society reaches a certain point, egalitarian decision-making can no longer cope. Too many people with too many conflicting interests overtax the capacity of face-to-face political processes. Here we see a crisis in social reproduction. At this point the crisis is resolved by the emergence of a new figure in human history, a *manager*, whose task it is to preserve the equitable distribution of food, work, and land. Fried, following Polanyi, has called these figures "egalitarian redistributors," people (usually men) who act as adjudicators, spokespersons, and repositories for the purpose of food redistribution. Harris notes that the way to identify who is the egalitarian redistributor in a given village is to seek out the *poorest hut*. The leader leads by example, and in primitive communal society virtue lies in generosity (Fried 1967:118; Polanyi 1944; Harris 1985:235–39).

The redistributor has very limited powers to keep people in line. He influences by persuasion and consensus. He may or may not pass on his "office" to his children. Part of his influence may derive from leadership in war, raiding, or intergroup conflict, or it may derive from his skills as a negotiator and a diplomat. Skills as a shaman, healer, or diviner may also play a role. Such leaders are found throughout the band and tribal world in North and South America, the Kalahari, Australia, and Southeast and Northeast Asia.

The next step is one about which we know very little. Yet the importance of this step cannot be doubted. At some point in the development of these redistributive societies there was an ideological shift of great magnitude, a changeover in the demeanor of leaders from modesty to self-aggrandizement, and from self-denial to self-praise. This shift removed a constraint on the behavior of leaders, lifting a ban that opened the way for the accumulation of power, prestige, and wealth for the first time.

Thus, we see in American Northwest Coast society chiefs living under the same roofs as commoners, but occupying a special place at feasts, wearing special regalia, and boasting of their prowess in war, of

238

their wealth, and of their ancestry. In Polynesia the deference toward chiefs was carried even further. The chiefs were almost godlike, with ritual constraints on their diet, toilet, and contact with commoners.

Not all advanced redistributive societies glorify their chiefs. In the big-man societies of New Guinea, the big-man is a "mover and shaker" with a larger house and more wives than the norm, but he has no "royal" prerogatives and no coercive powers. Among the Iroquois, the chiefs or *sachems* had to maintain a modest, temperate behavior in council and were subject to recall by the woman of their clan (see Trigger, this volume).

Social inequality thus seems to have its origins in the increasing scale of society, and in the development of productive forces. But there is not a perfect correlation between these variables and the degree of inequality. In some societies (e.g., West Africa), fairly large villages (100–2,000), will exist with modest social differentiation (e.g., Ibo), while in others (e.g., Northwest Coast, Tutchone), marked inequalities appear in relatively modest villages of 100–200 people. There is also considerable variation in the objective degree of inequality compared to its subjective perception. In some societies, the language and idioms of kinship and reciprocity may conceal large differences in wealth, while in others a discourse of masters and slaves, superiors and subordinates may be found in situations where rich and poor are not that far apart.

COURSES TOWARD INEQUALITY

Although examples of hierarchically organized foragers do exist (the Northwest Coast), the development of inequality is first and foremost a consequence of food production. Foragers directly appropriate from nature; farmers and herders by contrast depend far more on *improvements* upon nature and the *husbandry* of resources. Agricultural fields must be cleared, fenced, and weeded. Herds and flocks must be tended, watered, and protected from predators. The investment of labor in fields and herds adds value to the resource and sets it apart from the common store. In a word, farmers and herders depend for their livelihood on *property*, and new social groupings crystallize around the management of these properties. Let me cite three examples.

Lineage systems, found in West Africa and other parts of the world, tend to concentrate power in the hands of older men (elders) and disenfranchise the younger men (cadets) and women. As lineages grow

239

in size they tend to subdivide into senior and junior branches, and the oldest male of the most senior branch becomes the lineage head, a position which may become hereditary. Senior lineage segment heads get their pick of arable lands, and through their leverage within the lineage can concentrate wealth in land or cattle. In Polynesia social inequality is expressed through the ranked lineage or ramage. Senior members of senior segments of a ramage are chiefs who hold enormous power over the labor and lives of the junior members of the same social grouping.[12] The Lineage Mode of Production and the Polynesian ramage illustrate the point that the kin-ordered societies are capable of accommodating a considerable degree of inequality.

New Guinea big-men provide another example of the genesis of inequality.[13] In the great periodic ceremonials that brought together hundreds of people, big-men supervised lavish distributions of food and wealth in pigs, yams, and sweet potatoes. In hosting these feasts the big-man had to mobilize the resources of his clansmen and women. All the big-man's persuasive powers of oratory were necessary to get the people to part with their goods. The reward was the fame and renown that the big-man and his clan received for their largesse, though in precolonial times mobilizing neighboring groups as allies in war was a major function of these feasts.

Severe limitations acted as a brake on the self-aggrandizing big-man. He had no coercive powers, and if the demands placed upon his followers were too great, his supporters would melt away and attach themselves to the rising star of another big-man. The big-man thus might end his life in obscurity, just another member of the "rank and file." The dilemma of the big-man was the subject of a famous essay by Marshall Sahlins in which he contrasted the transitory fame of the Melanesian big-man with the inherited majesty and power of the Polynesian chief (1964).

Big-men systems exhibit the logic of communal society pushed to the breaking-point. Chiefdoms usher in for the first time the fundamental breach with the norms of communal society. The chief can command the obedience of his followers. His word is law. He can requisition goods and services in peace and war, and, perhaps most importantly, he can pass all this, the office and the wealth, on to one or more of his children.

Carneiro (1981), one of the most knowledgeable students of the chiefdom, has argued that the significance of the chiefdom lies in the fact that it is the first social form in history to transcend village

240

autonomy. In order to qualify as a chiefdom, the domain has to include two or more villages under a single rule. How do chiefdoms arise? Sahlins, following Polanyi, sees redistribution as the key to the chiefdom. The chief acts as a central force in concentrating, through labor and tribute, the economic wealth of society. The greater the level of production, the bigger the chiefdom. But where does the surplus come from? It is not natural; it has to be coerced. The chief and his retinue, through political means, coerce the subjects to produce more. Therefore, Carneiro concludes that political power leads to surplus production, and not the other way around.[14] The ultimate source of political power, argues Carneiro, is force. Therefore, the ultimate cause of the rise of chiefdoms is war.

Archaeological evidence of regional cultural florescences document the presence of warfare in sequences where the appearance of chiefdoms can be identified. Such sequences also exhibit evidence for population growth and environmental circumscription. However, not all cases of high warfare lead to chiefdoms. Tropical forest South America and highland New Guinea both exhibit high levels of warfare, but they have not produced chiefdoms. And not all chiefdoms are environmentally circumscribed. Some may be socially circumscribed (i.e., chiefdoms occurred on the islands of the Caribbean, but also on the adjacent mainland of South America and southeastern North America).

I doubt whether warfare alone will stand up as the principal "cause" of the chiefdom. It is difficult to disentangle warfare from the bundle of other forces in the economic and ideological spheres. Carneiro's argument *does* have the virtue of directing our attention to the political sphere, since the chiefdom, and for that matter the state, are primarily political institutions, and war, to paraphrase Clausewitz, is a form of politics.

Chiefs for the first time in history wear the mantle of legitimacy. They rule by right, a right society confers; there is the mystique of royal blood. There is an aura about the chief. We speak of chiefly bearing, or regal manner; this mystique is reinforced by speech forms, elaborate terms of respect, and by regalia, symbols of office. A second element of chiefdoms that is new is the retinue, the building up of a body of retainers, personal servants, bards, cooks, and bodyguards who owe loyalty to the chief and are not bound by family ties. These retainers may be relatives of the chief, but more often they are commoners recruited from the ranks, or outsiders specifically recruited to serve the ruler. Combining the symbols of legitimacy with the body of retainers, we see the emergence of a court and court life.[15] The court revolves around the person of the chief and the running of the affairs of the chiefdom. Here we see the dawn of bureaucracy and the dawn of civil society.

How is the retinue to be provisioned? How is the chief's need for resources to be satisfied? Here we come to another watershed in the evolution of social complexity: the transformation of redistribution into taxation. The first headmen were economic managers who helped communal society function on a larger and larger scale by acting as a focal point for food distribution and deployment of labor. Even with the changeover from the modesty of the egalitarian redistributor to the self-aggrandizement of the chief, the redistribution of goods at feasts and in times of hardship mainly benefited the people at large. With the rise of the chief's retinue, however, a larger and larger proportion of the tribute remained and was consumed at the center. Many anthropologists have suggested that the term redistribution needs refinement. What percentage of goods is redistributed, and to what percentage of the population? If the figures are high and a large proportion reap the benefits, it can be called redistribution, but if the figures are low, then that is properly called taxation.

Here in a nutshell is the key to the rise of the chiefdom and the key to "government": to build up and reproduce the center through greater exaction from the populace, while still retaining the loyalty (or at least acquiescence) of the same populace. It is at this point that the stage is set for the evolution of the state.[16]

WHAT IS THE CORE OF THE COMMUNAL MODE?

In the foregoing I have argued that a long sequence and a multiplicity of pathways link the communal mode with systems of inequality. And for an extended period, elements of communalism coexist with elements of hierarchy. Yet even in these transitional forms, the contours of the communal mode are visible to those who have eyes to see it. Because of this coexistence of communal and hierarchical forms, and because the dominant ideology in the capitalist West seeks to minimize or obscure the presence of communalism, the concept of primitive communism has received "bad press." Even among those who are sympathetic to Marxism, there is much resistance to the notion of a communal mode.

It is therefore appropriate that I conclude this inquiry with a hard look at what the communal mode is and is not.

First, the communal mode is *not* a system of perfect equality. Identity of subjects is not present; everybody is not the same. In communal societies wealth and status differences do occur, although to a limited degree. Second, primitive communism is not communism as currently constituted in the socialist world. The current socialist regimes are *state societies*, centrally administered and heavily bureaucratized. Whatever role the concept of primitive communism may play in their official ideologies, the "common" ownership of the means of production in these societies is of a fundamentally different character from that in the small-scale, communally organized *traditional* societies of interest here.

Third, the communal mode is neither utopian nor "pretty." *The members of these societies are real people with all the human frailties of people everywhere.* As I pointed out in *The !Kung San* (1979:458–61), communalism and sharing are achieved by the !Kung at considerable cost. A very rough form of joking and gossip is used to keep people in line. "Please" and "thank you" are not found in their vocabulary. And the impulse not to share (to hoard) is always present just beneath the surface. As Trigger points out (this volume), the capacity for altruism *and* selfishness are both present in the human make-up. Those who live by the communal mode are no more "noble" than the rest of us.

Fourth, and related, is the point that life in the communal mode is not peaceful. Violence, raiding, even warfare (but not conquest) can be observed among communal societies. Whether the levels of violence observed are higher, lower, or the same as those in state societies is a matter for discussion (cf. Lee 1979:396–400). But fierce or not, all communal societies (including the Yanomamo, to take one of the most dramatic examples) practiced the collective ownership of hunting lands and the law of hospitality.

Finally, the communal mode of production as observed in world ethnography is equivocal on gender relations. I agree with Leacock that band and tribal societies *overall* show less gender hierarchy and more equality between the sexes than do other levels of society (Leacock 1982). It is clear that the principles of communal organization do tend to protect women's status in crucial ways against the full weight of patriarchy (Lee and Daly 1987). However, there are many anomalies, cases where a degree of oppression of women coexists with a communal or semi-communal mode (epitomized by the Yanomamo, for example, and a number of highland New Guinea societies). This oppression is an important problem in need of further study.

Now that we have seen what the communal mode is not, we must ask what remains? What is the irreducible core of the communal mode of production? The key to this question lies in the remarkable institution of the leveling device. The rough form of joking that keeps people in line is part of a larger complex of behaviors and values that is as central to the reproduction of communal society as is the principle of private property and the right to profit in capitalist society. This can be characterized as a fierce adherence to egalitarianism, an abhorrence of the acceptance of status distinctions among them. This abhorrence persists even in some semicommunal societies with headmen and chiefs, where the leaders do hold office but only by virtue of continuing generosity to their "subjects."

But leveling devices are not simply aspects of value orientation. They also operate on the material plane to prevent both accumulation and destitution. The underlying principles can be modeled as follows: visualize two horizontal parallel lines. The upper line is a ceiling of accumulation of goods above which an individual cannot rise, and the lower line is a floor of destitution below which one cannot sink. In the communal mode the ceiling and the floor are closely connected; one cannot exist without the other. No one can have too much, and if there is any food in the camp, everybody in the camp is going to get some of it. The obligation to share food and the taboo against hoarding are no less strong and no less ubiquitous in the primitive world than the far more famous taboo against incest. But unlike the incest taboo, which persists to the present, the hoarding taboo became a casualty of social evolution. One of the key developments of social evolution is the lifting of the ceiling of accumulation. Animal domestication represents such a shift. Instead of shooting the animal and eating the meat, one brings the beast into the settlement and it sits there as property. Once the ceiling is raised, the possibility of wealth differences emerges. Someone could have no goats while another person had one; and if no goats and one goat is possible, then so is one goat and ten goats, or one goat and a hundred.

So far we have spoken of raising the ceiling, but at a crucial point in the evolution of societies we observe the lowering of the floor. I don't know exactly how that happens. In the communal mode if someone gets a little uppity, (s)he is leveled out. By the same token, those falling through the cracks are supported by the group. But when the floor is lowered, poverty for some becomes possible. The community safety net for some disappears. One of the elements of social evolution that is of great interest is how the cracks get wider. Do people fall through those cracks by neglect, or are they preyed upon? Does society devour itself by the rich preying upon the poor? (In ancient Greece, as some people got wealthier, they first took the land of their neighbors, then they enslaved them.) The ceiling and the floor are dialectically connected.

In the modern world, both floor and ceiling have disappeared. There are billionaires in one area and mass poverty and starvation in others. It is on the political agenda of both socialists and liberal capitalists to restore the floors and at least a semblance of the ceilings; both would stabilize at a much higher level of accumulation than that found in primitive communal formations. Primitive communism has existed within a narrow range at the bottom of a scale; future society would operate in a broader range at the top. But whatever the future may hold, it is the long experience of egalitarian sharing that has molded our past. Despite our seeming adaptation to life in hierarchical societies, there are signs that humankind retains a deep-rooted egalitarianism, a deep-rooted commitment to the norm of reciprocity, a deep-rooted desire for what Victor Turner has called *communitas,* the sense of community. All theories of justice revolve around these principles, and our sense of outrage at the violation of these norms indicates the depth of its gut-level appeal. That, in my view, is the core of primitive communism and the communal mode.

NOTES

Presented at an Advanced Seminar on "The Development of Political Systems in Prehistoric Sedentary Societies," School of American Research, Santa Fe, NM, April 20–25, 1987. I want to thank Steadman Upham, Bruce Trigger, Barbara Bender, and the other seminar members for their critical suggestions in the preparation of this chapter. Portions of the chapter are drawn from another work, *Kin Class and State: The Origins of Hegemony* (in preparation).

1. D. Legros has proposed an example of the latter, the Tutchone of the Southern Yukon. See Legros (1985).

2. Many "environmentalists" in archaeology are not unsympathetic to Marxist perspectives, while the bulk of Marxist scholarship in economics and

political science remains remarkably indifferent to the dynamics of precapitalist societies.

3. By adding the word "written" before "history" in the 1886 edition of the Manifesto.

4. My thinking on social reproduction has been influenced by Edholm, Harris, and Young (1977); and Luxton (1980).

5. The work of Carol Kramer comes to mind here (1982).

6. For a discussion of foraging as a mode of production see Lee (1981).

7. For full quotes, see my paper "Reflections on Primitive Communism" (in press).

8. Martin Whyte (1978) is one author who comes to mind.

9. It is worth noting here that Marx, in the "Formen" section of the *Grundrisse*, invokes population growth as a cause of social development. Where he parted company with Malthus was on the view of population growth as the main cause of human misery.

10. A more detailed sketch of this argument is presented in chapter 12 of *The !Kung San* (Lee 1979:320ff), where intensification of social life is examined in terms of concentration/dispersion settlement patterns, and of the increased labor demands of aggregated settlements.

11. But not entirely obscured; *pace* Wolf (1982a and 1982b).

12. For the lineage societies see Rey and Dupre (1973); and Meillassoux (1972). For Polynesia see Goldman (1970) and Sahlins (1958).

13. On the big-men see Meggitt (1974); Strathern (1971); Loman-Vayda (1976).

14. Sahlins (1958); Polanyi (1944); Carneiro (1981).

15. Court life as an evolutionary form is a theme developed by Norbert Elias (1982).

16. For a discussion of early Marxist theories of state formation see Lee (1985).

246

10
The dynamics of nonhierarchical societies

BARBARA BENDER

University College London

The average conference resembles a marketplace: somewhere to hawk your wares, to see what is on display, and to buy products for later consumption. Exchange is immediate; effect is delayed. The seminar at Santa Fe held in April, 1987, was different. Five entire days of intensive discussion made it possible to think about, question, and reformulate ideas *in situ*. It would be good to find a way of writing this chapter that gave a sense of that process. Lacking both skill and space, I observe that, as far as I am concerned, two issues were remolded before the seminar came to an end.

The first issue concerned the notion of "resistance." In my preseminar paper I questioned the notion of a step-like evolutionary process. I suggested that the independent emergence of states was a rare development, but that such states had major effects upon neighboring, and even quite distant, societies. I suggested that many kin-based social formations were part of a process of resistance to state formation. But the sense that came out of the seminar was of resistance not so much as a rear-guard action but as something positive: societies "holding to," rather than "holding on to," ways of being and ways of relating. Moreover resistance was not only about external pressures, but also about latent internal pressures that threatened social equality. And yet resistance to change is not, *pace* the functionalists, a recipe for stasis. The small-time, small-scale actions and interactions of people trying to maintain and enhance the status quo have their own, often unintended consequences. "Running to stand still" has its own dynamic.

The second issue had to do with the state of Marxist theory. Loosening-up the conception of base and superstructure, and giving greater priority to people's perceptions of their world and to their individual or group actions, carry the risk of becoming overly idealistic and relativistic, of losing sight of larger socioeconomic structures and historical trajectories. The seminar brought home to me the difficulty of maintaining a balance. In what follows, I focus on these two issues.

INEQUALITY, RESISTANCE, AND MIDDLE-RANGE SOCIETIES

In this section I examine two assumptions inherent in Upham's description (see chapter 1, this volume) of "middle-range" societies. First is the idea that there is a divide between gatherer-hunters and farmers. On one side of the divide are familial relations of the kin-oriented band, and on the other side are new forms of intergroup political relations. Second is the notion that small-scale, kin-based farming societies have emergent properties that provide the impetus toward greater social inequality and the development of increasingly ranked or stratified chiefdoms and states.

Does farming constitute a baseline?

The short answer to this question must be "no." Techno-environmental forces cannot in isolation determine how people gain a living or relate to one another. Thus, farming has little independent autonomy and is dependent upon prior and ongoing social relations. These relations are themselves tempered by environmental and technological constraints, but these constraints are socially mediated. There are, of course, limits to desert or arctic living where people are dependent upon wild resources. Yet, even in such extreme instances, what is taken from the environment, how it is taken and by which members of the community, how that community is constituted, and how the product is used cannot be "read off" from the environment. Gatherer-hunters do not reside in a

248

state of nature, and farming *per se* does not set the wheels of social evolution in motion, or even the wheels of social inequality.

Nonetheless there are aspects of a farming economy that play back into social relations, that can be used by individuals and groups to alter their relationships, both to each other and to the land. But again, the alterations will occur within the larger social matrix of what went before and will depend upon prior social relations, social perceptions, and divisions of labor.

The potential for social elaboration, including forms of social inequality, is present from very early prefarming times. It is embedded in the interlocking development of alliance, language, ideology, human labor that is socially constituted, and productivity that takes material form (Bender 1985b). Alliance is an early, necessary dimension to human relations. In order to secure a viable mating network, small gatherer-hunter bands key into a wider set of social relations. In very early time ranges, when population densities were very low, the network would have been open, but at some point in time (perhaps during the Middle Paleolithic), as population densities increased, a degree of social closure became possible (Wobst 1976). Population increase was only a precondition for closure; its adoption was due to longer-term strategies that placed a premium on sociability and communication. While the spatial extent of the alliance networks must, in part, respond to environmental and demographic factors, the variability, flexibility, and changeability in the form of alliance and exchange (and in the ways in which kith and kin are defined) also reflect social perceptions about how things should be done and what is necessary for social reproduction.

Alliance and exchange are part of the process by which human labor is socially created, evaluated, and differentially deployed. Because human productivity takes material form, that too becomes part of the same process. There is no such thing as a relationship between a person and an object, only relations between people. The material dimension of social relations has important repercussions, and much recent writing has refocused on the notion of the inalienability of objects in kin-based societies (Mauss 1954; Munn 1971, 1973, 1977; Sahlins 1972; Weiner 1985). Objects, even when given in exchange, remain tied to their creators and thus define differences between people, or qualities possessed by some but not by others (Rowlands 1987a). Because they

249

retain something of their maker, they permit the potential for social relations enduring beyond the immediate reciprocal transaction (Munn 1977). Exchanges, material and immaterial, cement and extend ties between people. They also foster dependencies between people that are open to negotiation or exploitation. They allow demands to be made upon other people's labor.

The social nature of human interaction, the way in which the identity of people and objects is culturally constituted, means that social relations and social standing are open to negotiation, manipulation, and reevaluation. Alliance and exchange form not only the social matrix from which smaller or more ephemeral units (base-camps, work-parties, etc.) are constituted and negotiated, but also the matrix for other divisions within society. Divisions of labor along gender or age lines are, for example, often assumed to be natural. "Man the hunter" and "woman the gatherer" supposedly relate to biological factors, such as physical strength or child-bearing. But if it were simply a biological imperative, such divisions would be fluid, changing according to different times in the male and female life cycle. In reality labor divisions are often very rigid, or are symbolically redefined so that the hunting of small game by women is seen as gathering. It seems likely that in early hominid societies, divisions would be flexible, but by the Middle or Late Paleolithic they would "harden," reflecting the increasing emphasis on social definition and differentiation. I have suggested that the creation of cave paintings and mobile art in the European Upper Paleolithic may have been part of a context in which distinctions based on kin-affiliation, age-set, and gender were sharpened and sanctified (Bender 1989). At certain times and places during the Upper Paleolithic, parts of the ideological repertoire deemed essential to social reproduction became increasingly inaccessible (both hidden and abstract), and access could be controlled by those "who knew" (the route, the code, the appropriate behavior). These particular European groups (in southwest France and northern Spain) were not sedentary, though they congregated in large numbers at certain times of year. Nor, to jump a continent and more than fifteen thousand years, were the Ohio Hopewell communities sedentary. Yet they too congregated at certain places and times of year, built ceremonial structures, created and exchanged goods within socially defined spheres, and negotiated social positions that were not open to everyone (Bender 1985a and 1985b; Braun and Plog 1982; Greber 1979).

250

These Hopewellian and southwest European social configurations were reproduced through alliances and exchanges that extended over wide areas and encompassed somewhat differently constituted social groupings. The effects of these linkages within the communal mode need further exploration. On a much smaller scale, there were degrees of unequal development within gatherer-hunter and small-scale farming societies long before the emergence of the state.[1]

The process of alliance and exchange, involving communication, ritual, congregation, and creation, made demands on people's time and labor, allowed the appropriation of certain people's labor and produce, and may well have fostered intensification of production (see Lourandos [1980] on the construction of eel runs to underwrite ritual gatherings in Victoria, Australia). But social differentiation need not automatically spiral. The situation described among the Iroquois by Trigger (this volume), where status positions were filled by different individuals with different priorities, creating a system of checks and balances, may be very widespread. The demands created by an ethos of generosity or the need to understate personal success (Lee, this volume) may also militate against the erosion of equality. Nonetheless, it is possible for there to be drift between an *ideology* based on an ethos of generosity, of status that has no material rewards, of demands made upon the individual in the name of the community, and a *reality* where demands become more onerous and less equally distributed, and power is displayed in terms of marital affiliation or ability to control esoteric knowledge. On the basis of the arguments presented in this book, it is clear that holding the balance is hard work. There are internal and external forces that create a dynamic tending toward inequality. In kin-based societies, however, the pattern is likely to be one of cycles rather than irreversible transformations.

The point is that the potential to manipulate social knowledge, to negotiate and renegotiate the networks of kith and kin, is in place among nonsedentary and sedentary gatherer-hunters. These social processes and the demands that they make on people's productivity may explain, at least in part, the move to food production. On the other hand, by increasing productivity over a large area, food production may make it easier for groups to move away and thus avoid social obligations. Early food production may have been fostered both by the demands of the social system, and by resistance to them.[2]

Socioeconomic developments in small-scale farming societies

The preceding discussion emphasises that there is no hard-and-fast division between gatherer-hunter and small-scale farmer. Examples of elders, leaders, chiefs, social differentiation, and gender inequality are all found within gatherer-hunter contexts. Although the more remarkable cases (e.g., the tribute-exacting Calusa chiefs in Florida) may, in part, reflect proximity to stratified societies, it is clear that even without food production the gamut of socioeconomic variability is considerable (Marquardt 1989). Is there, then, any way in which agricultural, small-scale, nonhierarchical societies are distinctive?

Authority, however minimally constituted, has a material dimension; it makes demands on the labor of those in power and those subordinate. Generosity, in both gatherer-hunter and small-scale farming societies, fuels social relations, and helps establish and maintain social position. Generosity often requires that one be more generous in return. Gifts and counter-gifts make demands on production. Most gatherer-hunter subsistence systems have considerable "slack" that can be picked up (Barker and Gamble 1986), free time that can be used to increase the resource harvest. Nonetheless, agricultural systems have the advantage: more labor investment will continue to augment supplies long after wild procurement strategies tail off. And, once the necessary technological improvements have occurred, investment can be made in areas that were not, in the first instance, particularly high yielding. Food production allows either the maintenance (the nonerosion) of the subsistence base for longer periods and over wider areas, or creates the possibility of intensifying labor and production, social conditions permitting. With higher productivity, certain individuals may be able to withdraw from direct subsistence activities and make demands upon others. This last point may be rephrased: Certain individuals can withdraw from direct labor and *depend upon* the labor of others. It is this dependency on others that explains the fragile basis of an authority not based on force or on the direct control of land or resources. The strong possibility of resistance exists if demands are felt to be onerous.

Some gatherer-hunter groups construct facilities and have to wait for the return. They have a stake in a specific patch. Or they stay put because resources are plentiful and tightly "packed." *All* agriculturists invest in the land and have to await a return. With rare exceptions,

252

farmers are sedentary, although the term is more relative than generally acknowledged. Small-scale swidden farmers stay put for a few years, but their investment is not very great, and mobility may remain an option in the face of unacceptable demands on their labor. Sedentism and labor investment can have important repercussions. Sedentism permits storage and facilitates the ironing out of seasonal and annual fluctuations in supplies. Thus, there may be a relaxation on birth-spacing. Labor investment creates inter-generational debts. Debts, increased population, and storage are all potentially exploitable. Storage may be used to permit unequal household accumulation; increased numbers may be encouraged because a larger household yields larger returns; increased sedentism may mean less fluid interaction and more formal gatherings that can be controlled by the elders (cf. Gamble 1986). Land may become property owned by a household or kin group, thus promoting unequal accumulation. Access to land and means of exploitation may be linked to prior exchanges, such as bridewealth payments. With farming, there is the potential for all these developments, but it is only *potential*. The shift from land as an object of production among gatherer-hunters to land as a means of production among farmers has to be nuanced. It is clear that over time farming lifts the level of the forces of production and removes some of the constraints on social interaction. The particular way in which the transformation takes place and the particular form of production, circulation, distribution, and consumption are powerfully constrained by the specific, historically constituted, socioeconomic configuration.

In both gathering-and-hunting and small-scale farming societies, kin and communality define and order social obligations and social distinctions within both the community and the larger social unit of reproduction. In this communal mode, kin-relations circumscribe the form, set limits on the ability to maneuver, and create the means of resistance.

Friedman and Rowlands (1978) have spelt out a potential trajectory which, whilst it might occur under certain environmentally optimal conditions amongst gatherer-hunters, will occur more widely amongst small-scale farmers. It pivots on the way in which depth of kin relations, expressed genealogically and in terms of ranking, can be equated with social distance. In the first instance, genealogical ranking turns on the acquisition and control of social knowledge: knowing how things should be done is referenced on the ancestors who, as repositories of knowledge, mediate between human beings and the supernatural. Thus, closeness to the ancestors legitimates social differences; "feasting" the ancestors creates and maintains social distance. Having the options to feast or give requires the exploitation of the household economy and any other debt relations. Slight inequalities in household composition or landholdings may have some significance, but it is the ability to convert mundane labor into something symbolically charged that permits social difference and ranking. Friedman and Rowlands indicate a series of possible feed-back loops between household inequalities, feasting and ceremony, control of marital negotiations and bridewealth, and creation of debt and labor obligations. They work through a trajectory in which the ancestral link is eventually bypassed and the paramount chief mediates directly with the gods.

A comparison of two examples from Papua New Guinea permits a contrast between a big-man system and a chiefly society. Briefly, in the western highlands of Papua New Guinea, there are big-men who appear, in the first instance, to have gained an advantage by exploiting the more productive swamplands. Surplus was converted into pig keeping, feasting, and ceremony, and, in that context, the big-men were able to control other exchanges. Even after the introduction of the sweet potato and the move from the swamplands, they maintained their position through controlling women's and "poor" men's labor (Golsen cited in White 1985). A reconstruction of Siassi society in the Vitiaz Straits in the early part of this century provides a contrast to the big-man system. Here, there were Marons, or chiefs, associated with peace and generosity; sorcerers who "forced the will"; and Dolman, who headed the men's houses, were authorities on genealogy and lore, and organized overseas trading expeditions (Lilley 1985). The position of both Maron and Dolman may have been inherited by the eldest son, and the Maron seems to come from a senior men's house, suggesting that there were a series of ranked lineages. Maron and Dolman were both involved in competitive trading, so that there was an overlap between ascribed leadership and achieved political and economic preeminence.

On first view the two cases might be placed in a neat evolutionary sequence, with a few intermediary stages still waiting to be filled. The sorcerer appears, as in many other societies, to play an ambiguous role, permitting an element of coercion to creep into a system otherwise based on peace and generosity (cf. Rowlands 1987b). It looks like the sort of trajectory plotted by Friedman and Rowlands (1978). Closer examination, however, suggests that something rather different was happening. The big-men of the western highlands seem to have had difficulty forcing the pace, and their attempts at intensifying external exchanges were apparently thwarted by the claims of kin, both real and fictive. Modjeska (cited in White 1985:57) suggests that "inequalities [had to] be contained in order to safeguard male solidarity which is the basic security of lineage and which ensures continuance of men's exploitation of women's labor." It may also be the case that some of the Papua New Guinea big-men systems are devolved chiefdoms. Intensive trade within chiefdoms seems to have led to a fragmentation of the original extensive system, and to trade-related status rivalry which undermined chiefly control (Friedman 1981). It is also possible that the Melanesian chiefdoms were not an indigenous development. They may have been a peripheral manifestation, a Melanesian reworking through contact or colonization, of the weakly stratified sociopolitical order of Southeast Asia. In other words, understanding a particular socioeconomic configuration may require the exploration of extensive spatial as well as temporal relationships.

The ability to cut loose from kin and to build upon some system of class exploitation, to commoditize at least some part of production, and to withdraw from direct subsistence production may be very problematic and rarely achieved (Gailey 1985); or if achieved, rarely sustained. It may be that pristine states are a rare phenomenon occurring only under quite special conditions (Mann 1984).[3] There may be no more than five or six such cases, and state formation should not, perhaps, be seen as a widely expected historical outcome. But while infrequent, state formations have expansionary tendencies, and many chiefdoms, from the fourth millennium B.C. in the Old World, or the first in the New, are the effect of encapsulation by or resistance to expansionary states (Fried 1975; Gailey and Patterson 1987; Rowlands 1984; Sherratt 1984).[4] Thus, the Melanesian case cited above, or the chiefdoms of East Polynesia and the American Northwest Coast may be "agents and victims of processes of political and economic expansion" (Wolf 1984:395).

Anthropologists may be better advised to examine the remarkable capacity of kin-based societies to resist divisions of labor leading to class formation, to resist the lifelong exploitation of one class by another, and to foment rebellions that may threaten or even destroy archaic states, rather than assume they exhibit an irresistible drive toward class and

255

state (Gailey and Patterson 1989). But the process of resistance also involves change. Two anthropologists (Gailey and Patterson) have recently discussed the effect of encapsulation of kin-based communities located on the edge of differently constituted states. They suggest that most of the social variability described by Marxists as the Germanic, Slave, Ancient, and Lineage Modes were generated under these conditions. The particular form depends largely upon the historical situation. If, for example,

the state is weak the autonomous kin societies on the periphery will retain communal control over production and reproduction but will have more rigid forms of kin-determined use-rights and marriage arrangements (Gailey and Patterson 1989).

A corollary to the above discussion is that notions of socioeconomic dynamics must be divorced from implications of unilineal change or progress, of steps that lead from band through tribe and chiefdom to state, of moves from incoherent homogeneity to coherent heterogeneity (Rowlands 1989). Such assumptions, as Rowlands has pointed out, are part of a pervasive meta-narrative, part of a dominant ideology that favors a modernizing ethos and the primacy of the West. It is quite possible to accept that there have been cumulative and irreversible social transformations over time; that qualitatively different social and cultural worlds have developed; that, among other things, the demographic and territorial scale of political integration through particular types of institutional arrangements or technologies of power has radically altered. But at the same time, it is necessary both to question whether there is any straightforward temporal axis of change and to suggest that the analytical and explanatory focus should be upon interconnected spatial developments (Gledhill 1989).

A MARXIST PERSPECTIVE

There have been a number of expositions dealing with the use and abuse of Marxist theory in anthropology and archaeology (Bender 1985b; McGuire 1985; Saitta 1988; Spriggs 1984; Tilley 1982; Trigger 1985). In this section I shall concentrate on a quite limited aspect of Marxist theory: recent discussions of power and ideology, and how these relate to earlier conceptualizations of forces and relations of production.

I take as a starting-point Upham's criticism of the notion that "technology in the largest sense of the word . . . is structured by social relations . . . and . . . reproduced by symbolic and ideological means" (chapter 1 this volume; see also Bender 1985a and 1985b). He suggests that if "all forms of sociopolitical organization are 'socially produced,' only ideographic interpretations are possible, since the unique social history of each group will condition its socially mediated response to the environment" (chapter 1, this volume).

Upham equates history with ideography and contrasts both with cross-cultural evolutionary processes. This comparison is reminiscent of Flannery's earliest processual manifesto (Flannery 1972a) and has been succinctly answered by Trigger (1985:116): "Marxism ignores the distinction between history and evolution, as well as that between history and science." But setting quotations eyeball to eyeball does not, in itself, answer the charge. It needs to be shown that history is both particular and general. To talk about dominant social relations or social mediation, to be concerned with people's perceptions of their world, their culture and ideology, does not involve a return to "an anthropology of the mind" or to the type of explanation that Binford (1968) berated as "vitalism" or Rowlands labeled "naive voluntarism."

Marxists do not construe culture or ideology purely as a text or a system of meaning. Rather, culture and ideology provide the impetus for social action: "Subjects draw upon their reflexive experience of the objective world . . . and act upon those same external conditions to reproduce and transform them" (Barrett cited in Leone 1986:416). Cultural perceptions place limits on what can be thought or done: "The coercion . . . of [a] potential fan of connotations to a few licensed imperative meanings . . . is a form of appropriation, alienation, theft" (Wolf 1984:396). And this appropriation is not only at the level of connotation or meaning but also at the level of active partisan manipulation and control. So, to misquote Keesing slightly, where symbolists find meaning, feminists and Marxists find oppression (Scholte 1986:9).

Marx's and Engels's writings were not immediately concerned with the relationship of culture to class or the problem of cultural transformation. In *German Ideology* and later writings they made a distinction between ideology as false consciousness – a tool by which the dominant class subverts reality and mystifies the process of exploitation – and corresponding forms of social consciousness (the equivalent of culture, although they did not use the term). Ideology was the public formulation; consciousness the presuppositions underlying these formulations. It was not until the 1920s that interest began to focus on the process, on the production of meaning and ideas. In anthropology, the Marxist revival began in the late sixties and seventies in France and Britain and tended to neglect the realm of social action, or the reflexive nature of culture and ideology. Instead, it focused on the social relations and on the feed-back (read tension) between the forces and relations of production and within social relations (Friedman 1974). The analysis of social relations concentrated on questions of production and appropriation (Who did what? How did they do it? How much did they produce? How was it allocated?). It is only recently that the discussion of social relations has broadened to include a more dynamic analysis of social action and ideology (Thompson 1978; Giddens 1979; Williams 1973; Foucault 1977; Bourdieu 1977). The spotlight on culture and ideology (Kus 1984; Leone 1986), combined with the impact of critical theory and the growing awareness of *our* subjectivity – our historically and socially situated vantage points (Trigger 1980, 1984b; Gero 1985) – creates the risk of our falling into an overly involuted and relativistic discourse. But the risk is worth taking if it allows us to create a diachronic perspective encompassing both the historically constituted social structures and the thought and activity of individuals who are both constrained by those structures *and* are the agents of their reformation and transformation.

Thus, Bourdieu's (1977) analysis of "habitus" focuses on the largely unreflective, conservative minutiae of daily living, yet permits cross-cultural generalizations about daily social and cultural negotiations, structural analyses of how household activities relate to other productive strategies, and historical analyses of the changing specificity (composition, scale, function, and perception) of the household. The latter allows us to understand how the perceived conservatism is contradicted by the forces of time. Miller (1982) underlines this contradiction in his discussion of emulation, whereby members of lower-order statuses pre-empt higher-order status symbols, which then have to be reconstituted. Again, Miller moves between the cross-cultural processes of negotiation and realignment, showing how they operate within a specific set of socioeconomic relations. He identifies "the ambiguity of time itself, in its expression always conservative, arising from the past, in its impression always new, irrevocably altering the future" (Miller 1982:96). Such studies clearly invalidate any attempt to isolate history from process.

258

Bourdieu and Miller focus on cultural perception, on the almost unspoken understanding of how the world is constituted and how things should be done, because that is how they are and always have been done. In contrast, ideology is that which is spoken, that which offers an internal logic, which purports to know why. Ideology is the domain in which justification and legitimation are offered, the domain of rhetoric (Bloch 1980). Ideology appears monolithic and timeless; but it is neither. It is collusive yet not all-pervasive. At one level there has to be an active complicity in all systems of dominance (Gilsenan 1986), but at another there will be negotiation and resistance. Those with power do not necessarily have identical interests, and people's positions alter during their lifetimes. There will be alternative readings and negotiation among the dominant, while the dominated may neither wish to understand nor fully accept that which is propagated. Nonetheless, alternative ideologies are counterpoints rather than genuine alternatives, for they are contained within the same socioeconomic system.

Ideology appears timeless, the rhetoric and ritual is full of incantation and references to times past, and yet they are open to subtle reworking, particularly where there is no written record (Webner 1977). Moreover, those in power may find themselves trammeled by their own rhetoric and ritual. When the ethos of generosity or of sanctity as the antithesis of wealth accumulation is violated by leader or chief it creates a weakness in the social fabric (Rowlands 1987b). Or it may be that "roles and legitimations taken in routinization and sedimentation of authority . . . become elaborated and eventually submerge the actual interests of the holders of office" (Miller 1989).

Ideology, like culture, has only limited autonomy. We have to ask, "How is this ideology reproduced? In which social exchanges, made in which cultural terms and vocabularies does such reproduction take place?" (Gilsenan 1986:20). Then we must move on to consider "the specific political and economic conditions which make certain rhetorical forms objectively possible, and authoritative" (Asad 1979:616).[5]

First, however, the link between ideology and power must be considered. Power does not have to be manipulative. It can be the "power to," the equivalent of social action – power to produce effects, to create resources. But "power to" can shade into "power over." Social action is socially circumscribed, and the "power to" may be available to everyone at some point in her or his life. More often, it will be available to some but not to others. It may be socially constituted power to control initiation, marital alliances, or the circulation and distribution of socially prized objects. "Power over" can shade into coercion, overt or masked. The generosity of the leader in small-scale societies often masks inequalities between leaders and juniors, or between males and females. Power is masked by being ideologically mystified and legitimated. "Power over" is justified, in kin-based societies, by "power from" the ancestors or the gods. It is this higher authority that confers value on certain people and certain objects. It is this power which allows the naming of things or makes it impossible to name them: "[things] never reflected on, not said, the key absence in the discourse" (Gilsenan 1986:20). There is a reflexivity, a dialectic, between action, ideas, and meaning, between imposition and resistance, maintenance and attrition.

Finally we return to the notion that ideology and power take their form and meaning from what is already there, from the specific, historically constituted political and economic conditions (Asad 1979). Giddens (1979) emphasizes that human beings are not to be treated as passive objects or as wholly free subjects, and Sahlins (1983:523) warns against a bourgeois ideology that expresses itself in the theory that "social outcomes are the cumulative expression of individual actions." Finally, Wolf (1984:399) explains that "cultural construction, reconstruction, deconstruction are ongoing processes, but they always take place within larger historical fields or arenas. These arenas are shaped, in their turn, by the operation of modes of mobilizing social labor and by the conflicts these generate internally and externally, within and between social constellations." Wolf has specified what he means by mobilizing social labor: "a specific, historically occurring set of social relations through which labor is deployed to wrest energy from the environment" (1982a:75).

Thus, we return to the social relations that interact with and dominate the forces of production, that dictate how and by whom the energy is wrested. The mobilization of social labor extends beyond wresting energy from the environment to encompass circulation and distribution. What is to be circulated and to whom? And who, in all these activities, is mobilized by whom? What we search for, and seem to find, are broad sets of social relations that Marx termed Communal, Archaic, Slave, Asiatic, Feudal, Capitalist. In the context of this volume, interest focuses on the communal mode: underwritten by alliance networks, constituted by kin relations (real or fictive), cross-cut by categories of age and gender (see Lee, this volume). Earlier, I discussed what activates relationships between people in this communal mode, and, in particular, the operation of alliance and exchange. To reiterate briefly, we start with biologically necessary alliance and perceive that the constitution of kin networks and the interlocking forms of exchange, people, things, and information (knowledge) are socially constructed. The form is constrained by the environment, but not determined. It reflects people's perceptions of themselves and of others, and of how things should be done within a world constituted by the perceptions and actions of preceding generations. The form may appear to be adaptive simply because it exists. Existence, however, is not a question of functional compatibility. Social existence involves a constant renegotiation of relations, a constant tension and flux. Social systems are not beaten into change, forced to adapt, because of external demographic or environmental forces. Such systems change, or remain relatively unchanged, because of the way they are internally structured, because of the unending contradictions between the way people relate to each other and the way they cognize those relationships. As Giddens (1979:131) puts it: "Don't look for the functions social practices fulfill, look for the contradictions they embody." Or "look for the ineradicable tension between the human urges for coherent life and thought and the limitation forced on us by our involvement in bodily, social, and historical existence" (Rabinow and Sullivan cited in Scholte 1986:10).

If there is demographic pressure, it will often be internally generated, and it will be perceived and acted upon within the terms of the social structure – as will environmental change, or change generated by the demands of neighboring or far distant communities. The contradictions are manifold, but in a system structured by kin relations the number of pathways to inequality are finite. One can make demands on kin, but one is bound by relations of reciprocity, even though reciprocity may involve an intangible return on something more material. One can demand kin labor, but only at great risk can one coerce it. Individuals within the community have use-rights to the land that are inalienable, and they are often self-sufficient so that the means of production cannot easily be controlled. Power and the ability to mobilize labor often derive not from the direct control of production but from the indirect control of social reproduction. And this is done, as we have seen above, by controlling access to and exchange of necessary knowledge or artifacts. Such exchanges are negotiated throughout the lifetime of the individual. Power and inequality derive from the inalienable nature of these exchanges that creates indelible liens between people. In the long reiteration of prestation and counter-prestation, prestige accrues to the giver of a fine axe, the dreamer of a fine dream. Often, axe and dream are ideologically dependent upon the labor of earlier generations; they are transformations of the ancestors, the creators of the world. So gift and giver are sanctified, and those with access to this world of knowledge and things have the power to make demands on people's labor. This aspect of the social system is the social and ideological substructure that is negotiated and transformed by each generation. "In the rough and tumble of social interaction, groups . . . exploit the ambiguities of inherited forms . . . impart new evaluations or valences to them . . . borrow forms more expressive of their interests . . . create new forms" (Wolf 1982b:387).

We cannot predict what will happen in social interaction; we can only attempt to work out historical sequences and explain the structure of that interaction. We have a structural model that attempts to identify fundamental relations that connect social groups in a given system of social relations. We watch the working out of "historically changing, imperfectly bounded, multiple and branching social alignments" (Wolf 1982b:387). In so doing we "seek not only to explain cross-cultural regularities but also the particularities, individual differences and specific contexts that distinguish one instance of social change from another" (Trigger 1985:116).

Like an amen, I end this chapter with a quotation from Marx. Our study is of "real individuals, their activity and their material conditions of life, including those which they already find in existence and those produced by their activity" (Marx 1964:10–11).

NOTES

I would like to thank John Gledhill, Danny Miller, Tom Patterson, and Mike Rowlands for reading and commenting on an earlier draft of this chapter, Felicity Edholm for moral (and intellectual) support when the notion of five days of intense discussion seemed altogether daunting, Jonathan Haas and the School of American Research for funding my participation, and the staff at the School for making life so comfortable. Most of all, I would like to thank my colleagues at the Advanced Seminar for making it possible to discuss and argue back and forth between past and present in a way that seemed far removed from what usually passes for academic discourse.

1. The effects of encapsulation by the state on contemporary gatherer-hunters has recently been discussed at some length by anthropologists (Schrire 1984; Woodburn 1989). But this is "history done to" rather than "history created by" gatherer-hunters. There has been greater reluctance to consider the interaction and resistance within communal formations.

2. Early agricultural production may not have been directly for food production. In coastal Peru, for example, gourds and cotton were the first important crops. They may have been used indirectly for food procurement, that is, for fish nets, containers and net-floats, or they may have played a role in ritual and exchange (Patterson, personal communication).

3. The notion of pristine state formations side-steps the question of whether they really are unitary phenomena, or whether they are the outcome of multisocietal interactions: highland/lowland, sedentary/pastoralist, gatherer-hunter/farmer (Boehm de Lameiras 1989).

4. The old evolutionary versus diffusionary argument risks rearing its hoary head. But earlier diffusionist theories failed to focus on the process of interaction and hid behind neutral terms like "contact situation" rather than acknowledging conflict, repression, and dissent.

5. Echoed in Miller's discussion of the ideological inversions of Carnival, in which "the political implications are contingent. In one social and economic context (carnivals) may be supportive of dominance, in another . . . the catalyst for revolution" (Miller 1989).

References

Abeles, Marc. 1981. In Search of the Monarch: Introduction of the State Among the Gamo of Ethiopia. In *Modes of Production in Africa: The Precolonial Era*, Donald Crummey and C. C. Stewart, eds. Pp. 35–67. Beverly Hills: Sage.

Adams, A. T. 1961. *The Explorations of Pierre Esprit Radisson.* Minneapolis: Ross & Haines.

Adams, Richard N. 1975. *Energy and Structure: A Theory of Social Power.* Austin: University of Texas Press.

Adams, Robert M. 1956. Some Hypotheses on the Development of Early Civilizations. *American Antiquity* 21:227–32.

Adams, Robert McC., and Hans J. Nissen. 1972. *The Uruk Countryside: The Natural Setting of Urban Societies.* Chicago: University of Chicago Press.

Alexander, J., and P. Alexander. 1982. Shared Poverty as an Ideology: Agrarian Relationships in Colonial Java. *Man* 17:597–619.

Alland, Alexander, Jr. 1975. Adaptation. *Annual Review of Anthropology* 4:59–73.

Althusser, Louis. 1971. *Lenin and Philosophy and Other Essays.* London: New Left Books.

1974. *For Marx.* New York: Vintage Press.

Amariglio, Jack. 1984. Forms of the Commune and Primitive Communal Class Processes. Association for Economic and Social Analysis Discussion Paper 19. Amherst: Department of Economics, University of Massachusetts.

264

References

Anderson, J. E. 1964. *The People of Fairty: An Osteological Analysis of an Iroquois Ossuary*. Ottawa: National Museum of Canada Bulletin 193:28–129.

Anderson, K. 1985. Commodity Exchange and Subordination: Montagnais–Naskapi and Huron Women, 1600–1650. *Signs, Journal of Women in Culture and Society* 11:48–62.

Anderson, P. 1974. *Passages from Antiquity to Feudalism*. London: New Left Books.

Anyon, R., S. Collins, and K. Bennett (editors). 1983. *Archaeological Investigations between Manuelito Canyon and Whitewater Arroyo, Northwest New Mexico*. 2 vols. Zuni Archaeological Program Report 185.

Ardrey, Robert. 1961. *African Genesis*. New York: Atheneum.
1966. *The Territorial Imperative*. New York: Atheneum.

Asad, T. 1979. Anthropology and the Analysis of Ideology. *Man* 14:607–27.

Atkinson, R. R. 1976. State Formation and Development in Western Acholi. In *The Central Lwo During the Aconya*, J. Onyango-Ku-Odongo and J. B. Webster, eds. Pp. 262–90. Nairobi: East African Literature Bureau.

Axelrod, Robert. 1984. *The Evolution of Cooperation*. New York: Basic Books.

Bargatsky, Thomas. 1984. Culture, Environment, and the Ills of Adaptationism. *Current Anthropology* 25:399–415.

Barker, G. and C. Gamble. 1986. Beyond Domestication: A Strategy for Investigating the Process and Consequence of Social Complexity. In *Beyond Domestication in Prehistoric Europe*, G. Barker and C. Gamble, eds. Pp. 1–31. London: Academic Press.

Barlett, Peggy F. 1976. Labor Efficiency and the Mechanism of Agricultural Evolution. *Journal of Anthropological Research* 32:124–40.
1987. Industrial Agriculture in Evolutionary Perspective. *Cultural Anthropology* 2:137–54.

Barry, Brian and Russell Hardin. 1982 (eds.). *Rational Man and Irrational Society?* Beverly Hills, CA: Sage.

Barth, F. 1961. *Nomads of South Persia: The Basseri Tribe of the Khamseh Confederacy*. New York: Humanities Press.

Bastien, J. W. 1978. *Mountain of the Condor*. Prospect Heights, IL: Waveland Press.

Bates, Daniel G., and Susan H. Lees. 1979. The Myth of Population Regulation. In *Evolutionary Biology and Human Social Behavior*, N. A. Chagnon and W. Irons, eds. North Scituate, MA: Duxbury Press.

Bayliss-Smith, T. P. 1982. *The Ecology of Agricultural Systems*. Cambridge, England: Cambridge University Press.

Becker, Gary S. 1981. *A Treatise on the Family*. Cambridge, MA: Harvard University Press.

265

Befu, H. 1968a. Ecology, Residence and Authority: The Corporate Household in Central Japan. *Ethnology* 7:25–42.

1968b. Origin of Large Households and Duolocal Residence in Central Japan. *American Anthropologist* 70:309–20.

Bender, Barbara. 1978. Gatherer-Hunter to Farmer: A Social Perspective. *World Archaeology* 10(2):204–22.

1985a. Emergent Tribal Formation in the American Midcontinent. *American Antiquity* 50(1):52–62.

1985b. Prehistoric Developments in the American Midcontinent and in Brittany, Northwest France. In *Prehistoric Hunter-Gatherers: The Emergence of Cultural Complexity*, T. Douglas Price and James A. Brown, eds. Pp 21–57. New York: Academic Press.

1986. *The Archaeology of Brittany, Normandy, and the Channel Islands*. London: Faber & Faber.

1989. The Roots of Inequality. In *Domination and Resistance*, D. Miller, M. Rowlands, and C. Tilley, eds. London: Hyman Unwin.

Bender, B. and B. Morris. in press. Introduction. In *History, Evolution and Social Change in Hunter-Gatherer Societies*, T. Ingold, D. Riches, and T. Woodburn, eds. London: Berg Publishers.

Bennett, John W. 1969. *Northern Plainsmen: Adaptive Strategy and Agrarian Life*. Chicago: Aldine.

Bentley, Jeffrey W. 1986. Ethnographic Study of a Rural Parish in Northwest Portugal. Ph.D. dissertation, Department of Anthropology, University of Arizona.

Bern, J. 1986. Is the Premise of Egalitarianism Inequality? Essays in Honor of Chandra Jayawardena. MS.

Berthoud, G. and F. Sabelli. 1979. Our Obsolete Production Mentality: The Heresy of the Communal Formation. *Current Anthropology* 20:745–60.

Binford, Lewis R. 1962. Archaeology as Anthropology. *American Antiquity* 28:217–25.

1968a. Post-Pleistocene Adaptations. In *New Perspectives in Archaeology*, S. and L. Binford, eds. Pp. 313–41. Chicago: Aldine.

1968b. Some Comments on Historical versus Processual Archaeology. *Southwestern Journal of Anthropology* 24:267–75.

1982. Objectivity, Explanation, Archaeology 1981. In *Theory and Explanation in Archaeology*, C. Renfrew, M. Rowlands, and B. Segraves, eds. Pp. 126–43. New York: Academic Press.

1983. *In Pursuit of the Past*. London: Thames & Hudson.

Binford, Lewis R., and W. J. Chasko, Jr. 1976. Nunamiut Demographic History: A Provocative Case. In *Demographic Anthropology*, E. B. W. Zubrow, ed. Pp. 63–143. Albuquerque: Univeresity of New Mexico Press.

Binswanger, Hans P., and Mark R. Rosenzweig. 1982. *Production Relations in Agriculture*. Report No. ARU5. Research Unit,

References

Agriculture and Rural Development Department, Operational Policy
Staff, World Bank.

Blair, E. H. 1911–12 (ed). *The Indian Tribes of the Upper Mississippi
Valley and Region of the Great Lakes.* 2 vols. Cleveland: Clark.

Blanton, Richard E. 1975. The Cybernetic Analysis of Human Population
Growth. In *Studies in Archaeology and Biological Anthropology: A
Symposium*, A. C. Swedlund, ed. Pp. 116–26. Memoirs of the
Society for American Archaeology 30.

Blanton, Richard E., S. Kowalewski, G. Feinman, and J. Appel. 1981.
Ancient Mesoamerica: A Comparison of Change in Three Regions.
Cambridge, England: Cambridge University Press.

Blasi, Joseph R. 1986. *The Communal Experience of the Kibbutz.* New
Brunswick, NJ: Transaction Books.

Blau, Peter M. 1977. *Inequality and Heterogeneity.* New York: Free Press.

Bloch, Maurice. 1980. Ritual Symbolism and the Nonrepresentation of
Society. In *Symbols as Sense*, M. LeCron Foster and S. Brandes, eds.
Pp. 93–102. New York: Academic Press.

   1983. *Marxism and Anthropology.* Oxford: Oxford University Press.

Boas, Franz. 1966 [1897]. *Kwakiutl Ethnography.* Chicago: University of
Chicago Press.

Boehm de Lameiras, B. 1989. In *State and Society: The Emergence and
Development of Social Hierarchy and Political Centralization*,
J. Gledhill, B. Bender, and M. Larson, eds. Pp. 231–46. London:
Hyman Unwin.

Bohannan, Laura. 1952. A Genealogical Charter. *Africa* 22:301–15.

Bohannan, P. 1954. The Migration and Expansion of the Tiv. *Africa*
24:2–16.

Boserup, Ester. 1965. *The Conditions of Agricultural Growth.* Chicago:
Aldine.

   1970. Present and Potential Food Production in Developing Countries.
In *Geography and a Crowding World*, W. Zelinsky, L. A. Kosinski,
R. Mansell Prothero, eds. London: Oxford University Press.

   1981. *Population and Technological Change: A Study of Long Term
Trends.* Chicago: University of Chicago Press.

   1985. Economic and Demographic Interrelationships in Sub-Saharan
Africa. *Population and Development Review* 11:383–97.

Bottomore, Thomas B., Laurence Harris, V. G. Kiernan, and Ralph
Miliband. 1983 (eds). *A Dictionary of Marxist Thought.* Cambridge,
MA: Harvard University Press (Leacock quote, p. 394).

Bourdieu, P. 1977. *Outline of a Theory of Practice.* Cambridge, England:
Cambridge University Press.

Boyd, Robert and Peter J. Richerson. 1985. *Culture and the Evolutionary
Process.* Chicago: University of Chicago Press.

Bradfield, M. 1971. The Changing Patterns of Hopi Agriculture. Occasional Papers of the Royal Anthropological Institute, no. 30. London.

Bradley, Richard J. 1982. The Destruction of Wealth in Later Prehistory. *Man* 17:108–22.

Bradley, Richard J., and Ian Hodder. 1979. British Prehistory: An Integrated View. *Man* 14:93–104.

Braidwood, R. J., and L. J. Braidwood. 1953. The Earliest Village Communities of Southwestern Asia. *Journal of World History* 1:278–310.

Braun, David P. 1985. Absolute Seriation: A Time-Series Approach. In *For Concordance in Archaeological Analysis*, C. Carr, ed. Pp. 509–39. Kansas City: Westport Publishers.

    1989. Are there Cross-Cultural Regularities in Tribal Social Practices? In *Between Bands and States*, Susan Gregg, ed. Southern Illinois University, Center for Archaeological Investigations, Occasional Paper no. 9, in press. Carbondale, Illinois.

Braun, David P., and Stephen Plog. 1982. Evolution of "Tribal" Social Networks: Theory and Prehistoric North American Evidence. *American Antiquity* 47:504–25.

Braun, Rudolf. 1978. Early Industrialization and Demographic Changes in the Canton of Zurich. In *Historical Studies of Changing Fertility*, Charles Tilly, ed. Pp. 289–334. Princeton: Princeton University Press.

Brookfield, H. C. 1968. New Directions in the Study of Agricultural Systems in Tropical Areas. In *Evolution and Environment*, E. T. Drake, ed. Pp. 413–39. New Haven: Yale University Press.

Brookfield, H. C., and D. Hart. 1971. *Melanesia: A Geographical Interpretation of an Island World*. London: Methuen.

Brose, D. S. 1970. *The Summer Island Site*. Cleveland: Case Western Reserve University Studies in Anthropology 1.

Brown, J. 1970. Economic Organization and the Position of Women Among the Iroquois. *Ethnohistory* 17:151–67.

Brown, J., and T. D. Price. 1985. Complex Hunter-Gatherers: Retrospect and Prospect. In *Prehistoric Hunter-Gatherers: The Emergence of Cultural Complexity*, T. Price and J. Brown, eds. Pp. 221–53. Orlando: Academic Press.

Brown, Paula and A. Podolefsky. 1976. Population Density, Agricultural Intensity, Land Tenure, and Group Size in the New Guinea Highlands. *Ethnology* 15:211–38.

Brumfiel, Elizabeth. 1976. Specialization and Exchange in the Late Postclassic (Aztec) Community of Huexotla, Mexico. Ph.D. dissertation, Department of Anthropology, University of Michigan. Ann Arbor: University Microfilms.

Brumfiel, Elizabeth, and Timothy Earle. 1987. Specialization, Exchange, and Complex Societies: An Introduction. In *Specialization, Exchange, and Complex Society*, E. Brumfiel and T. Earle, eds. Pp. 1–9. Cambridge, England: Cambridge University Press.

Brush, Stephen B. 1977. *Mountain, Field and Family: The Economy and*

268

Human Ecology of an Andean Valley. Philadelphia: University of Pennsylvania Press.

Buell, N. S. 1979. The Proto-Iroquoian Homeland. Master's thesis, Department of Anthropology, State University of New York at Albany.

Burger, Richard. 1978. The Occupation of Chavin, Ancash in the Initial Period and Early Horizon. Ph.D. dissertation, University of California, Berkeley. Ann Arbor: University Microfilms.

Burnham, Philip. 1980. *Opportunity and Constraint in a Savanna Society.* New York: Academic Press.

Cabral, Amilcar. 1972. The Weapon of Theory. In *Return to the Source: Selected Speeches.* Pp. 61–86. New York and London: Monthly Review Press.

Cain, Mead T. 1980. The Economic Activities of Children in a Village in Bangladesh. In *Rural Household Studies in Asia,* H. P. Binswanger, R. E. Evenson, C. A. Florencia, B. N. F. White, eds. Pp. 218–47. Singapore: Singapore University Press.

Carneiro, Robert L. 1926. Scale Analysis as an Instrument for the Study of Cultural Evolution. *Southwestern Journal of Anthropology* 18:149–69.

   1963. The Application of Scale Analysis to the Study of Cultural Evolution. *Transactions of the New York Academy of Sciences,* Series II, 26(2):196–207.

   1970. A Theory of the Origin of the State. *Science* 169:733–38.

   1981. The Chiefdom: Precursor of the State. In *The Transition to Statehood in the New World,* Grant D. Jones and Robert R. Dantz, eds. Pp. 37–79. Cambridge, England: Cambridge University Press.

Cashdan, Elizabeth A. 1980. Egalitarianism among Hunters and Gatherers. *American Anthropologist* 82:116–20.

   1985. Coping with Risk: Reciprocity among the Basarwa of Northern Botswana. *Man* 20:454–74.

Champlain, Samuel de. 1922–36. *The Works of Samuel de Champlain.* 6 vols. H. P. Biggar, ed. Toronto: The Champlain Society.

Chayanov, A. V. 1966. *The Theory of Peasant Economy.* D. Thorner, B. Kerblay, R. E. F. Smith, eds. Homewood, IL: American Economic Association.

Childe, E. Gordon. 1951 [1936]. *Man Makes Himself.* New York: New American Library.

Clastres, Pierre. 1977. *Society Against the State.* New York: Urizen Books.

Clermont, Norman. 1980. L'Augmentation de la population chez les iroquoiens préhistoriques. *Recherches amérindiennes au Quebec* 10:159–63.

Cohen, M. N. 1977. *The Food Crisis in Prehistory: Overpopulation and the Origins of Agriculture.* New Haven: Yale University Press.

Conkey, M. W. 1978. Style and Information in Cultural Evolution:

269

Toward a Predictive Model for the Paleolithic. In *Social Archaeology: Subsistence and Dating*, C. Redman et al., eds. Pp. 61–85. New York: Academic Press.

1980. Context, Structure and Efficacy in Paleolithic Art and Design. In *Symbols as Sense*, M. L. Foster and S. H. Branndes, eds. Pp. 225–48. New York: Academic Press.

Conklin, H. C. 1961. The Study of Shifting Cultivation. *Current Anthropology* 2:27–61.

1980. *Ethnographic Atlas of Ifugao: A Study of Environment, Culture, and Society in Northern Luzon.* New Haven: Yale University Press.

Connelly, John C. 1979. Hopi Social Organization. In *Handbook of North American Indians*, vol. 9, A. Ortiz, ed. Pp. 539–53. Washington DC: Smithsonian Institution Press.

Cook, Scott. 1977. Beyond the Foremen: Towards a Revised Marxist Theory of Pre-Capitalist Formations and the Transition to Capitalism. *Journal of Peasant Studies* 4:360–89.

Cordell, Linda S. 1984a. *Prehistory of the Southwest*. Orlando: Academic Press.

1984b. Southwestern Archaeology. *Annual Review of Anthropology* 13:301–32.

Cordell, Linda S., and Fred Plog. 1979. Escaping the Confines of Normative Thought: A Reevaluation of Puebloan Prehistory. *American Antiquity* 44:405–29.

Corning, Peter A. 1983. *The Synergism Hypothesis: A Theory of Progressive Evolution.* New York: McGraw-Hill.

Costin, Cathy L. 1984. The Organization and Intensity of Spinning and Cloth Production among the Late Prehispanic Huanca. Paper presented at the 24th Annual Meeting of the Institute for Andean Studies, Berkeley, CA.

1986. From Chiefdom to Empire State: Ceramic Economy among the Prehispanic Wanka of Highland Peru. Ph.D. dissertation, Anthropology Department, University of California, Los Angeles. Ann Arbor: University Microfilms.

Cowgill, G. L. 1975. On Causes and Consequences of Ancient and Modern Population Changes. *American Anthropologist* 77:505–25.

Cross, J. 1983. Organizational Options for Non-Subsistence Production in the Late Archaic. Paper presented at the 48th Annual Meeting of the Society for American Archaeology, Pittsburgh.

Dahl, R. A., and E. R. Tufte. 1973. *Size and Democracy*. Stanford, California: Stanford University Press.

Dalton, George. 1977. Aboriginal Economies in Stateless Societies. In *Exchange Systems in Prehistory*, T. Earle and J. Ericson, eds. Pp. 191–212. New York: Academic Press.

Damas, D. 1969 (ed.). *Ecological Essays*. Ottawa: National Museum of Canada Bulletin 230.

Dean, J., R. Euler, G. Gumerman, F. Plog, R. Hevly, and T. Karlstrom.

1985. Human Behavior, Demography, and Paleoenvironment on the Colorado Plateau. *American Antiquity* 50:537–54.

DeGarmo, Glen. 1976. Identification of Prehistoric Intrasettlement Exchange. In *Exchange Systems in Prehistory*, T. Earle and J. Ericson, eds. Pp. 153–70. New York: Academic Press.

Diamond, Stanley. 1974. *In Search of the Primitive: A Critique of Civilization*. New Brunswick, NJ: Transaction Books.

Diener, Paul, Donald Nonini, and Eugene E. Robkin. 1980. Ecology and Evolution in Cultural Anthropology. *Man* 15:1–31.

Dincauze, D. F. and R. J. Hasenstab. 1986. Explaining the Iroquois: Tribalization on a Prehistoric Periphery. Paper prepared for precirculation for the session on "Center–Periphery Relations" in the topic "Comparative Studies in the Development of Complex Societies." Southampton, England: World Archaeological Congress.

Dobyns, H. F. 1983. *Their Number Became Thinned: Native American Population Dynamics in Eastern North America*. Knoxville: University of Tennessee Press.

Dodd, C. F. 1984. *Ontario Iroquois Tradition Longhouses*. Ottawa: Archaeological Survey of Canada, Mercury Series 124:181–437.

Drennan, Robert D. 1984a. Long-Distance Transport Costs in Prehispanic Mesoamerica. *American Anthropologist* 88(1):105–14.

1984b. Long-Distance Movement of Goods in the Mesoamerican Formative and Classic. *American Antiquity* 49(1):27–43.

Drucker, C. B. 1977. To Inherit the Land: Descent and Decision in Northern Luzon. *Ethnology* 16:1–20.

Dunnell, Robert C. 1978. Style and Function: A Fundamental Dichotomy. *American Antiquity* 43:192–202.

1980. Evolutionary Theory and Archaeology. *Advances in Archaeological Method and Theory* 3:35–99.

1982. Science, Social Science, and Common Sense: The Agonizing Dilemma of Modern Archaeology. *Journal of Anthropological Research* 38:1–25.

1986. Methodological Issues in Americanist Archaeology. In *PSA 1984*, vol. 2, P. D. Asquity and P. Kitchner, eds. Pp. 717–44. E. Lansing, MI: Philosophy of Science Association.

Durham, William H. 1982. Interactions of Genetic and Cultural Evolution: Models and Examples. *Human Ecology* 10:289–323.

Durkheim, Emile. 1963 [1895]. *Primitive Classification*. Chicago: University of Chicago Press.

Dyson-Hudson, Rada, and Eric A. Smith. 1978. Human Territoriality: An Ecological Reassessment. *American Anthropologist* 80:21–41.

Earle, Timothy K. 1978. Economic and Social Organization of a Complex Chiefdom. Anthropological Paper 63. Ann Arbor: Museum of Anthropology, University of Michigan.

1981. Comments on Rice, Evolution of Specialized Production, a Trial Model. *Current Anthropology* 22(3):230–31.

1987. Specialization and the Production of Wealth: Hawaiian Chiefdoms and the Inka Empire. In *Specialization, Exchange, and Complex Societies*, E. Brumfiel and T. Earle, eds. Pp. 64–75, Cambridge, England: Cambridge University Press.

Earle, Timothy K., and Andrew L. Christenson. 1980 (eds.). *Modeling Change in Prehistoric Subsistence Economies*. New York: Academic Press.

Earle, Timothy K., Terence D'Altroy, Christine Hastorf, Catherine Scott, Cathy Costin, Glenn Russell, and Elsie Sandefur. 1987. *The Effects of Inka Conquest on the Wanka Domestic Economy*. Los Angeles: Institute of Archaeology, University of California.

Earle, Timothy K., Terence D'Altroy, Catherine LeBlanc, Christine Hastorf, and Terry LeVine. 1980. Changing Settlement Pattern in the Yanamarca Valley, Peru. *Journal of New World Archaeology* 4(1):1–93.

Eder, James F. 1982. *Who Shall Succeed? Agricultural Development and Social Inequality on a Philippine Frontier*. Cambridge, England: Cambridge University Press.

Edholm, F., O. Harris, and K. Young. 1977. Conceptualizing Women. *Critique of Anthropology* nos. 8 and 9.

Eggan, F. 1950. *Social Organization of the Western Pueblos*. Chicago: University of Chicago Press.

Ekholm, K. 1972. *Power and Prestige: The Rise and Fall of the Kongo Kingdom*. Uppsala: Akademisk Avhandling.

Elias, N. 1982. *Power and Civility: The Civilizing Process*. Vol. II. New York: Pantheon Books.

Ellen, Roy. 1982. *Environment, Subsistence and System: The Ecology of Small-Scale Social Formations*. Cambridge, England: Cambridge University Press.

Ember, Carol R. 1983. The Relative Decline in Women's Contribution to Agriculture with Intensification. *American Anthropologist* 85:285–304.

Ember, M. 1973. An Archaeological Indicator of Matrilocal versus Patrilocal Residence. *American Antiquity* 38:177–82.

Ember, M., and Carol R. Ember. 1983 (eds.). *Marriage, Family, and Kinship: Comparative Studies of Social Organization*. New Haven: HRAF Press.

Engelbrecht, W. E. 1974. The Iroquois: Archaeological Patterning on the Tribal Level. *World Archaeology* 6:52–65.

1986. New York Iroquois Political Development. In *Cultures in Contrast*, W. N. Fitzhugh, ed. Pp. 163–83. Washington DC: Smithsonian Institution Press.

1987. Factors Maintaining Low Population Density among the Prehistoric New York State Iroquois. *American Antiquity* 52:13–27.

Engels, F. 1972 [1884]. *The Origin of the Family, Private Property, and the State*. E. Leacock, ed. New York: International Publishing Co.

Erasmus, Charles. 1956. Culture, Structure and Process: The Occurrence

272

and Disappearance of Reciprocal Farm Labor. *Southwestern Journal of Anthropology* 12:444–69.

Evans-Pritchard, E. E. 1951. *Kinship and Marriage among the Nuer.* London: Oxford University Press.

Euler, Robert C., George J. Gumerman, Thor N. V. Karlstrom, Jeffrey S. Dean, and Richard H. Hevly. 1979. The Colorado Plateau: Cultural Dynamics and Paleo-Environment. *Science* 205:1089–1101.

Fallers, Lloyd. 1973. *Inequality: Social Stratification Reconsidered.* Chicago: University of Chicago Press.

Fecteau, R. D. 1985. The Introduction and Diffusion of Cultivated Plants in Southern Ontario. Master's thesis, Department of Geography, York University.

Feinman, G., and J. Neitzel. 1984. Too Many Types: An Overview of Sedentary Prestate Societies in the Americas. In *Advances in Archaeological Method and Theory*, vol. 7, M. B. Schiffer, ed. Pp. 39–102. New York: Academic Press.

Fenton, W. N. 1941. *Iroquois Suicide: A Study in the Stability of a Culture Pattern.* Washington: Bureau of American Ethnology Bulletin 128:79–138.

1957. Seneca Indians by Asher Wright [1859]. *Ethnohistory* 4:302–21.

1978. Northern Iroquoian Cultural Patterns. In *Handbook of North American Indians*, vol. 15, *Northeast*, ed. B. G. Trigger. Pp. 296–321. Washington DC: Smithsonian Institution Press.

Finlayson, W. D. 1985. *The 1975 and 1978 Rescue Excavations at the Draper Site: Introduction and Settlement Patterns.* Ottawa: Archaeological Survey of Canada, Mercury Series 130.

Flannery, Kent V. 1967. Culture History v. Culture Process: A Debate in American Archaeology. *Scientific American* 217(2):119–22.

1968. The Olmec and the Valley of Oaxaca: A Model for Interregional Interaction in Formative Times. In *Dumbarton Oaks Conference on the Olmec*, E. Benson, ed. Pp. 79–110. Washington DC: Dumbarton Oaks.

1969. Origins and Ecological Effects of Early Domestication in Iran and the Near East. In *The Domestication and Exploitation of Plants and Animals*, P. J. Ucko and G. W. Dimbleby, eds. Pp. 73–100. Chicago: Aldine-Atherton, Inc.

1972a. Culture History v. Culture Process: A Debate in American Archaeology. In *Contemporary Archaeology*, M. Leone, ed. Pp. 102–107. Carbondale and Edwardsville: Southern Illinois University Press.

1972b. The Cultural Evolution of Civilization. *Annual Review of Ecology and Systematics* 3:399–426.

1972c. The Origins of the Village as a Settlement Type in Mesoamerica and the Near East: A Comparative Study. In *Man, Settlement and Urbanism*, P. U. Ucko, R. Tringham, and G. W. Dimbleby, eds. Pp. 321–36. London: Duckworth.

1973. The Origins of Agriculture. *Annual Review of Anthropology* 2:271–310.

Flannery, Kent V., A. V. T. Kirkby, M. J. Kirkby, and A. W. Williams. 1967. Farming Systems and Political Growth in Oaxaca. *Science* 158:445–54.

Flannery, Kent V., and Joyce Marcus. 1976a. Evolution of the Public Building in Formative Oaxaca. In *Cultural Continuity and Change*, C. E. Cleland, ed. Pp. 205–32. New York: Academic Press.
    1976b. Formative Oaxaca and the Zapotec Cosmos. *American Scientist* 64:374–83.

Flannery, Kent V., Joyce Marcus, and Stephen A. Kowalewski. 1981. The Preceramic and Formative of the Valley of Oaxaca. In *Supplement to the Handbook of Middle American Indians*, vol. 1, J. A. Sabloff, ed. Pp. 164–86. Austin: University of Texas Press.

Flannery, Kent V., and Marcus C. Winter. 1976. Analysis on the Household Level. In *The Early Mesoamerican Village*, Kent V. Flannery, ed. Pp. 13–31. New York: Academic Press.

Folbre, Nancy. 1984. Household Production in the Philippines: A Non-Neoclassical Approach. *Economic Development and Cultural Change* 32:303–30.

Ford, Richard I. 1968. Jemez Cave and its Place in an Early Horticultural Settlement Pattern. Paper presented at the 33rd Annual Meeting of the Society for American Archaeology, Santa Fe, New Mexico.
    1974. Northeastern Archaeology: Past and Future Directions. *Annual Review of Anthropology* 3:385–413.
    1984. Ecological Consequences of Early Agriculture in the Southwest. In *Papers on Archaeology of Black Mesa, Arizona*, vol. 2, S. Plog and S. Powell, eds. Pp. 34–48. Carbondale: Southern Illinois University Press.

Forde, D. 1947. The Anthropological Approach in Social Science. *Advances in Science* 4:213–24.

Fortes, Meyer. 1945. *The Dynamics of Clanship among the Tallensi*. London: Oxford University Press.
    1969. *Kinship and the Social Order*. Chicago: Aldine.

Fortes, Meyer, and E. E. Evans-Pritchard. 1940. *African Political Systems*. London: Oxford University Press.

Foster, Brian L. 1977. Trade, Social Conflict, and Social Integration: Rethinking Some Old Ideas on Exchange. In *Economic Exchange and Social Interaction in Southeast Asia*, K. Hutterer, ed. Pp. 111–31. Michigan Papers on South and Southeast Asia 13.

Foster-Carter, A. 1976. The Modes of Production Controversy. *New Left Review* 107:47–77.

Foucault, Michel. 1977. *Discipline and Punish*. New York: Vintage Books.
    1984. Truth and Power. In *Foucault Reader*, P. Rabinow, ed. Pp. 51–75. New York: Pantheon Books.

References

Frankenstein, S., and M. Rowlands. 1978. *The Internal Structure and Regional Context of Early Iron Age Society in South West Germany.* London: Institute of Archaeology Bulletin 15:73–112.
Freeman, J. D. 1955. *Iban Agriculture.* Colonial Research Studies 18. London: Colonial Office.
Fried, Morton. 1967. *The Evolution of Political Society: An Essay in Political Anthropology.* New York: Random House.
   1975. *The Notion of Tribe.* Menlo Park, CA: Cummings Publishing Co.
Friedman, Jonathan. 1974. Marxism, Structuralism and Vulgar Materialism. *Man* 9:444–69.
   1975. Tribes, States and Transformations. In *Marxist Analyses and Social Anthropology*, M. Bloch, ed. Pp. 161–201. London: Malaby.
   1979a. Hegelian Ecology: Between Rousseau and the World Spirit. In *Social and Ecological Systems.* P. Burnham and R. F. Ellen, eds. Pp. 253–70. New York: Academic Press.
   1979b. *System, Structure and Contradiction in the Evolution of "Asiatic" Social Formations.* Copenhagen: National Museum of Denmark.
   1981. Notes on Structure and History in Oceania. *Folk* 23:275–95.
   1982. Catastrophe and Continuity in Social Evolution. In *Theory and Explanation in Archaeology: The Southampton Conference,* C. Renfrew, M. J. Rowlands, and B. A. Segraves, eds. Pp. 175–96. New York: Academic Press.
Friedman, Jonathan, and M. J. Rowlands. 1978 (eds.). *The Evolution of Social Systems.* Pittsburgh: University of Pittsburgh Press.
Fuller, Peter. 1980. *Beyond the Crisis in Art.* London: Writers and Readers.
Gailey, C. 1985. The Kindness of Strangers: Transformations of Kinship in Precapitalist Class and State Formation. *Culture* 5:3–16.
Gailey, Christine W. and Thomas C. Patterson. 1987. Power Relations and State Formation. In *Power Relations and State Formation.* Thomas C. Patterson and Christine W. Gailey, eds. Pp. 1–25. Washington DC: American Archaeological Association.
   1989. State Formation and Uneven Development. In *State and Society. The Emergence and Development of Social Hierarchy and Political Centralization.* J. Gledhill, B. Bender, and M. T. Larson, eds. Pp. 77–90. London: Hyman Unwin.
Gall, P. and A. H. Saxe. 1977. The Ecological Evolution of Culture: The State as Predator in Succession Theory. In *Exchange Systems in Prehistory*, T. K. Earle and J. E. Ericson, eds. Pp. 255–68. New York: Academic Press.
Gamble, Clive. 1982. Leadership and "Surplus" Production. In *Ranking and Exchange, Aspects of the Archaeology of Early European Society,* C. Renfrew and S. Shennan, eds. Pp. 100–105. Cambridge, England: Cambridge University Press.

1986. Hunter-Gatherers and the Origin of States. In *States in History*, J. Hall, ed. Pp. 22–47. Oxford: Basil Blackwell.

Gearing, Fred. 1962. *Priests and Warriors*. Memoirs of the American Anthropological Association 93.

Geertz, Clifford. 1963. *Agricultural Involution*. Berkeley: University of California Press.

1972. The Wet and the Dry: Traditional Irrigation in Bali and Morocco. *Human Ecology* 1:23–40.

Geras, Norman. 1983. *Marx and Human Nature: Refutation of a Legend*. London: Verso.

Gero, J. 1985. Socio-Politics and the Woman-at-Home Ideology. *American Antiquity* 50:342–50.

Gibbon, Guy. 1984. *Anthropological Archaeology*. New York: Columbia University Press.

Giddens, Anthony. 1979. *Central Problems in Social Theory*. London: Macmillan.

Gilsenan, M. 1986. Domination as Social Practice. *Critique of Anthropology* VI:17–37.

Gleave, M. B., and H. P. White. 1969. Population Density and Agricultural System in West Africa. In *Environment and Land Use in Africa*, M. F. Thomas and G. W. Whittington, eds. Pp. 273–300. London: Methuen.

Gledhill, John. 1978. Formative Development in the North American Southwest. In *Social Organization and Settlement*, D. Green, C. Haselgrove, and M. Spriggs, eds. Oxford: British Archaeological Reports, International Series 47:241–90.

1981. Time's Arrow: Anthropology, History, Social Evolution and Marxist Theory. *Critique of Anthropology* 16:3–30.

1986. Evolution and the Triumph of Homology, or Why History Matters. *American Scientist* 74:60–69.

1989. Introduction: The Comparative Analysis of Social and Political Transitions. In *State and Society: The Emergence and Development of Social Hierarchy and Political Centralization*, J. Gledhill, B. Bender, and M. Larsen, eds. London: Hyman Unwin.

Gluckman, Max. 1960. The Rise of a Zulu Empire. *Scientific American*. April, 1960. Pp. 157–68.

1962 (ed.). *Essays on the Ritual of Social Relations*. Manchester, England: Manchester University Press.

Goddard, A. D. 1972. Land Tenure, Land Holding and Agricultural Development in the Sokoto Close-Settled Zone. *Savanna* 1:29–41.

Goddard, A. D., M. J. Mortimore, and D. W. Norman. 1975. Some Social and Economic Implications of Population Growth in Rural Hausaland. In *Population Growth and Socio-Economic Change in West Africa*, J. C. Caldwell, ed. Pp. 321–36. New York: Columbia University Press.

References

Godelier, Maurice. 1978. Territory and Property in Primitive Society. *Social Science Information* 17:399–426.

Goldman, I. 1970. *Ancient Polynesian Society*. Chicago: University of Chicago Press.

Goodenough, Ward H. 1965. Rethinking "Status" and "Role": Toward a General Model of the Cultural Organization of Social Relationships. In *The Relevance of Models for Social Anthropology*. M. Banton, ed. Pp. 1–24. ASA Monograph 1.

Goody, Jack. 1977. Population and Polity in the Voltaic Region. In *The Evolution of Social Systems*, J. Friedman and M. J. Rowlands, eds. Pp. 535–45. London: Duckworth.

Gorman, Frederick J. E., and S. Terry Childs. 1981. Is Prudden's Unit Type of Anasazi Settlement Valid and Reliable? *North American Archaeologist* 2:153–92.

Gould, Stephen J. 1982. Darwinism and the Expansion of Evolutionary Theory. *Science* 216:380–87.

1986. Evolution and the Triumph of Homology, or Why History Matters. *American Scientist* 74:60–69.

Gould, Stephen J., and Richard C. Lewontin. 1978. The Spandrels of San Marco and the Panglossian Paradigm. *Proceedings of the Royal Society of London*, 1978. Pp. 581–98.

1984. Reprint of Gould and Lewontin [1978], in *Conceptual Issues in Evolutionary Biology: An Anthology*, E. Sober, ed. Pp. 252–70. Cambridge, MA: MIT Press.

Graber, Robert B. 1984. Circumscription as the Cause of Social Growth: A Mathematical Interpretation. Paper presented at the 83rd Annual Meeting of the American Anthropological Association, Denver, CO.

Gramly, R. M. 1977. Deerskins and Hunting Territories: Competition for a Scarce Resource of the Northeastern Woodlands. *American Antiquity* 42:601–605.

Graves, M., S. Holbrook, and W. Longacre. 1982. Aggregation and Abandonment at Grasshopper Pueblo: Evolutionary Trends in the Late Prehistory of East-Central Arizona. In *Multidisciplinary Research at Grasshopper Pueblo, Arizona*, W. Longacre, S. Holbrook, and M. Graves, eds. Pp. 110–22. Anthropological Papers of the University of Arizona 40.

Gray, R. F. 1963. *The Sonjo of Tanganyika*. London: Oxford University Press.

Greber, N. 1979. A Comparative Study of Site Morphology and Burial Patterns at Edwin Harness Mound and Siep Mounds 1 & 2. In *Hopewell Archaeology: The Chillicothe Conference*, D. Bross and N. Greber, eds. Pp. 27–38. Kent: Kent State University.

Greenhalgh, Susan. 1985. Is Inequality Demographically Induced? The Family Cycle and the Distribution of Income in Taiwan. *American Anthropologist* 87:571–94.

277

Greenwood, Davydd J. 1985. Egalitarian Hierarchies in the Spanish Basque Country: The Mondragon Cooperatives. Paper presented at the 84th Annual Meeting of the American Anthropological Association, Washington DC.

Gregory, C. A. 1980. Gifts to Men and Gifts to God: Gift Exchange and Capital Accumulation in Contemporary Papua. *Man* 15:626–52.

Grigg, David. 1979. Ester Boserup's Theory of Agrarian Change: A Critical View. *Progress in Human Geography* 3:64–84.

Guillet, David. 1979. *Agrarian Reform and Peasant Economy in Southern Peru*. Columbia, MO: Univerity of Missouri Press.

Haas, J. 1982. *The Evolution of the Prehistoric State*. New York: Columbia University Press.

Hall, R. L. 1979. In Search of the Ideology of the Adena–Hopewell Climax. In *Hopewell Archaeology: The Chillicothe Conference*, D. S. Brose and N. Greber, eds. Pp. 258–65. Kent: Kent State University Press.

Hamell, George. 1983. Trading in Metaphors: The Magic of Beads. In *Proceedings of the 1982 Glass Trade Bead Conference*, C. F. Hayes III, ed. Pp. 5–28. Rochester: Rochester Museum and Science Center, Research Records 16.

Hammel, E. A., and Nancy Howell. 1987. Research in Population and Culture: An Evolutionary Framework. *Current Anthropology* 28(2):141–60.

Handsman, Russell. 1985. History and Communal Class Struggles among Early Gatherer-Hunters. Paper presented at the 84th Annual Meeting of the American Anthropological Association, Washington DC.

Hanks, L. M. 1972. *Rice and Man: Agricultural Ecology in Southeast Asia*. Chicago: Aldine.

Hantman, Jeffrey L. 1983. Stylistic Distributions and Social Networks in the Prehistoric Plateau Southwest. Ph.d. dissertation, Department of Anthropology, Arizona State University. Ann Arbor: University Microfilms.

   1984. Regional Organization of the Northern Mogollon. *American Archaeology* 4:171–80.

Harner, Michael J. 1970. Population Pressure and the Social Evolution of Agriculturalists. *Southwestern Journal of Anthropology* 26:67–86.

Harris, Marvin. 1968. *The Rise of Anthropological Theory: A History of Theories of Culture*. New York: Thomas Y. Crowell Company.

   1977. *Cannibals and Kings: The Origin of Culture*. New York: Random House.

   1985. *Culture, People, Nature: An Introduction to General Anthropology*. New York: Harper & Row.

Hart, Gillian. 1980. Patterns of Household Labor Allocation in a Javanese Village. In *Rural Household Studies in Asia*, H. P. Binswanger, R. E. Evenson, A. Florencio, B. N. F. White, eds. Pp. 188–217. Singapore: Singapore University Press.

1986. *Power, Labor, and Livelihood: Processes of Change in Rural Java.* Berkeley: University of California Press.

Harvey, David. 1973. *Social Justice and the City.* London: Arnold.

Hastorf, Christine A. 1983. Prehistoric Agricultural Intensification and Political Development in the Jauja Region of Central Peru. Ph.D. dissertation, Anthropology Department, University of California, Los Angeles. Ann Arbor: University Microfilms.

n.d. Resources to Power. Manuscript in possession of the author.

Hastorf, Christine A., and Michael DeNiro. 1985. A New Isotopic Method Used to Reconstruct Prehistoric Food Plants and Cooking Practices. *Nature* 315:429–91.

Hastorf, Christine A., and Timothy Earle. 1985. Intensive Agriculture and the Geography of Political Change in the Upper Mantaro Region of Central Peru. In *Prehistoric Intensive Agriculture in the Tropics,* I. Farrington, ed. British Archaeological Reports, International Series 232:569–95.

Hastorf, Christine, Timothy Earle, Herbert Wright, Glen Russell, Cathy Costin, and Elsie Sandefur. 1986. Longterm Sausa Cultural Development: Excavations at Pancan and Regional Site Survey in the Upper Mantaro Valley Region. Preliminary report submitted to the National Institute of Culture, Lima.

Hayden, Brian. 1976. Corporate Groups and the Late Iroquoian Longhouse. *Ontario Archaeology* 28:3–16.

1978. Bigger is Better? Factors Determining Ontario Iroquois Site Sizes. *Canadian Journal of Archaeology* 2:107–16.

1979 (ed.). *Settlement Patterns of the Draper and White Sites: 1973 Excavations.* Burnaby: Simon Fraser University, Department of Archaeology, Publication 6.

Hegmon, Michelle. 1985. Exchange in Social Integration and Subsistence Risk: A Computer Simulation. Doctoral qualifying paper, Department of Anthropology, University of Michigan.

1986. Sharing as Social Integration and Risk Reduction: A Computer Simulation Involving the Hopi. Manuscript, Museum of Anthropology, University of Michigan.

Heidenreich, C. E. 1971. *Huronia: A History and Geography of the Huron Indians, 1600–1650.* Toronto: McClelland & Stewart.

Helms, Mary W. 1970. Matrilocality, Social Solidarity, and Culture Contact: Three Case Histories. *Southwestern Journal of Anthropology* 26:197–212.

1979. *Ancient Panama: Chiefs in Search of Power.* Austin: University of Texas.

Hill, James N. 1970. Broken K Pueblo: Prehistoric Social Organization in the American Southwest. Anthropological Papers of the University of Arizona 18.

1977 (ed.). *Explanation of Prehistoric Change.* Albuquerque: University of New Mexico Press.

279

Hindess, B., and P. Hirst. 1975. *Pre-Capitalist Modes of Production.* London: Routledge & Kegan Paul.

Hitchcock, R. K. 1982. Patterns of Sedentism among the Basarwa of Eastern Botswana. In *Politics and History in Band Societies,* E. Leacock and R. B. Lee, eds. Pp. 223–68. Cambridge, England: Cambridge University Press.

Hobsbawm, E. J. 1964. Introduction. In *Pre-Capitalist Economic Formation,* by Karl Marx. London: Lawrence & Wishart.

1965. *Marx's Pre-Capitalist Economic Formation.* New York: International Publishers.

Hodder, Ian. 1979. Economic and Social Stress and Material Culture Patterning. *American Antiquity* 44:446–54.

1982. *Symbols in Action.* Cambridge, England: Cambridge University Press.

1985. Postprocessual Archaeology. *Advances in Archaeological Method and Theory* 8:1–26. New York: Academic Press.

Hoskins, W. G. 1957. *The Midland Peasant.* London: Macmillan.

Howell, Nancy. 1976. Toward a Uniformitarian Theory of Human Paleodemography. In *The Demographic Evolution of Human Populations,* R. H. Ward and K. M. Weiss, eds. Pp. 25–40. New York: Academic Press.

1979. *Demography of the Dobe !Kung.* New York: Academic Press.

Hughes, D. 1975. Urban Growth and Family Structure in Medieval Genoa. *Past and Present* 66:13–17.

Hunt, Robert E., and Eva Hunt. 1976. Canal Irrigation and Local Social Organization. *Current Anthropology* 17:389–98.

Isbell, Billie Jean. 1978. *To Defend Ourselves: Ecology and Ritual in an Andean Village.* Austin: University of Texas Press.

Jackes, Mary. 1986. The Mortality of Ontario Archaeological Populations. *Canadian Journal of Anthropology* 5(2):33–48.

Jochim, Michael A. 1976. *Hunter-Gatherer Subsistence and Settlement,* A *Predictive Model.* New York: Academic Press.

1981. *Strategies for Survival: Cultural Behavior in an Ecological Context.* New York: Academic Press.

Johnson, Allen. 1972. Individuality and Experimentation in Traditional Agriculture. *Human Ecology* 1:149–59.

Johnson, Allen, and Timothy Earle. 1987. *The Evolution of Human Society.* Stanford: Stanford University Press.

Johnson, Gregory A. 1973. Local Exchange and Early State Development in Southwestern Iran. Anthropological Paper 51. Ann Arbor: Museum of Anthropology, University of Michigan.

1978. Information sources and the Development of Decision-Making Organizations. In *Social Archaeology: Beyond Subsistence and Dating,* C. Redman et al., ed. Pp. 87–112. New York: Academic Press.

1982. Organization Structure and Scalar Stress. In *Theory and Explanation in Archaeology: The Southampton Conference,*

References

C. Renfrew, M. J. Rowlands, and B. A. Segraves, eds. Pp. 89–421. New York: Academic Press.

1983. Decision-Making Organization and Pastoral Nomad Camp Size. *Human Ecology* 11:175–99.

1984. Dynamics of Southwestern Prehistory: Far Outside, Looking In. Paper presented at the Advanced Seminar on Dynamics of Southwestern Prehistory. Sante Fe, NM: School of American Research.

Johnson, R. B. 1968. The Archaeology of the Serpent Mounds Site. Toronto: Royal Ontario Museum, Occasional Paper 10.

JR, *see* Thwaites 1896–1901.

Keat, R., and J. Urry. 1981. *Social Theory as Science*. Second edition. London: Routledge & Kegan Paul.

Keene, Arthur S. 1981. *Prehistoric Foraging in a Temperate Forest: A Linear Programming Model*. New York: Academic Press.

1986. Stories We Tell: Gatherer-Hunters as Ideology. Paper presented at the 4th International Congress on Hunter-Gatherers, London.

Kelly, Raymond. 1968. Demographic Pressure and Descent Group Structure in the New Guinea Highlands. *Oceania* 30:36–63.

Kenyon, K. M. 1959. Some Observations on the Beginnings of Settlement in the Near East. *Journal of the Royal Anthropological Institute* 89(1):35–43.

Kenyon, W. A. 1982. The Grimsby Site: A Historic Neutral Cemetery. Toronto: Royal Ontario Museum, Occasional Paper 14.

Kidd, K. E. 1953. The Excavation and Historical Identification of a Huron Ossuary. *American Antiquity* 18:359–79.

Kintigh, Keith. 1984. Late Prehistoric Agricultural Strategies and Settlement in the Zuni Area. In *Prehistoric Agricultural Strategies in the Southwest*. S. Fish and P. Fish, eds. Pp. 215–32. Arizona State University Anthropological Research Paper 33.

1985. Settlement, Subsistence and Society in Late Zuni Prehistory. Anthropological Papers of the University of Arizona 44.

Kirby, Anne V. T. 1973. *The Use of Land and Water Resources in the Past and Present Valley of Oaxaca*. University of Michigan: Memoirs of the Museum of Anthropology 5.

Kirch, Patrick V. 1980. The Archaeological Study of Adaptation: Theoretical and Methodological Issues. *Advances in Archaeological Method and Theory* 3:101–56.

Kluckhohn, Clyde, and Dorothea Leighton. 1962. *The Navaho*. Garden City: Natural History Library.

Knowles, Nathaniel. 1940. The Torture of Captives by the Indians of Eastern North America. *Proceedings of the American Philosophical Society* 82:151–225.

Kohl, Philip. 1981. Materialist Approaches in Prehistory. *Annual Review of Anthropology* 10:89–118.

Konner, M., and C. Worthman. 1980. Nursing Frequency, Gonadal

Function, and Birth Spacing Among !Kung Hunter-Gatherers. *Science* 207:788–91.

Kottak, C. P. 1980. *The Past in the Present: History, Ecology, and Cultural Variation in Highland Madagascar.* Ann Arbor: University of Michigan Press.

Krader, Lawrence. 1968. *Formation of the State.* Englewood Cliffs: Prentice-Hall.

——— 1979. The Ethnological Notebooks of Karl Marx: A Commentary. In *Toward a Marxist Anthropology.* Stanley Diamond, ed. Pp. 153–84. The Hague: Mouton.

Kramer, C. 1982. *Village Ethnoarchaeology: Rural Iran in Archaeological Perspective.* New York: Academic Press.

Krauthammer, C. 1986. The Joy of Analog. *Time* 129(21):84.

Krippendorf, Klaus. 1971. Communication and the Genesis of Structure. *General Systems* 16:171–85.

Kristiansen, Kristian. 1982. The Formation of Tribal Systems in Later European Prehistory: Northern Europe, 4000–500 B.C. In *Theory and Explanation in Archaeology: The Southampton Conference,* C. Renfrew, M. J. Rowlands, and B. A. Segraves, eds. Pp. 241–80. New York: Academic Press.

——— 1984. Ideology and Material Culture: An Archaeological Perspective. In *Marxist Perspectives in Archaeology,* M. Spriggs, ed. Pp. 72–100. Cambridge, England: Cambridge University Press.

Kus, S. 1984. The Spirit and its Burden: Archaeology and Symbolic Activity. In *Marxist Perspectives in Archaeology,* M. Spriggs, ed. Pp. 101–107. Cambridge, England: Cambridge University Press.

Lafitau, Joseph-François. 1974–77 [1724]. *Customs of the American Indians.* 2 vols. William N. Fenton and Elizabeth Moore, trans. and eds. Toronto: The Champlain Society. Translation of Lafitau, Joseph-François, S. J. *Moeurs des sauvages amériquains, comparées aux moeurs des premiers temps.* Vol. II. Paris: Saugrain l'aîné.

Lagemann, Johannes. 1977. *Traditional African Farming Systems in Eastern Nigeria: An Analysis of Reaction to Increasing Population Pressure.* Munich: Weltforum Verlag.

Laslett, Peter. 1965. *The World We Have Lost.* New York: Scribner's.

Latta, M. A. 1971. Archaeology of the Penetang Peninsula. In *Paleoecology and Ontario Prehistory II,* W. M. Hurley and C. E. Heidenreich, eds. Pp. 116–36. University of Toronto: Department of Anthropology, Research Report 2.

Leach, Edmund R. 1954. *Political Systems of Highland Burma.* Cambridge, MA: Harvard University Press.

——— 1976. *Culture and Communication: The Logic by which Symbols are Connected.* Cambridge, England: Cambridge University Press.

Leacock, Eleanor B. 1954. *The Montagnais "Hunting Territory" and the Fur Trade.* Menasha, WI: American Anthropological Memoir 78.

——— 1975. Class, Commodity, and Status of Women. In *Women Cross-*

Culturally: Change and Challenge, R. Rohrilich-Leavitt, ed. Pp. 601–18. The Hague: Mouton.

1978. Women's Status in Egalitarian Society: Implication for Social Evolution. *Current Anthropology* 19(2):247–76.

1981. *Myths of Male Dominance.* New York and London: Monthly Review Press.

1982. Relations of Production in Band Society. In *Politics and History in Band Societies.* E. Leacock and R. B. Lee, eds. Pp. 159–70. Cambridge, England: Cambridge University Press.

1983. *See* Bottomore et al.

Leacock, Eleanor, and Richard B. Lee. 1982 (eds.). *Politics and History in Band Societies.* Cambridge, England: Cambridge University Press.

Leaf, Murray J. 1973. Peasant Motivation, Ecology, and Economy in Punjab. In *Contributions to Asian Studies 3*, K. Ishwaran, ed. Leiden: E. J. Brill.

LeBlanc, Catherine J. 1981. Late Prehispanic Huanca Settlement Patterns in the Yanamarca Valley, Peru. Ph.D. dissertation, Anthropology Department, University of California, Los Angeles. Ann Arbor: University Microfilms.

LeBlanc, Steven A. 1986. Aspects of Southwestern Prehistory: A.D. 900–1400. In *Ripples in the Chichimec Sea*, F. J. Mathien and R. H. McGuire, eds. Pp. 105–34. Carbondale: Southern Illinois University Press.

LeCount, L. J. 1987. Toward Defining and Explaining Fundamental Variation in Sausa Ceramics from the Upper Mantaro Valley, Peru. M.A. Thesis, Anthropology Department, University of California at Los Angeles. Los Angeles.

Lee, Richard B. 1972a. !Kung Spatial Organization: An Ecological and Historical Perspective. *Human Ecology* 1(2):125–47.

1972b. Population Growth and the Beginnings of Sedentary Life Among !Kung Bushmen. In *Population Growth: Anthropological Implications*, B. Spooner, ed. Pp. 343–50. Cambridge, MA: MIT Press.

1979. *The !Kung San.* Cambridge, England and New York: Cambridge University Press.

1981. Is there a Foraging Mode of Production? *Canadian Journal of Anthropology* 2(1):13–19.

1984. *The Dobe !Kung.* New York: Holt, Rinehart, & Winston.

1985. Greeks and Victorians: A Reexamination of Engels' Theory of the Athenian Polis. *Culture* 5(1):63–74.

in press. Reflections on Primitive Communism. In *Essays in Honor of Stanley Diamond*, C. Gailey et al., eds. New York: Columbia UP

Lee, Richard B., and Richard H. Daly. 1987. Man's Domination and Women's Oppression: The Search for Origins. In *Beyond Patriarchy*, Michael Kaufman, ed. Pp. 46–67. Toronto: Oxford University Press.

Lee, Richard B., and Irven DeVore. 1968 (eds.). *Man the Hunter.* Chicago: Aldine.

Lee, Ronald D. 1986a. Malthus and Boserup: A Dynamic Synthesis. In *The State of Population Theory*, David Coleman and Roger Schofield, eds. Pp. 96–130. Oxford: Basil Blackwell.

　　1986b. Was Malthus Right? Diminishing Returns, Homeostasis and Induced Technological Change. Program in Population Research Working Paper 21. Berkeley: University of California.

Leeds, Anthony. 1969. Ecological Determinants of Chieftainship among the Yaruro Indians of Venezuela. In *Environment and Cultural Behavior: Ecological Studies in Cultural Anthropology*. A. P. Vayda, ed. Pp. 377–94. New York: Natural History Press.

Legros, D. 1985. Wealth, Poverty and Slavery among 19th-Century Tutchone Athapaskans. *Research in Economic Anthropology 7*.

Lenig, Donald. 1965. *The Oak Hill Horizon and its Relation to the Development of Five Nations Iroquois Culture*. Buffalo: New York State Archaeological Association, Researches and Transactions 15(1).

Leonard, R. D., and G. T. Jones. 1987. Elements of an Inclusive Evolutionary Model for Archaeology. *Journal of Anthropological Archaeology* 6:199–219.

Leone, M. 1986. Symbolic, Structural, and Critical Archaeology. In *American Archaeology Past and Future*, D. Meltzer, D. Fowler, and J. Sabloff, eds. Pp. 415–38. Washington DC: Smithsonian Institution Press.

Lévi-Strauss, Claude. 1966. *The Savage Mind*. Chicago: University of Chicago Press.

Levine, D. 1977. *Family Formation in an Age of Nascent Capitalism*. New York: Academic Press.

Lewin, Kurt. 1935. *A Dynamic Theory of Personality*. New York: McGraw-Hill.

Lewontin, Richard C. 1978. *Adaptation*. Scientific American 239(3):213–30.

　　1984. Adaptation. In *Conceptual Issues in Evolutionary Biology: An Anthology*, E. Sober, ed. Pp. 235–51. Cambridge, MA: MIT Press.

Lightfoot, Kent. 1984. *Prehistoric Political Dynamics: A Case Study from the American Southwest*. Dekalb: Northern Illinois University Press.

Lilley, I. 1985. Chiefs Without Chiefdoms. *Archaeology in Oceania* 20:60–65.

Lofgren, Orvar. 1974. Family and Household among Scandinavian Peasants: An Exploratory Essay. *Ethnologia Scandinavica* 74:1–52.

Loman-Vayda, C. 1976. Maring Big Men. *Mankind* 32:21–46.

Longacre, William. 1966. Changing Patterns of Social Integration: A Prehistoric Example from the American Southwest. *American Anthropologist* 68:94–102.

Loucky, James. 1979. Production and Patterning of Social Relations and Values in Two Guatemalan Villages. *American Ethnologist* 6:702–23.

Lounsbury, F. G. 1978. Iroquoian Languages. In *Handbook of North*

American Indians, vol. 15, *Northeast*, B. G. Trigger, ed. Pp. 334–43. Washington DC: Smithsonian Institution Press.

Lourandos, H. 1980. Change or Stability? Hydraulics, Hunter-Gatherers and Population in Temperate Australia. *World Archaeology* 11:245–64.

Lowie, Robert H. 1963 [1954]. *Indians of the Plains*. Garden City: Natural History Library.

Luxton, M. 1980. *More than a Labor of Love: Three Generations of Women's Work in the Home*. Toronto: Women's Press.

MacDonald, R. I. 1986. The Coleman Site (AiHd-7): a Late Prehistoric Iroquois Village in the Waterloo Region. Master's thesis, Department of Anthropology, Trent University.

Macfarlane, Alan. 1970. *Witchcraft in Tudor and Stuart England*. London: Routledge & Kegan Paul.

McGuire, Randall. 1983. Breaking Down Cultural Complexity; Inequality and Heterogeneity. *Advances in Archaeological Methods and Theory* 6:91–142.

1985. The Muddle over Modes. Paper presented at the 50th Annual Meetings of the Society for American Archaeology, Denver, Colorado.

McGuire, Randall, and Robert McC. Netting. 1982. Leveling Peasants: The Maintenance of Equality in a Swiss Alpine Community. *American Ethnologist* 9:269–90.

McIlwain, C. H. 1915 (ed.). *An Abridgement of the Indian Affairs . . .* , by Peter Wraxall. Cambridge, MA: Harvard Historical Studies 21.

MacNeish, R. S. 1964. Ancient Mesoamerican Civilization. *Science* 143:531–7.

McPherron, Alan. 1967. On the Sociology of Ceramics: Pottery Style Clustering, Marital Residence, and Cultural Adaptations of an Algonkian–Iroquoian Border. In *Iroquois Culture, History, and Prehistory*, E. Tooker, ed. Pp. 101–107. Albany: The University of the State of New York.

Madden, Marcie. 1984. Social Network Systems amongst Hunter-Gatherers Considered within Southern Norway. In *Ideology, Power, and Prehistory*, D. Miller and C. Tilley, eds. London: Cambridge University Press.

Mann, M. 1984. The Autonomous Power of the State: Its Origins, Mechanisms and Results. *Archives Européenes de sociologie* XXV:185–213.

Marcus, Joyce. 1976. The Size of the Early Mesoamerican Village. In *The Early Mesoamerican Village*, K. V. Flannery, ed. Pp. 79–88. New York: Academic Press.

Marquardt, W. 1989. Politics and Production among the Calusa of South Florida. In *History, Evolution and Social Change in Hunter-Gatherer Societies*, T. Ingold, D. Riches, and J. Woodburn, eds. London: Berg Publishers.

Martin, D. L., G. J. Armelagos, A. H. Goodman, and D. P. Van
    Gerven. 1984. The Effects of Socioeconomic Change in Prehistoric
    Africa: Nubia as a Case Study. In *Paleopathology at the Origins of
    Agriculture*, M. N. Cohen and G. J. Armelagos, eds. Pp. 193–214.
    Orlando: Academic Press.
Marx, Karl. 1964 [1857–58]. *Pre-Capitalist Economic Formations*.
    London: Lawrence & Wishart.
    1971 [1867]. *Capital*, vol. 1: *A Critical Analysis of Capitalist
    Production*. Moscow: Progress Publishers.
    1972 [1857]. *The Grundrisse*. David McClellan, trans. and ed. New
    York: Harper & Row.
Marx, Karl, and F. Engels. 1964. *German Ideology*. London: Lawrence &
    Wishart.
Matlon, Peter J., and Dunstan S. Spencer. 1984. Increasing Food
    Production in Sub-Saharan Africa: Environmental Problems and
    Inadequate Technological Solutions. *American Journal of Agricultural
    Economics* 66:671–6.
Mauss, M. 1954. *The Gift*. Illinois: Free Press.
    1967 [1925]. *The Gift*. New York: Norton.
Mayhew, B. H. 1973. System Size and Ruling Elites. *American
    Sociological Review* 38:468–75.
Mayhew, B. H., and R. L. Levinger. 1976. On the Emergence of
    Oligarchy in Human Interaction. *American Journal of Sociology*
    81:1017–1049.
Meek, R. L. 1953. *Marx and Engels on Malthus*. London: Lawrence &
    Wishart.
Meggers, B. J. 1954. Environmental Limitation on the Development of
    Culture. *American Anthropologist* 56:801–24.
Meggitt, M. J. 1965. *The Lineage System of the Mae-Enga of New
    Guinea*. Edinburgh: Oliver & Boyd.
    1967. The Pattern of Leadership among the Mae-Enga. *Anthropological
    Forum* 2:20–35.
    1972. System and Subsystem: The Te Exchange Cycle among the Mae-
    Enga. *Human Ecology* 1:111–23.
    1974. Pigs are our Hearts: The Te Exchange Cycle among the Mae-
    Enga of New Guinea. *Oceania* 44(3):165–203.
Meillassoux, C. 1972. From Reproduction to Production: A Marxist
    Approach to Economic Anthropology. *Economy and Society*
    1:93–105.
    1981. *Maidens, Meal and Money Capitalism and the Domestic
    Economy*. Cambridge, England: Cambridge University Press.
Michels, R. 1915. *Political Parties*. Translated by F. Paul and C. Paul.
    New York: Hearst's International Library.
Miller, C. L., and G. R. Hamell. 1986. A New Perspective on Indian–
    White Contact: Cultural Symbols and Colonial Trade. *Journal of
    American History* 73:311–28.

Miller, D. 1982. Structures and Strategies: An Aspect of the Relationship between Social Hierarchy and Cultural Change. In *Symbolic and Structural Archaeology*, I. Hodder, ed. Pp. 80–98. Cambridge, England: Cambridge University Press.

    1989. The Limits of Dominance. In *Domination and Resistance*, D. Miller, M. Rowlands, and C. Tilley, eds. Pp, 63–79. London: Hyman Unwin.

Miller, Daniel, and Christopher Tilley. 1984 (eds.). *Ideology, Power and Prehistory*. Cambridge, England: Cambridge University Press.

Miller, James G. 1978. *Living Systems*. New York: McGraw-Hill.

Minnis, Paul E. 1984. Peeking under the Tortilla Curtain: Regional Exchange and Integration on the Northeast Periphery of Cases Grandes. *American Archaeology* 4:181–93.

    1985. *Social Adaptation to Food Stress: A Prehistoric Southwestern Example*. Chicago: University of Chicago Press.

Mithun, Marianne. 1984. The Proto-Iroquoians: Cultural Reconstruction from Lexical Materials. In *Extending the Rafters: Interdisciplinary Approaches to Iroquoian Studies*, M. K. Foster, et al., eds. Pp. 259–81. Albany: State University of New York Press.

Mitterauer, Michael, and Reinhard Sieder. 1979. The Development Process of Domestic Groups: Problems of Reconstruction and Possibilities of Interpretation. *Journal of Family History* 4:257–84.

Molto, J. E. 1983. *Biological Relationships of Southern Ontario Woodland Peoples: The Evidence of Discontinuous Cranial Morphology*. Ottawa: Archaeological Survey of Canada, Mercury Series 117.

Moore, James A. 1981. The Effects of Information Networks in Hunter-Gatherer Societies. In *Hunter-Gatherer Foraging Strategies: Ethnographic and Archaeological Analyses*, B. Winterhalder and E. A. Smith, eds. Pp. 194–217. Chicago: University of Chicago Press.

    1983. The Trouble with Know-It-Alls: Information as Social and Ecological Resource. In *Archaeological Hammers and Theories*, J. Moore and A. Keene, eds. Pp. 173–91. New York: Academic Press.

Moran, Emilio F. 1982. *Human Adaptability: An Introduction to Ecological Anthropology*. Boulder, CO: Westview Press.

    1984 (ed.). *The Ecosystem Concept in Anthropology*. AAAS Selected Symposium 92. Boulder, CO: Westview Press.

Morantz, Toby. 1983. *An Ethnohistoric Study of Eastern James Bay Cree Social Organization, 1800–1850*. Ottawa: National Museums of Canada.

Morgan, Lewis Henry. 1851. *League of the Ho-de-no-sau-nee, or Iroquois*. Rochester: Sage.

    1963 [1877]. *Ancient Society*. E. Leacock, ed. New York: World Publishing Co.

    1965 [1881]. *Houses and House-Life of the American Aborigines*. Chicago: University of Chicago Press.

Morgan, W. B. 1953. Farming Practice, Settlement Pattern and

Population Density in Southeastern Nigeria. *Geographical Journal* 121:320–33.

Mortimore, M. J. 1972. Land and Population Pressure in the Kano Close-Settled Zone, Northern Nigeria. In *People and Land in Africa South of the Sahara*, R. M. Prothero, ed. Pp. 60–70. New York: Oxford University Press.

Most, Rachel, and A. Trinkle Jones. 1983. Environmental and Organizational Variability on the Colorado Plateau. Paper presented at the 48th Annual Meeting of The Society for American Archaeology, Pittsburgh.

Munn, N. 1971. The Transformation of Subjects into Objects in Walbiri and Pitjantjatjara Myth. In *Australian Aboriginal Anthropology*, R. Berndt, ed. Pp. 141–63. Australian Institute of Aboriginal Studies.

1973. The Spatiotemporal Transformations of Gawa Canoes. *Societé des oceanistes* 33:39–52.

1977. *Walbiri Iconography*. Ithica: Cornell University Press.

Murdock, George P. 1967. *Ethnographic Atlas*. Pittsburgh: University of Pittsburgh Press.

Murra, John V. 1980 [1965]. *The Economic Organization of the Inca State*. Greenwich, CT: JAI Press.

Nadel, Sigfried F. 1957. *The Theory of Social Structure*. Glencoe, IL: The Free Press.

Nag, Moni, B. N. F. White, and R. C. Peet. 1978. An Anthropological Approach to the Study of the Economic Value of Children in Java and Nepal. *Current Anthropology* 19:293–306.

Naroll, R. 1956. A Preliminary Index of Social Development. *American Anthropologist* 56:687–715.

Nash, Manning. 1961. The Social Context of Economic Choice in a Small Society. *Man* 61:186–91.

Netting, Robert McC. 1965a. A Trial Model of Cultural Ecology. *Anthropology Quarterly* 38:81–96.

1965b. Household Organization and Intensive Agriculture: The Kofyar Case. *Africa* 35:422–29.

1968. *Hill Farmers of Nigeria: Cultural Ecology of the Kofyar of the Jos Plateau*. Seattle: University of Washington Press.

1969. Ecosystems in Process: A Comparative Study of Change in Two West African Societies. In *Ecological Essays*, David Damas, ed. *National Museum of Canada Bulletin* 230.

1972. Sacred Power and Centralization: Some Notes on Political Adaptation in Africa. In *Population Growth: Anthropological Implications*, Brian Spooner, ed. Pp. 219–44. Cambridge, MA: MIT Press.

1973. Fighting, Forest, and the Fly: Some Demographic Regulators among the Kofyar. *Journal of Anthropological Research* 29:164–79.

1974a. Agrarian Ecology. *Annual Review of Anthropology* 3:21–56. Palo Alto: Annual Reviews.

1974b. Kofyar Armed Conflict: Social Causes and Consequences. *Journal of Anthropological Research* 30:139–63.

1976. What Alpine Peasants have in Common: Observations on Communal Tenure in a Swiss Village. *Human Ecology* 4:135–46.

1977. Maya Subsistence: Mythologies, Analogies, Possibilities. In *The Rise of Maya Civilization*, Richard Adams, ed. Pp. 299–333. Albuquerque: University of New Mexico Press.

1979. Household Dynamics in a Nineteenth-Century Swiss Village. *Journal of Family History* 4:39–58.

1981. *Balancing on an Alp: Ecological Change and Continuity in a Swiss Mountain Community.* Cambridge, England: Cambridge University Press.

1982a. Territory, Property and Tenure. In *Behavioral and Social Science Research: A National Resource.* Pp. 446–502. Washington: National Academy Press.

1982b. Some Home Truths on Household Size and Wealth. *American Behavioral Scientist* 25:641–62.

Netting, Robert McC., David Cleveland, and Frances Stier. 1980. The Conditions of Agricultural Intensification in the West African Savannah. In *Sahelian Social Development*, Stephen P. Reyna, ed. Abidjan: USAID.

Netting, Robert McC., Richard Wilk, and Eric Arnould. 1984 (eds.). *Households: Comparative and Historical Studies of the Domestic Group.* Berkeley: University of California Press.

Niemczycki, M. A. P. 1986. The Genesee Connection: The Origins of Iroquois Culture in West-Central New York. *North American Archaeologist* 7:15–44.

Niemi, R. G., and H. F. Weisberg. 1972. The Effects of Group Size on Collective Decision-Making. In *Probability Models of Collective Decision-Making*, R. G. Niemi and H. F. Weisberg, eds. Pp. 125–48. Columbus, Ohio: Merrill.

Noell, J. J. 1974. On the Administrative Sector of Social Systems. *Social Forces* 52:549–58.

Norman, David White. 1972. An Economic Study of Three Villages in Zaria Province. Samaru Miscellaneous Papers 37 and 38. Zaria: Institute for Agricultural Research, Ahmadu Bello University.

1977. Economic Rationality in Traditional Hausa Dryland Farmers in the North of Nigeria. In *Tradition and Dynamics in Small-Farm Agriculture*, R. D. Stevens, ed. Pp. 63–91. Ames: Iowa State University Press.

Norman, David W., E. B. Simmons, and H. M. Hays. 1982. *Farming Systems in the Nigerian Savanna.* Boulder: Westview.

Northern Algonquian Land Tenure Systems. 1985. Symposium. Canadian Ethnology Society/American Ethnological Society Annual Congress. Organizer: Toby Morantz.

Oberg, Kalervo. 1955. Types of Social Structure among the Lowland

Tribes of South and Central America. *American Anthropologist* 57:472–87.

Olmstead, Judith. 1975. Agricultural Land and Social Stratification in the Gamu Highland of Southern Ethiopia. In *Proceedings of the First United States Conference on Ethiopian Studies*, Harold G. Marcus, ed. Pp. 223–33. East Lansing: African Studies Center, Michigan State University.

Orans, M. 1966. Surplus. *Human Organization* 25:24–32.

Parker Pearson, Michael. 1984. Economic and Ideological Change: Cyclical Growth in the Pre-State Societies of Jutland. In *Ideology, Power and Prehistory*, D. Miller and C. Tilley, eds. Pp. 69–92. Cambridge, England: Cambridge University Press.

Parsons, Jeffery. 1978. El complejo hidraulico de Tunanmarca: canales, acueductos y reservorios. In *El hombre y la cultura andina: actas y trabajos del III Congresco*, tomo II, R. Matos M., ed. Pp. 556–66. Lima: Universidad Nacional Mayor de San Marcos.

Parsons, Jeffrey, and Ramiro Matos Mendieta. 1978. Asentamientos prehispánicos en el Mantaro, Perú: informe preliminar. In *El hombre y la cultura andina: actas y trabajos del III Congreso*, tomo II, R. Matos M., ed. Pp. 539–55. Lima: Universidad Nacional Mayor de San Marcos.

Patterson, Thomas. 1971. Chavin: An Interpretation of its Spread and Influence. In *Dumbarton Oaks Conference on Chavin*, E. Benson, ed. Pp. 29–48. Washington DC: Dumbarton Oaks.

in press. Class and State Formation: The Case of Pre-Incaic Peru. In *State and Society: The Emergence and Development of Social Hierarchy and Political Centralization*, J. Gledhill, B. Bender, and M. Larsen, eds. London: Hyman Unwin.

Pearce, R. J. 1984. Mapping Middleport: A Case Study in Societal Archaeology. Ph.D. dissertation, Department of Anthropology, McGill University.

Peebles, Christopher S., and Susan M. Kus. 1977. Some Archaeological Correlates of Ranked Societies. *American Antiquity* 42:421–48.

Plog, Fred. 1973. Diachronic Anthropology. In *Research and Theory in Current Archaeology*, C. Redman, ed. Pp. 181–98. New York: Wiley.

1974. *The Study of Prehistoric Change*. New York: Academic Press.

1977. Explaining Change. In *The Explanation of Prehistoric Change*, J. N. Hill, ed. Pp. 17–57. Albuquerque: University of New Mexico Press.

1979. Alternative Models of Prehistoric Change. In *Transformations: Mathematical Approaches to Culture Change*, C. Renfrew and K. L. Cooke, eds. Pp. 221–36. New York: Academic Press.

1983. Political and Economic Alliances on the Colorado Plateaus, A.D. 400 to 1450. *Advances in World Prehistory* 2:289–302.

Plog, Fred, and Steadman Upham. 1983. The Analysis of Prehistoric Political Organization. In *The Development of Political Organization*

290

in Native North America, E. Tooker and M. Fried, eds. Pp. 199–
213. Washington DC: American Ethnological Society.

Plog, Stephen. 1980. Village Autonomy in the American Southwest: An
Evaluation of the Evidence. *Society for American Archaeology Papers*
1:135–46.

1986a. Change in Regional Trade Networks. In *Spatial Organization
and Exchange*, S. Plog, ed. Pp. 282–309. Carbondale: Southern
Illinois University Press.

1986b. Understanding Culture Change in the Northern Southwest. In
Spatial Organization and Exchange, S. Plog, ed. Pp. 310–38.
Carbondale: Southern Illinois University Press.

1987. Sociopolitical Implications of Southwestern Stylistic Variation. In
The Use of Style in Archaeology, M. W. Conkey and C. A. Hastorf,
eds. Pp. 56–73. Cambridge, England: Cambridge University Press.

Plog, Stephen, and Jeffrey H. Hantman. 1986. Multiple Regression
Analysis as a Dating Method in the American Southwest. In *Spatial
Organization and Exchange*, S. Plog, ed. Pp. 87–113. Carbondale:
Southern Illinois University Press.

1987. Chronology Construction and the Study of Culture Change.
Manuscript, Department of Anthropology, University of Virginia.

Polanyi, K. 1944. *The Great Transformation*. New York: Farrar, Straus.

Pozorski, T., and S. Pozorski. 1987. Chavin, the Early Horizon and the
Initial Period. In *The Origins and Development of the Andean State*,
J. Haas, S. Pozorski, and T. Pozorski, eds. Pp. 36–46. Cambridge,
England: Cambridge University Press.

Prudden, T. Mitchell. 1903. The Prehistoric Ruins of the San Juan
Watershed of Utah, Arizona, Colorado and New Mexico. *American
Anthropologist* 5:224–88.

Pryor, Frederic L. 1977. *The Origins of the Economy: A Comparative
Study of Distribution in Primitive and Peasant Economies*. New York:
Academic Press.

1985. The Invention of the Plow. *Comparative Studies in Society and
History* 27:727–43.

1986. The Adoption of Agriculture: Some Theoretical and Empirical
Evidence. *American Anthropologist* 88:879–97.

Pryor, Frederic L., and Stephen B. Maurer. 1982. On Induced Economic
Change in Precapitalist Economies. *Journal of Development
Economics* 10:325–53.

Quain, Buell. 1937. The Iroquois. In *Cooperation and Competition
among Primitive Peoples*, Margaret Mead, ed. Pp. 240–81. New York:
McGraw-Hill.

Radcliffe-Brown, A. R. 1922. *The Andaman Islanders*. London:
Cambridge University Press.

Ramenofsky, A. F. 1987. *Vectors of Death*. Albuquerque: University of
New Mexico Press.

Ramsden, P. G. 1977. A *Refinement of Some Aspects of Huron Ceramic*

Analysis. Ottawa: Archaeological Survey of Canada, Mercury Series 63.

Rands, R. L., and C. L. Riley. 1958. Diffusion and Discontinuous Distribution. *American Anthropologist* 60:274–97.

Rappaport, Roy A. 1968. *Pigs for the Ancestors*. New enlarged edition. New Haven: Yale University Press.

1979. *Ecology, Meaning, and Religion*. Richmond, CA: North Atlantic Books.

Rathje, William. 1971. The Origin and Development of Lowland Classic Maya Civilization. *American Antiquity* 36(3):275–85.

1972. Praise the Gods and Pass the Metates: A Hypothesis of the Development of Lowland Rainforest Civilizations in Mesoamerica. In *Contemporary Archaeology*, M. Leone, ed. Pp. 365–92. Carbondale: Southern Illinois University Press.

1975. The Last Tango in Mayapan: A Tentative Trajectory of Production–Distribution Systems. In *Ancient Civilization and Trade*, J. Sabloff and C. C. Lamberg-Karlovsky, eds. Pp. 409–48. Albuquerque: University of New Mexico Press.

Rawski, E. S. 1972. *Agricultural Change and the Peasant Economy of South China*. Cambridge, MA: Harvard University Press.

Renfrew, C. 1974. Beyond a Subsistence Economy: The Evolution of Social Organization in Prehistoric Europe. In *Reconstructing Complex Societies*, C. B. Moore, ed. Pp. 69–85. Cambridge, MA: American School of Oriental Research.

Resnick, Stephen, and Richard D. Wolff. 1982. Marxist Epistemology: The Critique of Economic Determinism. *Social Text* 6:31–72.

1987. *Knowledge and Class*. Chicago: University of Chicago Press.

Rey, P. P., and G. Dupre. 1973. Reflections on the Relevance of a Theory of the History of Exchange. *Economy and Society* 2(2):131–63.

Richards, Cara. 1967. Huron and Iroquois Residence Patterns, 1600–1650. In *Iroquois Culture, History and Prehistory*, E. Tooker, ed. Pp. 51–56. Albany: The University of the State of New York.

Richards, Paul. 1983. Farming Systems and Agrarian Change in West Africa. *Progress in Human Geography* 7:1–39.

1985. *Indigenous Agricultural Revolution, Ecology, and Food Production in West Africa*. London: Hutchinson.

Richter, D. K. 1983. War and Culture: The Iroquois Experience. *William and Mary Quarterly* 40:528–59.

Rindos, David. 1984. *The Origins of Agriculture*. New York: Academic Press.

1985. Darwinian Selection, Symbolic Variation, and the Evolution of Culture. *Current Anthropology* 26:65–88.

1986. The Genetics of Cultural Anthropology: Toward a Genetic Model for the Origin of the Capacity for Culture. *Journal of Anthropological Archaeology* 5:1–38.

References

Ritchie, W. A. 1965. *The Archaeology of New York State*. Garden City: Natural History Press.

Ritchie, W. A., and R. E. Funk. 1973. *Aboriginal Settlement Patterns in the Northeast*. Albany: New York State Museum and Science Service, Memoir 20.

Roberts, Frank H. H. 1929. *Shabik'eschee Village, a Late Basket Maker Site in the Chaco Canyon, New Mexico*. Bureau of American Ethnology Bulletin 92. Washington DC: Government Printing Office.

Robertson, Linda. 1983. Achiya: Dekyap'bowa: Alliance and Polity in the Development of Cibola. Doctoral dissertation, Department of Anthropology, Brown University, Providence.

Robinson, Geroid T. 1932. *Rural Russia under the Old Regime*. London: Longmans, Green.

Robinson, W., and A. Schutjer. 1984. Agricultural Development and Demographic Change: A Generalization of the Boserup Model. *Economic Development and Cultural Change* 32:355–66.

Roosevelt, Anna G. 1984. Population, Health and the Evolution of Subsistence. In *Paleopathology at the Origins of Agriculture*, M. N. Cohen and G. J. Armelagos, eds. Pp. 559–83. Orlando: Academic Press.

Rowe, John. 1962. *Chavin Art: An Inquiry into its Form and Meaning*. New York: Museum of Primitive Art.

Rowlands, Michael J. 1980. Kinship, Alliance, and Exchange in the European Bronze Age. In *Settlement and Society in the British Late Bronze Age*, J. Barrett and R. Bradley, eds. Pp. 15–55. Oxford: British Archaeological Reports, British Series 83.

——— 1982. Processual Archaeology as Historical Social Science. In *Theory and Explanation in Archaeology: The Southampton Conference*, C. Renfrew, M. J. Rowlands, and B. A. Segraves, eds. Pp. 155–74. New York: Academic Press.

——— 1984. Conceptualizing the European Bronze and Early Iron Age. In *European Social Evolution*, J. Bintliff, ed. Pp. 147–56. Bradford: University of Bradford.

——— 1987a. Center and Periphery: A Review of a Concept. In *Center and Periphery in the Ancient World*. M. Rowlands, M. Larsen, and K. Kristiansen, eds. Cambridge, England: Cambridge University Press.

——— 1987b. Power and Moral Order in Precolonial West-Central Africa. In *Specialization, Exchange, and Complex Societies*, E. Brumfiel and T. Earle, eds. Pp. 52–63. Cambridge, England: Cambridge University Press.

——— 1989. A Question of Complexity. In *Domination and Resistance*, D. Miller, M. Rowlands, and C. Tilley, eds. Pp. 29–40. London: Hyman Unwin.

Rowley-Conwy, P. 1984. Sedentary Hunters: The Ertebolle Example. In *Hunter-Gatherer Economy in Prehistory*, G. Bailey, ed. Pp. 111–26. Cambridge, England: Cambridge University Press.

Sackett, J. R. 1985. Style and Ethnicity in the Kalahari: A Reply to Wiessner. *American Antiquity* 50:154–59.

Sacks, Karen. 1979. *Sisters and Wives: The Past and Future of Sexual Equality.* Urbana: University of Illinois Press.

Sagard, Gabriel. 1939. *The Long Journey to the Country of the Hurons.* Toronto: The Champlain Society.

Sahlins, Marshall D. 1957. Lane Use and the Extended Family in Moala, Fiji. *American Anthropologist* 59:449–62.

   1958. *Social Stratification in Polynesia.* Seattle: University of Washington Press.

   1961. The Segmentary Lineage: An Organization of Predatory Expansion. *American Anthropologist* 63:332–45.

   1964. Poor Man, Rich Man, Big-Man, Chief. *Comparative Studies in Society and History* 5:285–303.

   1968. *Tribesmen.* Englewood Cliffs, NJ: Prentice-Hall.

   1972. *Stone Age Economics.* Chicago: Aldine.

   1972 [1965]. The Sociology of Primitive Exchange. In *Stone Age Economics.* Pp. 185–276. Chicago: Aldine.

   1976. *Culture and Practical Reason.* Chicago: University of Chicago Press.

   1983. Other Times, Other Customs: The Anthropology of History. *American Anthropologist* 85:517–44.

Saile, David. 1977. "Architecture" in Prehispanic Pueblo Archaeology: Examples from Chaco Canyon, New Mexico. *World Archaeology* 9:157–73.

Saitta, Dean J. 1983. On the Evolution of "Tribal" Social Networks. *American Antiquity* 48:820–24.

   1987a. Dialectics, Critical Inquiry and Archaeology. In *Critical Traditions in Contemporary Archaeology: Essays in the Philosophy and History of Archaeology,* V. Pinsky and A. Wylie, eds. Cambridge, England: Cambridge University Press.

   1987b. Economic Integration and Social Development in Zuni Prehistory. Doctoral dissertation, Department of Anthropology, University of Massachusetts, Amherst.

   1988. Marxism, Prehistory, and Primitive Communism. *Rethinking Marxism* 1(4):147–68.

Saitta, Dean, and Arthur Keene. 1985. Concepts of Surplus and the Primitive Economy: A Critique and Reformation. Paper presented at the 50th Annual Meeting of the Society for American Archaeology, Denver, Colorado.

Salamon, Sonya. 1985. Ethnic Communities and the Structure of Agriculture. *Rural Sociology* 50:323–40.

Sandefur, Elsie. 1987. Correspondence, June 15, 1987.

Sanders, William. 1956. The Central Mexican Symbiotic Region: A Study in Prehistoric Settlement Patterns. In *Prehistoric Settlement Patterns in the New World,* G. Willey, ed. Pp. 115–27. New York: Wenner–Gren Foundation.

References

Sanders, William, and Barbara Price. 1968. *Mesoamerica: Evolution of a Civilization*. New York: Random House.

Sanders, W. T., and D. L. Webster. 1978. Unilinealism, Multilinealism, and the Evolution of Complex Societies. In *Social Archaeology: Beyond Subsistence and Dating*, C. Redman, ed. Pp. 249–302. New York: Academic Press.

Schelling, Thomas C. 1978. *Micromotives and Macrobehavior*. New York: Norton.

Schiffer, Michael B. 1981. Some Issues in the Philosophy of Archaeology. *American Antiquity* 46:899–908.

Schlanger, Sarah Helen. 1985. Prehistoric Population Dynamics in the Dolores Area, Southwestern Colorado. Ph.D. dissertation, Department of Anthropology, University of Colorado. Ann Arbor: University Microfilms.

Schneider, Jane. 1975. Peacocks and Penguins: The Political Economy of European Cloth and Colors. *American Ethnologist* 5:413–47.

Scholl, Theresa O., M. E. Odell, and Francis E. Johnston. 1976. Biological Correlates of Modernization in a Guatemalan Highland Municipio. *Annals of Human Biology* 3:23–32.

Scholte, Bob. 1981. Critical Anthropology since its Reinvention. In *The Anthropology of Precapitalist Societies*, J. Kahn and J. Llobera, eds. Pp. 148–84. London: Macmillan.

    1986. The Charmed Circle of Geertz's Hermeneutics. *Critique of Anthropology* VI:5–15.

Schrire, C. 1982. *Past and Present in Hunter-Gatherer Studies*. New York: Academic Press.

Service, Elman R. 1962. *Primitive Social Organization*. New York: Random House.

    1985. *A Century of Controversy: Ethnological Issues from 1860 to 1960*. Orlando: Academic Press.

Sherratt, A. 1984. Social Evolution: Europe in the Later Neolithic and Copper Ages. In *European Social Evolution*, J. Bintliff, ed. Pp. 123–34. Bradford: University of Bradford.

Shipton, Parker M. 1984. Strips and Patches: A Demographic Dimension in Some African Land-Holding and Political Systems. *Man* 19:613–34.

Silverblatt, Irene. 1987. *Moon, Sun and Witches: Gender Ideologies and Class in Inca and Colonial Peru*. Princeton, NJ: Princeton University Press.

Simon, Herbert A. 1957. *Models of Man*. New York: Wiley.

Simon, Julian L. 1981. *The Ultimate Resource*. Princeton: Princeton University Press.

Simpson, G. G. 1944. *Tempo and Mode in Evolution*. New York: Columbia University Press.

    1952. Periodicity in Vertebrate Evolution. *Journal of Paleontology* 26:359–70.

1953. *The Major Features of Evolution*. New York: Columbia University Press.

Skipp, V. 1978. *Crisis and Development: An Ecological Case Study of the Forest of Arden 1570–1674*. Cambridge, England: Cambridge University Press.

Sklar, Harald O. 1982. *The Warm Valley People: Duality and Land Reform among the Quechua Indians of Highland Peru*. Oslo: Universitetsforlaget, and New York: Columbia University Press.

Slobodkin, Lawrence B., and Anatol Rapoport. 1974. An Optimal Strategy of Evolution. *Quarterly Review of Biology* 49:181–200.

Smith, B. 1978. Variation in Mississippian Settlement Patterns. In *Mississippian Settlement Patterns*, B. Smith, ed. Pp. 479–502. New York: Academic Press.

Smith, P. E. L. 1972. Land-Use, Settlement Patterns and Subsistence Agriculture: A Demographic Perspective. In *Man, Settlement and Urbanism*, P. J. Ucko et al., eds. Pp. 409–25. London: Duckworth.
   1976. *Food Production and its Consequences*. Second edition. Menlo Park: Cummings.

Smith, Thomas C. 1959. *The Agrarian Origins of Modern Japan*. Stanford: Stanford University Press.

Smith, W. M. 1970. A Reappraisal of the Huron Kinship System. *Anthropologica* 12:191–206.

Snow, D. R. 1985. The Mohawk Valley Project. *De Nieu Nederlanse Marcurius* 1(3):3–4.

Sober, Elliot. 1984. *The Nature of Selection*. Cambridge, MA: MIT Press.

Speck, Frank G. 1915. The Family Hunting Band as the Basis of Algonkian Social Organization. *American Anthropologist* 17:289–305.

Spence, M. W. 1984. Another Way of Telling: Marxist Perspectives in Archaeology. In *Marxist Perspectives in Archaeology*, M. Spriggs, ed. Pp. 1–9. Cambridge, England: Cambridge University Press.
   1986. Band structure and Interaction in Early Southern Ontario. *Canadian Journal of Anthropology* 5(2):83–95.

Spence, M. W., W. D. Finlayson, and R. H. Phil. 1979. Hopewellian Influences on Middle Woodland Cultures in Southern Ontario. In *Hopewell Archaeology: The Chillicothe Conference*, D. S. Brose and N. Greber, eds. Pp. 115–21. Kent: Kent State University Press.

Spencer, Herbert. 1866. *The Principles of Biology*. New York: D. Appleton.

Spencer, R. 1959. *The North Alaskan Eskimo*. Washington: Bureau of American Ethnology Bulletin 171.

Spooner, Brian. 1972 (ed.). *Population Growth: Anthropological Implications*. Philadelphia: University of Pennsylvania Press.
   1974. Irrigation and Society: The Iranian Plateau. In *Irrigation's Impact on Society*, T. E. Downing and M. Gibson, eds. Papers of the Arizona State Museum 25. Tucson, AZ: University of Arizona Press.

References

Spriggs, Matthew. 1984 (ed.). *Marxist Perspectives in Archaeology.*
  Cambridge, England: Cambridge University Press.
Stark, Barbara. 1981. The Rise of Sedentary Life. In *Supplement to the Handbook of Middle American Indians,* J. A. Sabloff, ed. Pp. 86–103. Austin: University of Texas Press.
Steponaitis, V. 1978. Location Theory and Complex Chiefdoms: A Mississippian Example. In *Mississippian Settlement Patterns,* B. Smith, ed. Pp. 417–53. New York: Academic Press.
Stevenson, Robert F. 1968. *Population and Political Systems in Tropical Africa.* New York: Columbia University Press.
Steward, Julian H. 1937. Ecological Aspects of Southwestern Society. *Anthropos* 32:87–104.
  1948. The Circum-Caribbean Tribes: An Introduction. In *Handbook of South American Indians,* vol. 4, J. H. Steward, ed. Pp. 1–41. Bureau of American Ethnology Bulletin 143.
  1949. Cultural Causality and Law: A Trial Formulation of Early Civilization. *American Anthropologist* 5(1):1–27.
  1955. *Theory of Cultural Change.* Urbana: University of Illinois Press.
  1968. Causal Factors and Processes in the Evolution of Pre-Farming Societies. In *Man the Hunter,* R. B. Lee and I. DeVore, eds. Pp. 321–34. Chicago: Aldine.
Steward, Julian H., and Louis C. Faron. 1959. *The Native Peoples of South America.* New York: McGraw-Hill.
Stocking, George W., Jr. 1987. *Victorian Anthropology.* New York: The Free Press.
Stone, G. D., Priscilla Johnson-Stone, and Robert McC. Netting. 1984. Household Variability and Inequality in Kofyar Subsistence and Cash Cropping Economics. *Journal of Anthropological Research* 40:90–108.
Stothers, D. M. 1977. *The Princess Point Complex.* Ottawa: Archaeological Survey of Canada, Mercury Series 58.
Strathern, Andrew. 1971. *The Rope of Moka: Big Men and Ceremonial Exchange in Mount Hagen, New Guinea.* Cambridge, England: Cambridge University Press.
Stuart, David, and Rory Gauthier. 1984. *Prehistoric New Mexico: Background for Survey.* Santa Fe: New Mexico Historic Preservation Bureau.
Sullivan, N. C. 1983. Some Comments on John A. Dickinson's "The Precontact Huron Population: A Reappraisal" *Ontario History* 75:187–90.
Suttles, Wayne. 1968. Coping with Abundance: Subsistence on the Northwest Coast. In *Man the Hunter,* R. Lee and I. DeVore, eds. Pp. 56–58. Chicago: Aldine.
Taylor, D. 1975. Some Locational Aspects of Middle-Range Hierarchical Societies. Unpublished doctoral dissertation, Department of Anthropology, The City University of New York, New York.

Testart, Alain. 1982. *Les Chasseurs-cueilleurs ou L'Origine des inégalites.* Paris: Société d'Ethnographie, Mémoires 26.

1985. *Le Communisme primitif: I. Economie et ideologie.* Paris: Editions de la Maison des Sciences de l'Homme.

Thompson, E. A. 1965. *The Early Germans.* Oxford: Clarendon Press.

Thompson, E. P. 1963. *The Making of the English Working Class.* New York: Pantheon.

1978. *The Poverty of Theory and Other Essays.* London: Merlin Press.

Thwaites, R. G. 1896–1901. *The Jesuit Relations and Allied Documents.* 73 vols. Cleveland: Burrows Brothers.

Tibbetts, Paul. 1986. The Sociology of Scientific Knowledge: The Constructivist Thesis and Relativism. *Philosophy of Social Science* 16:39–57.

Tilley, C. 1982. Social Formation, Social Structures and Social Change. In *Symbolic and Structural Archaeology*, I. Hodder, ed. Pp. 26–38. Cambridge, England: Cambridge University Press.

Timmins, Peter. 1985. *Analysis and Interpretation of Radiocarbon Dates in Iroquoian Archaeology.* London: Museum of Indian Archaeology, Research Report 19.

Titiev, Mischa. 1944. *Old Oraibi: A Study of the Hopi Indians of Third Mesa.* Papers of the Peabody Museum of American Archaeology and Ethnology 22. Cambridge, MA: Harvard University Press.

Toledo, Francisco de. 1940 [1570]. Información hecha por orden de Don Francisco de Toledo en su visita de las provincias del Perú, en la que declaran indios ancianos sobre el derecho de los caciques y sobre el gobierno que tienen aquellos pueblos antes que los Incas los conquistasen. In *Don Francisco de Toledo, supremo organizador del Perú, su vida, su obra 1515–1582,* vol. II, R. Levillier, ed. Pp. 14–37. Buenos Aires: Espasa-Calpe.

Toll, H. Wolcott. 1985. Pottery, Production, Public Architecture, and the Chaco Anasazi System. Ph.D. dissertation, Department of Anthropology, University of Colorado. Ann Arbor: University Microfilms.

Tooker, Elisabeth. 1970. Northern Iroquoian Sociopolitical Organization. *American Anthropologist* 72:90–97.

1978. The League of the Iroquois: Its History, Politics, and Ritual. In *Handbook of North American Indians,* vol. 15, *Northeast,* B. G. Trigger, ed. Pp. 418–41. Washington DC: Smithsonian Institution Press.

1984. Women in Iroquois Society. In *Extending the Rafters: Interdisciplinary Approaches to Iroquoian Studies,* M. K. Foster et al., eds. Pp. 109–23. Albany: State University of New York Press.

1985a (ed.). *An Iroquois Source Book,* vol. 1, *Political and Social Organization.* New York: Garland.

1985b (ed.). *An Iroquois Source Book,* vol. 2, *Calendric Rituals.* New York: Garland.

References

1985c (ed.). *An Iroquois Source Book*, vol. 3, *Medicine Society Rituals*. New York: Garland.

Tosi, Maurizio. 1984. The Notion of Craft Specialization and its Representations in the Archaeological Record of Early States in the Turanian Basin. In *Marxist Perspectives in Archaeology*, M. Spriggs, ed. Pp. 22–52. Cambridge, England: Cambridge University Press.

Trigger, Bruce G. 1963. Order and Freedom in Huron Society. *Anthropologica* 5:151–69.

1970. The Aims of Prehistoric Archaeology. *Antiquity* 44:26–37.

1973. The Future of Archaeology is the Past. In *Research and Theory in Current Archaeology*, C. Redman, ed. Pp. 95–112. New York: Wiley.

1974. The Archaeology of Government. *World Archaeology* 6:95–106.

1976. *The Children of Aataentsic: A History of the Huron People to 1660*. 2 vols. Montreal: McGill–Queen's University Press.

1978a. Iroquois Matriliny. *Pennsylvania Archaeologist* 47(1–2):55–65.

1978b. *Time and Traditions*, Edinburgh: Edinburgh University Press.

1980. Archaeology and the Image of the American Indian. *American Antiquity* 45:662–78.

1982. Archaeological Analysis and Concepts of Causality. *Culture* 2(2):31–42.

1984a. Alternative Archaeologies: Nationalist, Colonialist, Imperialist. *Man* 19:355–70.

1984b. Archaeology at the Crossroads: What's New? *Annual Review of Anthropology* 13:275–300.

1984c. The Road to Affluence: A Reassessment of Early Huron Responses to European Contact. In *Affluence and Cultural Survival*, R. F. Salisbury and E. Tooker, eds. Pp. 12–25. Washington: The American Ethnological Society.

1985a. Marxism in Archaeology: Real or Spurious? Reviews in *Anthropology* 24:114–23.

1985b. *Natives and Newcomers: Canada's "Heroic Age" Reconsidered*. Montreal: McGill–Queen's University Press.

Tuck, J. A. 1971. *Onondaga Iroquois Prehistory: A Study in Settlement Archaeology*. Syracuse: Syracuse University Press.

Turner, B. L., and W. E. Doolittle. 1978. The Concept and Measure of Agricultural Intensity. *Professional Geographer* 30:297–301.

Turner, B. L., R. Q. Hanham, and A. V. Portararo. 1977. Population Pressure and Agricultural Intensity. *Annals of the Association of American Geographers* 67:384–96.

Tyyska, A. E. 1968. *Settlement Patterns at Cahiague*. Toronto: Report submitted to the Archaeological and Historic Sites Board of the Province of Ontario.

Udo, R. K. 1965. Disintegration of Nucleated Settlement in Eastern Nigeria. *Geographical Review* 55:53–67.

Upham, Steadman. 1982. *Polities and Power: An Economic and Political History of the Western Pueblo*. New York: Academic Press.

1987. A Theoretical Consideration of Middle Range Societies. In *Archaeological Reconstructions and Chiefdoms in the Americas*, R. Drennan and C. Uribe, eds. Pp. 345–68. New York: University Press of America.

van der Leeuw, Sander. 1976. *Studies in the Technology of Ancient Pottery*. Amsterdam: s.n.

Vayda, Andrew P. 1961. Expansion and Warfare among Swidden Agriculturalists. *American Anthropologist* 63:346–58.

1971. Phases of the Process of War and Peace among the Marings of New Guinea. *Oceania* 42:1–24.

Vayda, Andrew, P., and Bonnie McKay. 1975. New Directions in Ecology and Ecological Anthropology. *Annual Review of Anthropology* 4:293–306.

von Gernet, Alexander. 1982. Analysis of Intrasite Artifact Spatial Distributions: The Draper Site Smoking Pipes, Master's thesis, Department of Anthropology, McGill University.

Waddell, E. 1972. *The Moundbuilders*. Seattle: University of Washington Press.

Wagley, Charles. 1969. Cultural Influences on Population: A Comparison of Two Tupi Tribes. In *Environment and Cultural Behavior: Ecological Studies in Cultural Anthropology*, A. Vayda, ed. Pp. 268–80. New York: Natural History Press.

Wallace, A. F. C. 1958. Dreams and Wishes of the Soul: A Type of Psychoanalytic Theory among the Seventeenth Century Iroquois. *American Anthropologist* 60:234–68.

1969. *The Death and Rebirth of the Seneca*. New York: Knopf.

Wallerstein, I. 1974. *The Modern World System*. New York: Academic Press.

Warrick, Gary. 1984. Reconstructing Ontario Iroquoian Village Organization. Ottawa: Archaeological Survey of Canada, Mercury Series 124:1–180.

1989. A Population History of the Huron-Petun, A.D. 900–1650. Ph.D. dissertation, Department of Anthropology, McGill University.

Watson, P. J., S. LeBlanc, and C. Redman. 1971. *Explanation in Archaeology: An Explicitly Scientific Approach*. New York: Columbia University Press.

1980. Aspects of Zuni Prehistory: Preliminary Report on Excavation and Survey in the El Morro Valley of New Mexico. *Journal of Field Archaeology* 7:201–18.

1984. *Archaeological Explanation*. Cambridge, England: Cambridge University Press.

Webb, S. S. 1984. *1676: The End of American Independence*. Cambridge, MA: Harvard University Press.

Weber, Max. 1968. *Economy and Society*. New York: Bedminster Press.

Webner, R. 1977. The Argument in and about Oratory. *African Studies* 36:141–44.

References

Weiner, A. 1985. Inalienable Wealth. *American Ethnologist* 12:210–27.

Whalen, Michael E. 1976. Zoning within an Early Formative Community in the Valley of Oaxaca. In *The Early Mesoamerican Village*, K. V. Flannery, ed. Pp. 75–78. New York: Academic Press.

Whallon, Robert, Jr. 1968. Investigations of Late Prehistoric Social Organization in New York State. In *New Perspectives in Archaeology*, S. R. and L. R. Binford, eds. Pp. 223–44. Chicago: Aldine.

White, L. 1949. *The Science of Culture*. New York: Grove Press.

1959. *The Evolution of Culture*. New York: McGraw-Hill.

White, J. P. 1985. Digging out Big-Men? *Archaeology in Oceania* 20:57–60.

Whiteley, Peter M. 1985. Unpacking Hopi "Clans:" Another Vintage Model out of Africa? *Journal of Anthropological Research* 41:359–74.

1986. Unpacking Hopi "Clans," II: Further Questions about Hopi Descent Groups. *Journal of Anthropological Research* 42:69–79.

Whyte, M. K. 1978. *The Status of Women in Pre-Industrial Societies*. Princeton: Princeton University Press.

Wiessner, Pauline W. 1977. Hxaro: A Regional System of Reciprocity for Reducing Risk among the !Kung San. Ph.D. dissertation, University of Michigan. Ann Arbor: University Microfilms.

1982. Risk, Reciprocity, and Social Influence on !Kung San Economies. In *Politics and History in Band Societies*, E. Leacock and R. Lee, eds. Pp. 61–84. London: Cambridge University Press.

1983. Style and Social Information in Kalahari San Projectile Points. *American Antiquity* 48:253–76.

1985. Styles or Isochrestic Variation? A Reply to Sackett. *American Antiquity* 50:160–66.

Wilcox, David R., and Charles Sternberg. 1983. *Hohokam Ballcourts and their Distribution*. Arizona State Museum Archaeological Series 160.

Wilk, Richard R. 1984. Households in Process: Agricultural Change and Domestic Transformation among the Kekchi Maya of Belize. In *Households: Comparative and Historical Studies of the Domestic Group*. R. McC. Netting, R. R. Wilk, and E. J. Arnould, eds. Pp. 217–44. Berkeley: University of California Press.

Wilk, Richard R., and Robert McC. Netting. 1984. Households: Changing Forms and Functions. In *Households: Comparative and Historical Studies of the Domestic Group*, R. McC. Netting, R. R. Wilk, and E. J. Arnould, eds. Pp. 1–28. Berkeley: University of California Press.

Wilk, Richard R., and William J. Rathje. 1982 (eds.). Household Archaeology. American Behavioral Scientist 25(6):617–39.

Wilkinson, R. 1973. *Poverty and Progress: An Ecological Perspective on Economic Development*. New York: Praeger.

Williams, R. 1973. *The Country and the City*. Oxford: Oxford University Press.

References

Williamson, R. F. 1985. Glen Meyer: People in Transition. Ph.D. dissertation, Department of Anthropology, McGill University.
Wills, Wirt H., and Thomas C. Windes. 1986. Shabik'eschee Village and the Basketmaker III Period in Chaco Canyon, New Mexico. Manuscript, Department of Anthropology, University of New Mexico.
Wilmsen, Edwin N. 1979. Diet and Fertility among Kalahari Bushmen. African Studies Center, Working Paper 14. Boston, MA: Boston University.
1982. Biological Variables in Forager Fertility Performance: A Critique of Bongaarts' Model. African Studies Center, Working Paper 60. Boston, MA: Boston University.
Winter, Marcus C. 1976. The Archaeological Household Cluster in the Valley of Oaxaca. In The Early Mesoamerican Village, K. V. Flannery, ed. Pp. 25–30. New York: Academic Press.
Winterhalder, Bruce. 1980. Environmental Analysis in Human Evolution and Adaptational Research. Human Ecology 8:135–70.
1986. Diet Choice, Risk, and Food Sharing in a Stochastic Environment. Journal of Anthropological Archaeology 5:369–92.
Wissler, Clark. 1966 [1940]. Indians of the United States. Garden City: Doubleday.
Wittfogel, Karl. 1957. Oriental Despotism. New Haven: Yale University Press.
Witthoft, John. 1959. Ancestry of the Susquehannocks. In Susquehannock Miscellany, John Witthoft and W. J. Kinsey III, eds. Pp. 16–60. Harrisburg: Pennsylvania Historical and Museum Commission.
Wobst, H. Martin. 1974. Boundary Conditions for Paleolithic Social Systems: A Simulation Approach. American Antiquity 39:147–78.
1976. Locational Relationships in Paleolithic Society. In The Demographic Evolution of Human Populations, R. Ward and K. Weiss, eds. Pp. 49–58. London: Academic Press.
1978. The Archaeo-Ethnology of Hunter-Gatherers or the Tyranny of the Ethnographic Record in Archaeology. American Antiquity 43:303–309.
Wolf, Eric R. 1966. Peasants. Englewood Cliffs, NJ: Prentice-Hall.
1982a. Europe and the People without History. Berkeley: University of California Press.
1982b. The Mills of Inequality. In Social Inequality, G. Berreman, ed. New York: Academic Press.
1984. Culture: Panacea or Problem? American Antiquity 49:393–400.
Wolf, Eric R., and Angel Palerm. 1955. Irrigation in the Old Acolhua Domain. Southwest Journal of Anthropology 11:265–81.
Wolpe, H. 1972. Capitalism and Cheap Labor Power in South Africa: From Segregation to Apartheid. Economy and Society 1(4):425–56.
Woodburn, James. 1981. Egalitarian Societies. Man 17:431–51.
1989. In History, Evolution and Social Change in Hunter-Gatherer

302

Societies, T. Ingold, D. Riches, and J. Woodburn, eds. London: Berg Publishers.

Wray, C. F. 1973. *Manual for Seneca Iroquois Archaeology*. Honeoye Falls: Cultures Primitive.

Wray, C. F., and H. L. Schoff. 1953. A Preliminary Report on the Seneca Sequence in Western New York, 1550–1687. *Pennsylvania Archaeologist* 23(2):53–63.

Wright, Henry. 1969. The Administration of Rural Production in an Early Mesopotamian Town. Anthropological Paper 38. Ann Arbor: Museum of Anthropology, University of Michigan.

Wright, Henry, and Melinda Zeder. 1977. The Simulation of a Linear Exchange System Under Equilibrium Conditions. In *Exchange Systems in Prehistory*, T. Earle and J. Ericson, eds. Pp. 233–53. New York: Academic Press.

Wright, J. V. 1966. *The Ontario Iroquois Tradition*. Ottawa: National Museum of Canada Bulletin 210.

1972. *Ontario Prehistory*. Ottawa: National Museum of Canada.

1984. The Cultural Continuity of the Northern Iroquoian-Speaking Peoples. In *Extending the Rafters: Interdisciplinary Approaches to Iroquoian Studies*, M. K. Foster et al., eds. Pp. 283–99. Albany: State University of New York Press.

Yang, M. C. 1965. *A Chinese Village: Taitou, Shantung Province*. New York: Columbia University Press.

Index

Index

cemeteries *and see* burial practices
  Iroquois Indians, 124
  Mesoamerica, 185–86, 188–89
ceramics, Sausa, 161–63, 168–69, 172
ceremonial space, Zuni, 221–22
change *and see* social change
  definition of, 64, 96–97
  directional, 229
  rates of, 94–97
  and social reproduction, 228–29
Chavinoid motifs, 154–55
chiefs and chiefdoms, 55–58, 60–61, 240–42
  Iroquois Indians, 133–35, 137, 143, 239
  powers of, 120, 134–35, 137, 143, 148
  social position, 133–34, 143, 238–39
  and warfare, 57–58, 135, 241
children
  in Iroquoian society, 130, 132
  and labor, 40–41
Chokfem, population density, 24
Christianity, and Iroquois Indians, 140
class structure
  Java, 44–45
  Sausa, 167–69
  and social organization, 120–21
communal mode, 242–45, 260–61
communal production, evolution of, 230–31
communal property, 49–50
communal society *and see* social organization, 10, 203–205
  abandonment of, 222–23
  definition of, 213–14
  and population growth, 237–38
  relationships within, 220–21
communism *and see* primitive communism, 233–34
community size, and decision-making, 83–84
competition, and adaptation, 67–68
compound cultivation, 29
confederacy, Iroquois Indians, 129–30
conflict, in nonhierarchical communities, 69–70
consensus, and adaptation, 68–69
continuous approach, 92–94
contraception, 124
cooperation, and adaptation, 67–68
cottage industry, 45–46
crafts, 43–44, 60, 156, 219
crop rotation, 23–25, 29
cropping index (CI), 25, 34
cultural selection, 79
culture, and social reproduction, 228
curing societies, 134–35
cycles, 76–77

decision-making, 10
  and community size, 83–84
  in nonhierarchical communities, 69–70
defense *and see* warfare, and agricultural efficiency, 57
defensive settlements, 58, 126–27, 165, 173
definitions *and see* specific term, 5–6
delayed debt, 152
delegation, and authority, 69–70
demography *and see* population, population density, population growth
  and agricultural intensity, 23–26, 38
  and environment, 195
  and political evolution, 8
  variability, 99–101
dendrochronology, 194
dialectical epistemology, 206–208
diet, 36, 187–88
digital approach, 91–97
directional change, 229

economic formations, 50–51
economic variability, 102–103
economics *and see* exchange, trade
  delayed debt, 152
  of households, 102–103
  and political power, 148
endogamy, 101, 128
Engels
  and economic formations, 50–51
  and exchange system, 102
  and land tenure, 50–51
  on Malthus, 35–36
  and population growth, 35–36
  'primitive' societies, 119–20
ensete gardens, 58
environment *and see* agriculture
  and agriculture, 34, 38, 159–60
  and demographic change, 195
  and human adaptive response, 7
  packed landscapes, 111
  and political systems, 177–99
  and population, 33–34
  and sedentism, 180–88
  and social change, 177–99
  and social organization, 209, 248–51
equality *and see* inequality, 235–36
evolutionary science, 63
exchange *and see* economics, generosity, gift-giving, trade, 8–9, 152–55, 186–87
  Engles's theory, 102
  exogenous, 152, 154–55
  generalized reciprocity, 234–35
  importance of, 249–50
  intra-group, 152–54
  local, 152–54

Index

longhouses, 123–24
  effect of Mississippian culture, 125–26
  political behavior, 137–39
  population, 124–25, 129
  prehistory of, 122–30
  religious beliefs, 123, 134–37, 140–43
  and resistance, 10
  social organization, 121–22, 128–30, 133,
    143
  town development, 123–24, 126–27
  and trade, 124, 127, 129, 135–36, 139–40
  warfare, 125–26, 135
  and women, 124–25, 130–33
irrigation systems, 55–56, 169
isochrestic variability, 104, 187

Java, 41, 43–45
Jesuits, view of Iroquois society, 141–42

Kekchi, and land tenure, 54
kibbutzim, 203–205
kin relations
  and labor, 261
  and social development, 253–56
kiva:room ratio studies, 191, 217–19, 222
knowledge *and see* information, as resource,
    66, 190–91, 197–98
Kofyar
  crop yields, 27
  distribution of labor, 39
  Gini index, 48
  household size, 42–43
  population density, 23–24
  and women as laborers, 41
!Kung San, 243
  inequality of, 236
  and resistance, 10

labor, 209–10
  and agriculture, 29–31, 39–41, 60
  and children, 40–41
  control of, 261–62
  costs of, 26–31, 44
  division of, 12–13, 250–51; Hausa, 45;
    and household groups, 39–41, 60;
    Iroquois Indians, 130–32, 139, 251;
    Java, 45; Kofyar, 39; and women, 41,
    250
  and kin relations, 261
  landless workers, 43
  and population density, 27–31
  reproduction of, 227
  returns per hour in rural occupations, 44
  scheduling of, 113–14
  surpluses, 8–9, 209–13
  and technological progress, 26–31

land tenure
  and agriculture, 46–54
  and Engels, 50–51
  and household size, 42–43
  inheritance, 51–54, 56, 58
  and land use, 47–48
  Marxist theory, 50–51
  and population density, 56
  privatization, 13
land use *and see* agriculture, 47–48, 197
Land Without Evil movement, 121
landless workers, 43
leveling devices, 243–45
lineage systems, 239–40
local exchange *and see* exchange, 152–54
longhouses, Iroquois Indian, 123–24
Luo, and land inheritance, 56

Madagascar, defensive settlements, 58
Mae-Enga, and land tenure, 53–54
maize, 161, 163, 170
Malthusian theory on population growth,
    32–38
manioc (cassava), 30
Mantaro Valley, defensive settlements, 58
Maori, and land tenure, 53
Marxist theory, 256–62
  and biological reproduction, 227
  and economic formations, 50–51
  and historical materialism, 208–11
  and land tenure, 50–51
  limitations of, 211–13
  and political development, 14
  population growth, 35–36
  and primitive communism, 226–29
  primitive societies, 119–20
  and production, 226–27
  and social reproduction, 227–28
  technology and social production, 6–7
Maya, and craftwork, 43
Mesoamerica
  archaeological data, 184–88
  burial, 186
  cemeteries, 185–86, 188–89
  comparison with Southwest, 194
  diet, 187–88
  exchange, 186–87
  food storage, 184–85
  households, 184–85, 189–91
  houses, 184–85
  population, 187
  public buildings, 186
  ritual behavior, 190–91
  style, 187
minifundistas, 43

307

Index

private property *and see* personal wealth, 12–13
processual approach, 5–6
production
    control of, 151–52
    and Marxist theory, 226–27
    surpluses, 8–9, 151, 155–57
productive specialization, 8–9, 157–59, 163
property, 12–13, 46–47
public buildings, 166, 186
Pueblos, 214–15

quantum effects, and rates of change, 94–97

ramage, 240
redistribution of goods, 198, 242
redistributors, 238–39
reference incomes, 35
religion
    and Iroquois Indians, 123, 134–37, 140–43
    and political power, 121
reproduction, control of, 124, 151–52, 227
resistance, 10, 247–49
resource exploitation, and adaptation, 66–67
resource sharing, 189–91
rice, and labor costs, 31
risk, 181
ritual
    and adaptation, 71–72
    and exchange, 153, 190–92
    knowledge, 197–98
room-set analysis, 217–19
rope production, 43

sachems, 239
sacrifice
    animal, 162
    human, 124–25
Sausa, 150–51, 159–75
    and agriculture, 159–63, 169–70
    animal bone data, 170
    ceramics, 161–63, 168–69, 172
    class structure, 167–69
    defensive sites, 165, 173
    environment of, 159–60
    households, 171
    houses, 166–67
    irrigation, 169
    political system, 146–75
    population, 164–65
    site location, 161–65, 169, 173
    trade, 170–72
    warfare, 165–66, 171, 173
scalar stress, 84–85
scheduling, of household tasks, 113–14

sedentism
    and agriculture, 110–11, 181–83, 252–53
    definition, 180–81
    and environment, 180–88
    and hierarchies, 110–11
    and social change, 188–93
selectionism, 79–85
semicommunal societies, 232
sequential hierarchy, 69
Shabik'eschee, 185
sharing, 189–91, 198, 242
simultaneous hierarchy, 69
sinchicuna, 165–66
social boundaries, 191–92
social change *and see* change, 228–29
    and environment, 177–99
    experimentation, 78
    and foragers, 237–38
    and population, 11, 236–38, 249
    and sedentism, 188–93
    and style, 104–107, 112–13, 187
social conflict, 198
social development, and kin relations, 253–56
social evolution, 63–64, 230
social inequality, 235–42
social organization *and see* communal society
    and adaptation, 65–66
    and class, 120–21
    and environment, 209, 248–51
    and food production, 251
    hierarchies, 69, 110–11
    Iroquois Indians, 121–22, 128–30, 133, 143
    leveling devices, 243–45
social production, and political evolution, 6–7
social reproduction, 228–31
    and Marxist theory, 227–28
social resources
    knowledge, 66, 190–91, 197–98
    people, 66–68
social stratification *and see* hierarchies, 148–49
social variability, 103–107
societal typology, 88–91
specialization, 157–59
style, and social change, 104–107, 112–13, 187
subsistence economy, and exchange, 102–103
Switzerland
    cottage industry, 46
    Gini index, 48
symbolic variability, 104–105, 112–13, 187

309